Grand Rapids

v i s i o n s
Highlighting Western Michigan

Written by: Rich DeVos

Stephen Hung, Publisher

Staff for Grand Rapids Visions
Art Director: Thad Pickett
Managing Editor: Julie Clark
Profile Writers: Kate Convissor, Laura Bennett-Kimble
Sales Manager: Henry Hintermeister
Staff Writers: Barbara Bellesi, Judith A. Fader

PAGODA GROUP
PUBLISHING SOLUTIONS

Brookline, Massachusetts
© 2007 Pagoda Group
All Rights Reserved

First Edition
ISBN: 0- 9759736-6-5

www.cityscapesbooks.com

Dust Jacket photo by: Thad Pickett

Table Of contents

Grand Rapids Visions

by Rich DeVos

The Right Climate

Falling snow was covering the streets in downtown Grand Rapids. But I told 2,500 people gathered for the grand opening of the DeVos Place convention center that our community enjoys the right climate. I was not referring to the wintry weather outside. I was describing the people gathered inside who create a special climate of philanthropy, teamwork, leadership, work ethic, and community spirit that makes West Michigan such a great place to live.

The new convention center we celebrated that evening was the latest in a long list of community improvements that have been changing the landscape of West Michigan during the past few decades and have led to a rebirth of our community. As I told the crowd that evening, the convention center was covered with the fingerprints of our leaders and residents who pitched in to contribute their time, talent, and treasures to present a gift to our community. The DeVos Place convention center was a typical unselfish West Michigan partnership of public and private resources that developed from a dream to reality. Yes, we have a great climate in West Michigan, and I love to live here.

I consider myself very fortunate to be both a typical West Michigan native and to have touched or been touched by most of the recent projects and progress that have reshaped our area from the major city of Grand Rapids to the smaller cities and communities that dot the nearby shore of Lake Michigan and the rural landscape. I'm proud to have worked side by side with so many fellow residents of this great community on the rebirth of downtown Grand Rapids, the growth and development of our colleges and universities, the advancement of our hospitals and medical centers, and the flourishing of our arts. For all of our progress, I'm also glad that we have not lost the values we hold dear: hard work, family, worship, volunteerism, philanthropy, and community.

The West Michigan founders and settlers were a unique combination of people seeking wealth and religious freedom. In 1826 Detroit-born Louis Campau, the official founder of Grand Rapids, built his cabin, trading post, and blacksmith shop on the east bank of the Grand River near the rapids. Campau returned to Detroit and came back a year later with his wife and $5,000 of goods to trade with the native tribes. Twenty-one years later, Albertus Van Raalte and his followers from Rotterdam in The

The Muskegon south pier lighthouse covered with ice. Photo by Marge Beaver

Netherlands established a colony on Lake Macatawa near Lake Michigan that became the city of Holland. Other Dutch immigrants soon followed, establishing the nearby city of Zeeland and crossroad farming communities named after Dutch provinces including Drenthe, Friesland, and Overijssel. The entrepreneurship of Campau and Christian virtues of the early Dutch settlers continue to strongly influence West Michigan. Two things immediately obvious to visitors are West Michigan's economic development and number of churches.

The special atmosphere of this community has been apparent to me since I was a boy growing up in Grand Rapids during the Great Depression. Like so many West Michigan residents, my family was of Dutch heritage—known for being conservative, thrifty, tidy, hard working, and church-going. Like many others, I also was shaped by humble beginnings. Because my father lost his job during the Depression, we lived with my grandparents. My grandfather sold vegetables door-to-door from his old truck. I was raised in a home where money was scare but love was abundant. My parents sacrificed to pay tuition to send me to Christian schools. Being in church every Sunday morning and evening was a given. The lessons I learned at home, at school and in church of persistence, confidence, family, and faith laid the foundation that

helped me co-found and build a successful business that employs thousands in West Michigan and more worldwide.

That's a typical West Michigan story. Even with a greater diversity of heritage and religions today, I still think we live in this same climate of— for lack of a better term—American values. These values have built and continue to build the businesses, schools, hospitals, and arts and recreation centers that make this a place that more than 1.3 million people feel blessed to call home.

Made in West Michigan

In 1959, Jay Van Andel and I started Amway in our homes on the Thornapple River near the tiny village of Ada. The company we built is now one of the largest employers in West Michigan. As the owner of a manufacturing company, when I think of West Michigan, I think of manufacturing and our community's work ethic. When I was growing up, Grand Rapids was known nationally as "Furniture City" because of the number of plants along the Grand River that manufactured fine residential furniture. The Grand Rapids area is still the nation's capital for office furniture, with major companies including Steelcase, Herman Miller, and Haworth.

With our close proximity to the Motor City, West Michigan also is home to a number of companies that manufacture and develop auto parts. Seven our top twenty-five employers are automotive companies. Despite national headlines about the decline of manufacturing, one in four people in our area still is employed in manufacturing, and our area ranks No. 1 in manufacturing employment among cities with labor markets of 500,000 or more.

Cities and Villages

Beyond manufacturing, commerce these days is most apparent in the growth of our cities, towns, and villages. Grand Rapids is beginning to offer the level of amenities associated with major cities, and surrounding urban centers are developing unique personalities that appeal to a variety of diversions and pleasures. From an evening of Broadway theater to enjoying an ice cream cone on a waters-edge boardwalk, West Michigan cities, towns, and villages have something for everyone. I've done everything in our towns from attend black-tie galas in glittering hotel ballrooms to docking a boat for a bite at a beachside bistro. Each experience is unique and wonderful, especially if shared with the friendly people of West Michigan who love to congregate in our wealth of public places.

Nearly four decades ago, I was asked to join an effort to revitalize downtown Grand Rapids, which like so many of our cities in the 1960s had deteriorated with the exodus to the suburbs.

Anyone who moved from the city then and returned today would not recognize Grand Rapids. The people of Grand Rapids rolled up their sleeves and opened their pockets to make their city shine again. We established Calder Plaza with its huge, red Alexander Calder stabile that has become the symbol of Grand Rapids. Jay Van Andel and I refurbished a crumbling Pantlind Hotel, brought it back to its former glory as the Amway Grand Plaza Hotel and added a modern 27-story tower. This new focal point for community in downtown Grand Rapids spurred a torrent of development including the Van Andel Museum Center, DeVos Performance Hall, Meijer Heart Center, Van Andel Arena, the Big Old Building ("The BOB") entertainment center, Rosa Parks Circle, DeVos Place convention center, a new Grand Rapids Art Museum, a refurbished Civic Theater, and a new 24-story JW Marriott hotel.

New restaurants seem to be opening monthly, and once-abandoned buildings are being transformed into luxury condominiums, stores, and businesses. The view at night from vehicles on the intersecting U.S. 131 and I-196 freeways is of a gleaming, modern skyline. Yes, we have a great climate in West Michigan.

Traveling a half hour west from Grand Rapids brings you to Holland, known nationally as the home of the Tulip Festival. Holland could easily have given in to the economic forces of the flight to shopping malls.

The Grand Haven lighthouse in winter. Photo by Marge Beaver

But the people of Holland banded together to build on its small-town Midwestern charm and Dutch character to create a desirable destination for shopping, art galleries, restaurants, or simply strolling its tree-lined sidewalks beneath 19th century brick buildings with touches of Dutch architecture.

Go north from Holland along Lake Michigan—I suggest the scenic route along the dunes on the tree-lined Lakeshore Drive—to Grand Haven. Where the Grand River flows into Lake Michigan is the perfect spot to stroll on the boardwalk, watch boats from the riverside park, or enjoy refreshments under an umbrella on a restaurant deck. South of Holland is another unique, water-front experience in the village of Saugatuck, an arts center on the Kalamazoo River with the feel of a Cape Cod town that fills with tourists each summer.

These same types of pleasures await visitors to any number of towns and villages found inland among the farms, forests, and rivers of West Michigan: Historic Rockford on the Rogue River with its annual Start of Summer Festival and Corner Bar famous for its hot dogs; East Grand Rapids, a town of large homes on tree-lined boulevards and yacht club on Reeds Lake; Zeeland, Holland's smaller cousin; and my home of Ada, the tiny village that boasts a historic covered bridge. And then there are the farming communities too numerous to mention that you come upon as just quick stops at a crossroads in the cornfields and that still host grain elevators, grange halls, or left behind one-room schoolhouses turned into family homes.

Caring for People

Wherever they live, people in West Michigan are cared for and care for one another. We work hard to enhance life and leave the world a better place. I've been privileged to be involved in a number of initiatives that provide people with improved medical care, higher education, and art.

The Michigan Street hill overlooking downtown Grand Rapids is becoming a medical corridor respected regionally and even nationally for the level and extent of its care. Through my involvement as a board member of Spectrum Health, I marvel at the dedication of our medical people from administrators and surgeons to nurses and staff. Thanks to the generosity and vision of the people of West Michigan, we have in just a few blocks the Van Andel Institute research center, the Butterworth Campus of Spectrum Health, the Cook-DeVos Health Building of Grand Valley State University, the Spectrum Health Meijer Heart Center, and soon the new Lemmen-Holton Cancer Center, Helen DeVos Children's Hospital and Michigan State University medical school.

We also believe in helping our young people succeed through education and have become a community of colleges and universities. Proud to have a state university in Allendale, the people of West Michigan have contributed to help Grand Valley State University grow to include a downtown campus, an enrollment of more than 20,000 students, national football championships, and growing academic quality. It's been a thrill to be involved with the growth of GVSU (within three decades) from its birth as four buildings on farmland to its stature as a leading university in less than three decades. We also boast two nationally recognized historic Christian colleges: Hope College in Holland and Calvin College in Grand Rapids—which incidentally have a basketball rivalry ranked as one of the best in the country by *Sports Illustrated*. Our young people can study art at Kendall College, business, technology, and health professions at the rapidly growing Davenport University with its new main campus; and a variety of subjects at several religious-affiliated private colleges and universities.

Arts and entertainment in West Michigan rival Chicago and other larger cities in our region. My wife, Helen, and I have been supporters of the Grand Rapids Symphony Orchestra for years and had the pleasure of seeing it perform a special concert in Carnegie Hall. Grand Rapids also boasts its own opera and ballet companies. There are more than a dozen theater companies, from the major Broadway Theater Guild and Civic Theater in Grand Rapids to community theaters throughout the area.

Nearly every family will sooner or later spend time in one of our area's attractions including the John Ball Park Zoo, Grand Rapids Museum, Gerald R. Ford Museum—housing the history of our native U.S. President—and some of our latest and greatest attractions: Meijer Gardens and Sculpture Park and Millennium Park, which is being developed on a parcel of land larger than Central Park in New York City. Of course, like people in most communities, we're sports enthusiasts and enjoy our Whitecaps baseball, Griffins hockey, and Rampage arena football teams.

Big-hearted Entrepreneurs

As a successful entrepreneur I may be biased, but I'm convinced that our community is special for its entrepreneurs, who not only succeed beyond their dreams but share their success to give us a better place to live. Successful business people are largely responsible for making our community successful – providing not only paychecks that mean livelihoods for thousands of families, but also philanthropic contributions that breathe life into our community with hospitals, arts and recreation

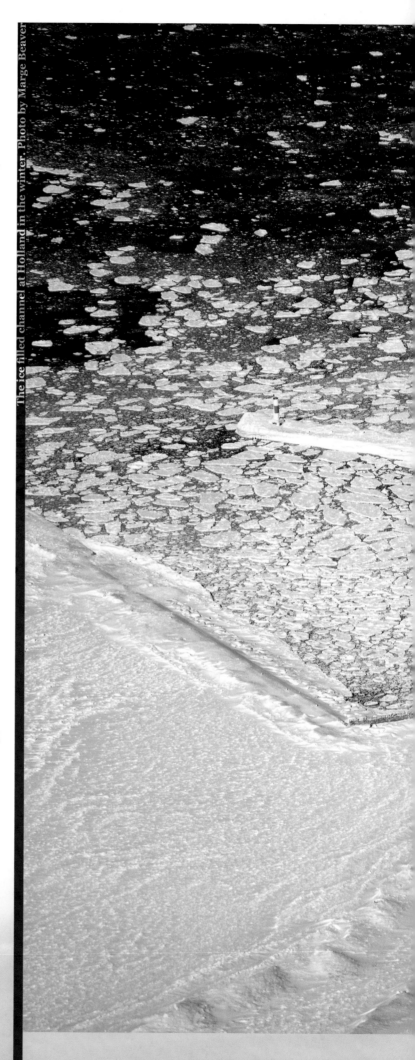

The ice filled channel at Holland in the winter. Photo by Marge Beaver

facilities, and colleges and universities. You need not travel far in our community to come upon any number of public facilities built with contributions totaling in the tens of millions of dollars. We are a community with a big heart.

Michigan's West Coast

Beyond all that residents have put into our area, West Michigan is perhaps most special for what was here before the first settlers arrived – formed by glaciers during an ice age thousands of years ago. Our area is promoted as "Michigan's West Coast." Even if Lake Michigan is seldom in sight to most residents, the "Big Lake" is seldom out of mind. The Great Lakes are a rare jewel in the world, and we in West Michigan feel fortunate to be bordered on the west by the Lake Michigan shoreline. Our harbors at Holland and Grand Haven are guarded by two of the Great Lakes' historic and picturesque lighthouses. "Big Red" in Holland and its smaller relative to the north are immediately recognizable in our community from hundreds of paintings and photographs.

We flock each summer to white sand beaches splashed by waves of crystal fresh water and take picnics to the shore to watch a blazing sun sink into the lake's horizon against a sky streaked with pink and purple. My family has enjoyed boating for years and has sailed throughout the world, but there is no sight quite like seeing

majestic dunes from a boat in Lake Michigan. We hoist huge trout and salmon from the lake, amble on piers and boardwalks, escape the routine and slow down on vacations in cottages, relax with summer reading on beach blankets, and beat the heat with a cool dip in the lake or a wild ride on water skis.

Inland is special, too. We have acres and acres of farms that provide an abundance of fruits and vegetables prominent at roadside stands in the summer. We produce more blueberries than any area in the world, and we wait all year for the homegrown tomatoes and sweet corn of late summer. Our fields and meadows are bordered by forests reminiscent of primitive Michigan with trees that turn brilliant yellow, orange, and red each fall. West Michigan is crisscrossed with rivers and streams and dotted with lakes—a paradise for outdoor enthusiasts whose passions include deer-hunting, boating, fishing, skiing, and snowmobiling.

Our proximity to Lake Michigan also produces "lake effect snow" and an unusual number of cloudy days. Our winters can be cold and summer can arrive late. As we say, if you don't like the weather here, wait a few minutes." So we can be excused for grumbling at times about our weather. But our people are warm and generous. As I told that crowd in Grand Rapids that snowy evening, we really do live in the right climate in West Michigan.

End of the day for the fisherman of Grand Heaven. Photo by Thad Pickett

Photo gallery

Grand Rapids Police directing traffic at the DeVos Performance Hall. Photo by Michael Buck

Speed and concentration mark the straight away to the finish line. Photo by John Corriveau

Ballet at the Grand Rapids' Festival of the Arts. Photo by Dianne Carroll Burdick

Tulipanes Festival in Holland, Michigan. Photo by Johnny Quirin

21

Chef Mitchell of The 1913 Room restaurant in the Amway Grand Plaza Hotel. Photo by Randa Bishop

Seared Norwegian salmon prepared by Chef Mitchell. Photo by Randa Bishop

Walking Bridge to Plaza Towers, Grand Rapids. Photo by Michael Buck

Sunrise on the Grand River. Photo by Thad Pickett

Artistic tree guards in Heartside. Photo by Randa Bishop

Artistic tree guards in Heartside. Photo by Randa Bishop

Rustic buildings of Heartside. Photo by Thad Pickett

Home of Lumber Baron, Charles Hackley in Muskegon. Photo by Frederic Reinecke

Photo by Thad Pickett

The Kirby House built in 1890 in Saugatuck. Photo by Randa Bishop

St. George Orthodox Church in Grand Rapids. Photo by Randa Bishop

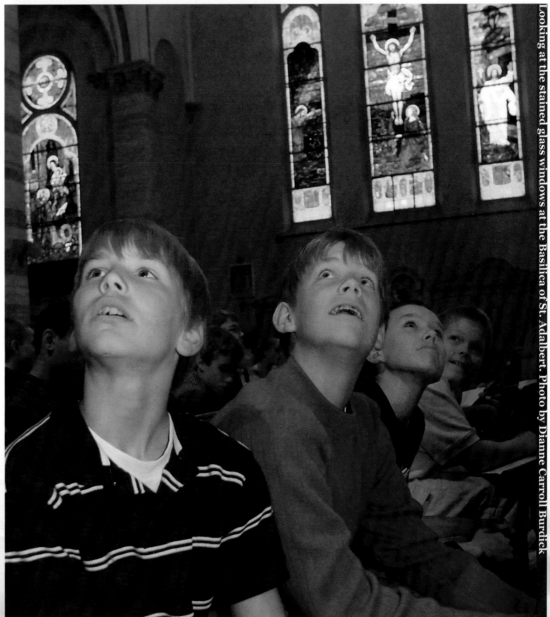

Signing the guest book at President Ford's funeral. Photo by Chris Tack

President Gerald R. Ford's funeral in Grand Rapids. Photo by Michael Buck

Amazing flowers of color at the Frederik Meijer Gardens & Sculpture Park in Grand Rapids. Photo by Thad Pickett

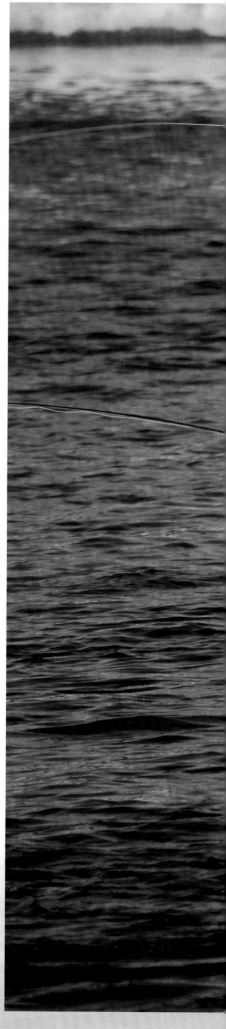

Lighthouse at Grand Heaven. Photo by Thad Pickett.

Holland Princess cruising by Holland Harbor Lighthouse "Big Red." Photo by Randa Bishop

Break wall at Muskegon's Pere Marquette Park. Photo by Frederic Reinecke

Reflection in a puddle in Grand Rapids. Photo by Julie K. Flietstra

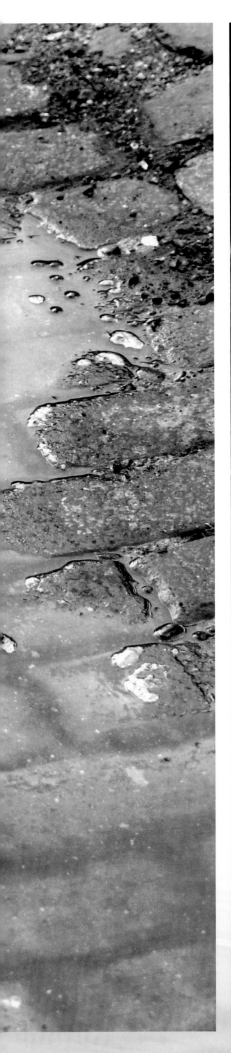

Downtown Grand Rapids. Photo by Lori Turner

Beach Volley Ball is popular throughout the summer at Pere Marquette Park in Muskegon. Photo by Frederic Reinecke

Pole vaulting beach event at Grand Haven City Beach in Grand Haven. Photo by Johnny Quirin

Sue Dow of Sue Chef from Ada. Photo by Dianne Carroll Burdick

Pastry Cook, Tyler Flaherty at Erika's. Photo by Dianne Carroll Burdick

Chocolate apricot sacher from The 1913 Room. Photo by Randa Bishop

Crab cake from Cygnus 27 restaurant. Photo by Randa Bishop

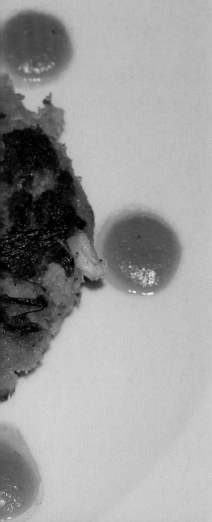

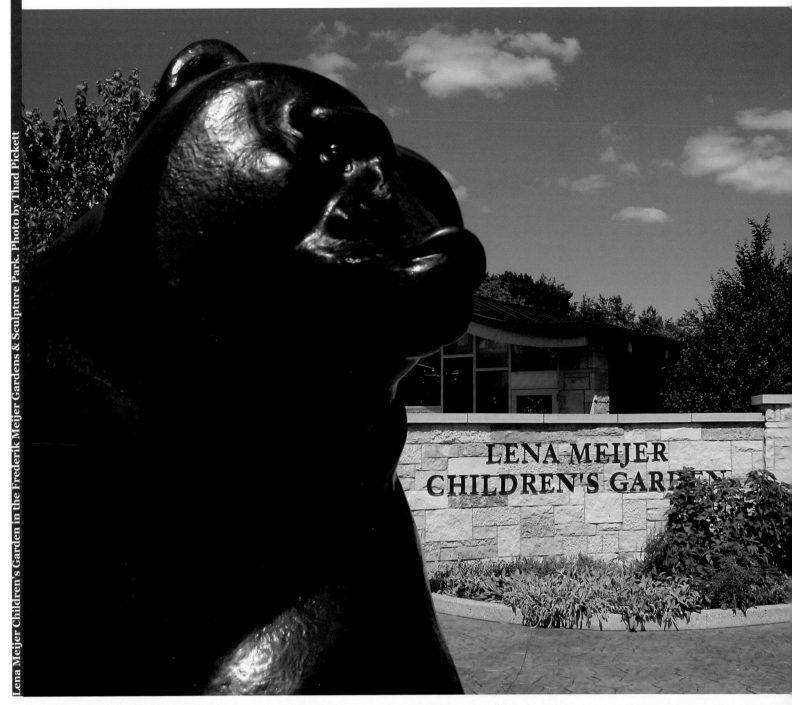

Lena Meijer Children's Garden in the Frederik Meijer Gardens & Sculpture Park. Photo by Thad Pickett

Photo by Thad Pickett

Architectural detail of McFadden's Restaurant and Saloon in Grand Rapids. Photo by Randa Bishop.

Young "Dutch" girl enjoying the beautiful Tulips of Holland. Photo by Julie K. Flietstra

Field of Tulips on Windmill Island. Photo by Lori Turner

Studio in Saugatuck. Photo by Thad Pickett

Artist Debra Reid Jenkins. Photo by Dianne Carroll Burdick

Polar Express backdrop to be used at the movie premiere party. Photo by John Corriveau

Sword Fighting demonstration at the Rockford Celtic Festival in Rockford, Michigan. Photo by Johnny Quirin

Photo by John Corriveau

Sound and fury mark the performance of medieval reanactors. Photo by John Corriveau

Oval Beach on Lake Michigan in Saugatuck. Photo by Randa Bishop

Rosy Mound Natural Area in Grand Haven. Photo by Johnny Quirin

One of the prime attractions of The Van Andel Museum Center is the lovingly reconstructed carousel. Photo by John Corriveau.

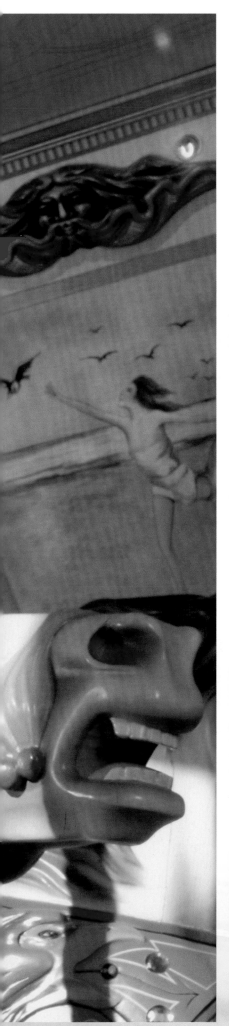

1928 Carousel in the Van Andel Museum Center. Photo by Randa Bishop

The snow and ice form lonely shapes during the winter months along Lake Michigan. Photo by Frederic Reinecke

The first snow of the season covers parts of Lamberton Creek. Photo by John Corriveau

Sunset at Holland State Park. Photo by Lori Turner

Veteran's Memorial Park in Grand Rapids. Photo by Michael Buck

1941
1945

1950
1953

THEY PERISHED
DEFENDING US

Listen to him play. Photo by Thad Pickett

Pop-folk band Cowboy Junkies. Photo by Randa Bishop

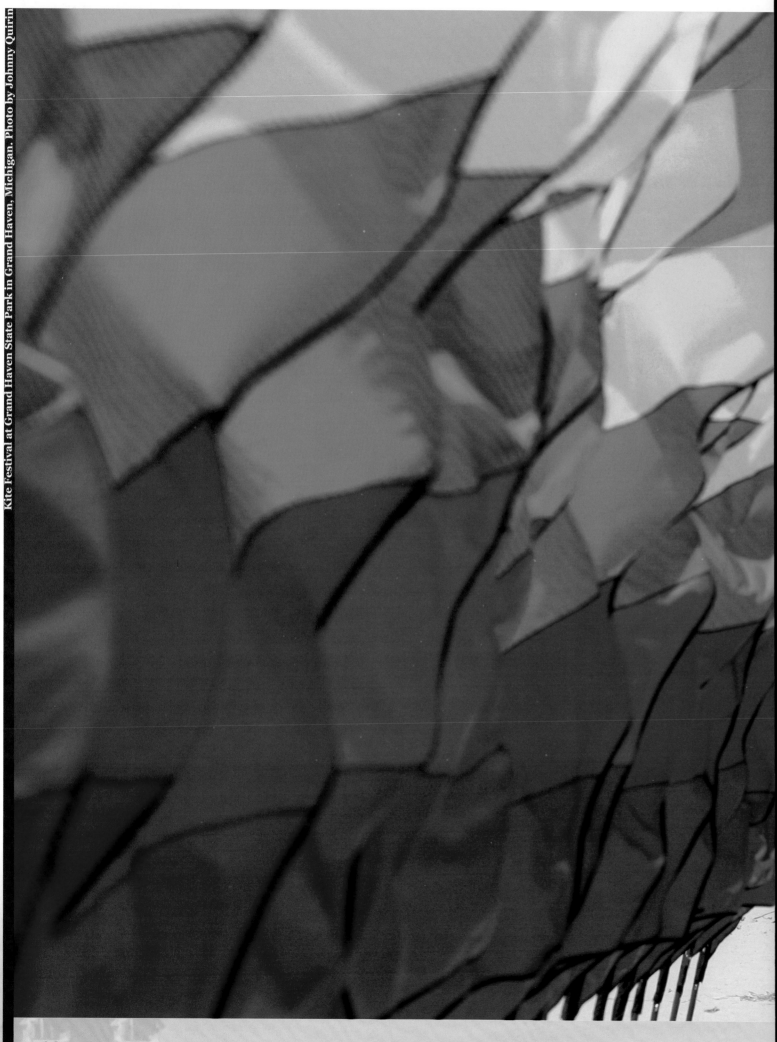

Kite Festival at Grand Haven State Park in Grand Haven, Michigan. Photo by Johnny Quirin

Ice Skating at Rosa Parks Circle in Grand Rapids. Photo by Michael Buck

Zamboni on Rosa Parks Circle. Photo by Michael Buck

Photos by Thad Pickett

Grand Rapids Children's Museum

Pop! Photos by Thad Picketti

Photo by Randa Bishop

Grand Rapids Children's Museum

Photo by Lori Turner

Carnival at John Ball Park. Photo by Julie K. Flietstra

Church steeple against a sunset sky in west Grand Rapids. Photos by Randa Bishop

Victorian mansion built for Carl G.A. Voigt in 1895. Photo by Randa Bishop

Photo by Thad Pickett

Photo by Thad Pickett

Voigt House in Grand Rapids, Photo by Michael Buck

Photo by Thad Pickett

Photo by Randa Bishop

The Gaslight District at night in Grand Rapids. Photos by Thad Pickett

Tall Ships "Parade of Sail" at Muskegon. Photo by Marge Beaver

A celebration of Tall Ships in Muskegon at Heritage Landing. Photo by Frederic Reinecke

Sunset on the masts of the Tall Ships. Photo by Frederic Reinecke

View of Grand Rapids skyline. Photo by Randa Bishop

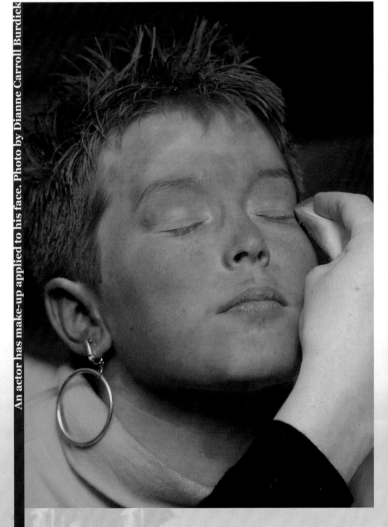

Community Circle Theatre. Photo by Dianne Carroll Burdick

An actor has make-up applied to his face. Photo by Dianne Carroll Burdick

Photo by John Corriveau

The cross lake ferry entering the Muskegon channel. Photo by Marge Beaver

The Lake Express high speed ferry. Photo by Frederic Reinecke

Reflections of Grand Rapids. Photo by Julie K. Flietsstra

Kayaks on the small interior waterway that runs around Windmill Island in Holland, Michigan, photo by Thad Pickett

Summer outdoor concerts at the Frederik Meijer Gardens & Sculpture Park in Grand Rapids. Photo by Randa Bishop

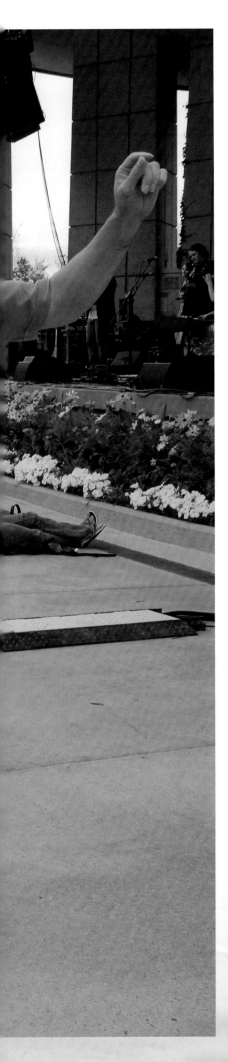

Dancing on Ionia Street in Grand Rapids. Photo by Michael Buck

A chicken makes a nice pet on Trillium Haven Farms in Jenison. Photo by John Corriveau

Exterior of the Meyer S. May house designed by Frank Lloyd Wright. Photo by Thad Pickett

Exclusive dining set by Frank Lloyd Wright for the May house. Photo by Randa Bishop

Young man doing tricks on his bicycle near the Grand River in Grand Rapids. Photo by Julie K. Flietstra

Leaves turn on the trees near Buchanan, Michigan. Photo by Johnny Quirin

Beach goers at Holland State Park. Photo by Johnny Quirin

Oval Beach on Lake Michigan in Saugatuck. Photo by Randa Bishop

Van Andel Arena in Grand Rapids. Photo by Michael Buck

DeVos Place and Convention Center interior in Grand Rapids. Photo by Randa Bishop.

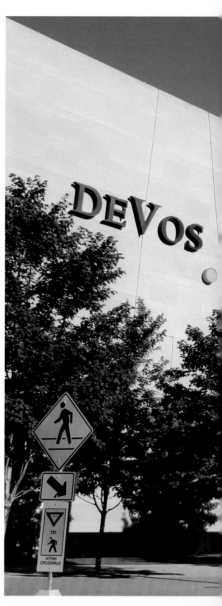

Exterior of Presidential Museum. Photo by Randa Bishop

Display of the Oval Office. Photo by Thad Pickett

Photo by Randa Bishop

129

Sunset on Grand Haven beach. Photo by Thad Pickett

Panoramic of Holland State Park. Photo by Lori Turner

131

George and Ben of G-Rad an online blogging community. Photo by Johnny Quirin

Jersey Junction ice cream parlor. Photo by Randa Bishop

Wall of candy at Jersey Junction. Photo by Thad Pickett

Craftsman restoring an antique book using tools that are over 100 years old. Photo by John Corriveau

"Tinker" fixes a stoneware jug at the Feast of the Strawberry Moon in Grand Haven, Michigan. Photo by Johnny Quirin

137

Fishing boats going out the Muskegon channel at sunrise. Photo by Marge Beaver

The Golden Angel street organ at the Dutch Village in Holland. Photo by Thad Pickett

Displaying a music book for the Golden Angel at the Dutch Village. Photo by Randa Bishop

Street organ from Amsterdam now played at Windmill Island. Photo by Randa Bishop

Music books for the street organ at the Dutch Village in Holland. Photo by Randa Bishop

Cleaning the windows on the fourth floor of the Monroe Street parking ramp in downtown Grand Rapids. Photo by John Corriveau

143

Evening on Ionia Street. Photo by Michael Buck

Old building on Ionia Street. Photo by Julie K. Flietstra

the sierra room

Old furniture company building now a restaurant, The Sierra Room, in Grand Rapids. Photo by Randa Bishop

Old red barn on the centennial farm of Fred C. Bowen, established in 1873 near Fallasburg, Michigan. Photo by Randa Bishop

Boy and his dog near the Manistee River. Photo by Lori Turner

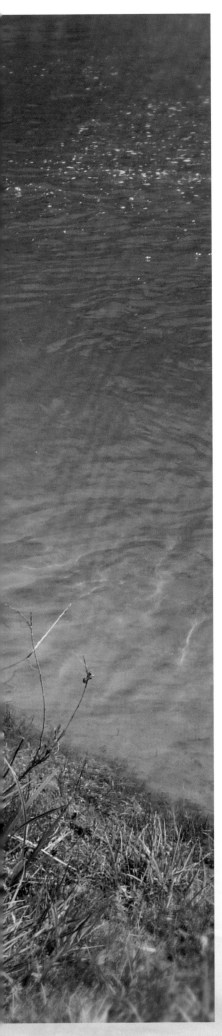

5 year old Kennedy runs through a sprinkler in early spring. Photo by Johnny Quirin

149

Dancing musical fountains featured on summer night in Grand Haven. Photo by Randa Bishop

Young couple dancing to the show of the musically illuminated fountain in Grand Heaven. Photo by Thad Pickett

Walking path in the shape of the United States in Hagar Park. Photo by Marge Beaver

Stainless steel sculpture of the earth in Ada, Michigan. Photo by Thad Pickett

Sunset view of the many bridges that span the Grand River in Grand Rapids. Photo by Randa Bishop

The Grand River that runs next to downtown Grand Rapids. Photo by Michael Buck

157

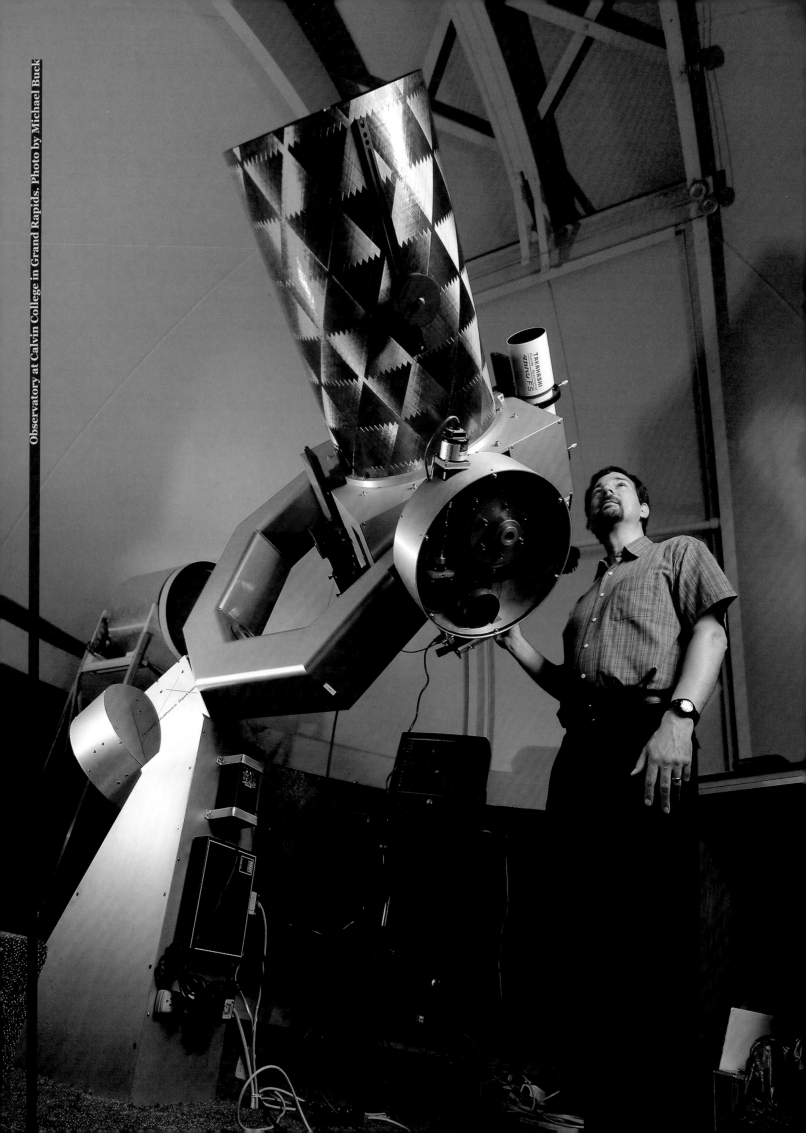

Fishermen line the outer break wall during the annual fall salmon run in Muskegon. Photo by Frederic Reinecke

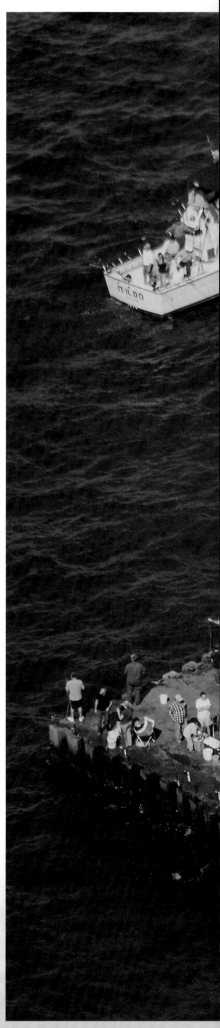

Beautiful butterfly at the Frederik Meijer Gardens & Sculpture Park. Photo by Julie K. Flietstra

Bono talks with Dave Van Andel. Photo by John Corriveau

Bono, lead singer for U2, spoke on the world poverty issue at the Economic Club of Grand Rapids 2006 annual dinner. Photo by John Corriveau

Picnicking before the start of a concert. Photo by Thad Pickett

Summer outdoor concert at the Frederik Meijer Gardens & Sculpture Park. Photo by Randa Bishop

GERALD R FORD PRESIDEN

GERALD R FORD MUSEUM

TERROR IN AMERICA 1776 to Today
ENEMY WITHIN

Displays at the Gerald R. Ford Presidential Museum. Photo by Thad Pickett

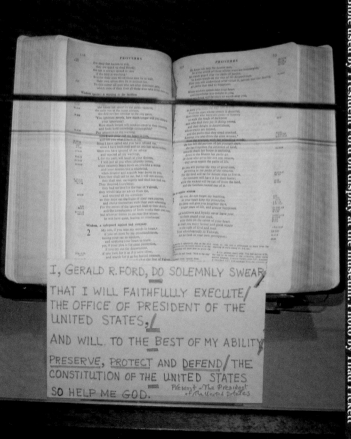

Bible used by President Ford on display at the museum. Photo by Thad Pickett

SURPLUS OFFICE FURNITURE

Seemingly trampled by The American Horse sculpture in the Frederik Meijer Gardens & Sculpture Park. Photo by Thad Pickett

Fresh vegetables at the Fulton Street Farmers Market. Photo by John Corriveau

Perspective buyer at the Grand Haven Arts Festival. Photo by Johnny Quirin

Stained glass art work at the Saugatuck Art Festival. Photo by Thad Pickett

Thousand Oaks Golf Course. Photo by Michael Buck

Sunset at Arcadia Bluffs Golf Course in Arcadia. Photo by Michael Buck

Arcadia Bluffs Golf Course. Photo by Michael Buck

The 16th. hole at the Wallinwood Golf Course in Jenison. Photo by Michael Buck

VAN ANDEL MUSEUM CENTER
PUBLIC MUSEUM OF GRAND RAPIDS

Playing the Japanese Koto in Grand Rapids. Photo by John Corriveau

Street performer in Holland. Photo by Lori Turner

Bagpiper at the Rockford Celtic Festival in Rockford. Photo by Johnny Quirin

Performer at the Rodeo in Grand Rapids. Photo by Johnny Quirin

Holland harbor lighthouse "Big Red" on Lake Macatawa inlet from Lake Michigan. Photo by Randa Bishop

Lighthouse lady gives a minute to talk about "Big Red" at Holland beach. Photo by Thad Pickett

Detail of "Big Red." Photo by Thad Pickett

Holland Lighthouse "Big Red" at sunset. Photo by Lori Turner

191

REWARD

$10.00 WHO & WHO'S DOG MESSES OUR SIDEWALK I WANT TO KNOW!!!

Cygnus 27 restaurant on the top of the Amway Grand Plaza hotel tower with a sunset view of the city. Photo by Randa Bishop

Skim boarding at South Heaven beach. Photo by Thad Pickett

Great Wolf Lodge in Traverse City. Photo by Michael Buck

Photo by Thad Pickett

197

Profiles
in excellence

WOOD TV8	1949
Unist, Inc.	1957
Alticor Inc.	1959
Master Finish Company	1959
Grand Valley State University	1960
Granger Construction	1960
Visser Brothers	1960
Erhardt Construction	1962
WZZM 13	1962
Hope Network	1963
Gerald R. Ford International Airport	1963
Gill Industries	1964
Prein&Newhof	1969
Porter Hills Retirement Communities & Services	1970
Monroe, LLC	1971
Trivalent Group	1971
ADAC Automotive	1972
Suspa, Inc.	1974
Competition Engineering, Inc.	1976
Robert Grooters Development Company	1977
Amway Grand Plaza Hotel	1978
Ferris State University Grand Rapids	1979
JR Automation Technologies, LLC	1980
Clean Rooms International, Inc.	1982
Cambridge Partners, Inc.	1985
The Right Place, Inc.	1985
Marsh USA Inc.	1986
S.J. Wisinski & Company	1986
Rockford Construction	1987
Parkland Properties	1988
Compatico, Inc.	1989
Dane Systems, LLC	1990
Founders Bank & Trust	1991
Michigan Fluid Power	1991
Reagan Marketing + Design	1991
Michigan Medical, P.C.	1995
Van Andel Institute	1996
Datum Industries, LLC	1997
The Bank of Holland	1998
West Michigan Strategic Alliance	2000
The Staybridge Suites, Grand Rapids	2001
WilliamCharles	2001
Arivium	2002
Lakeshore Advantage	2003
Residence Inn Holland	2003
Crayon Interface	2005
Boatwerks	2006

Since 1997, Spectrum Health has built a solid reputation for its commitment to bringing world-class health care to West Michigan. With more than 140 service sites in the area, Spectrum Health's service to the community is unsurpassed. As the largest not-for-profit integrated health system in the region, Spectrum Health has 13,000 employees, 1,400 physicians and more than 2,000 volunteers. Together they deliver high quality care to improve the health of the communities they serve.

Spectrum Health provides excellent health care value. Its hospitals are among the highest quality providers nationally. Its costs are in the lowest quartile compared with peers. Spectrum Health's Priority Health, is ranked one of the top health plans in the nation. Its health premiums are in the lowest quartile benchmarked against regional competitors.

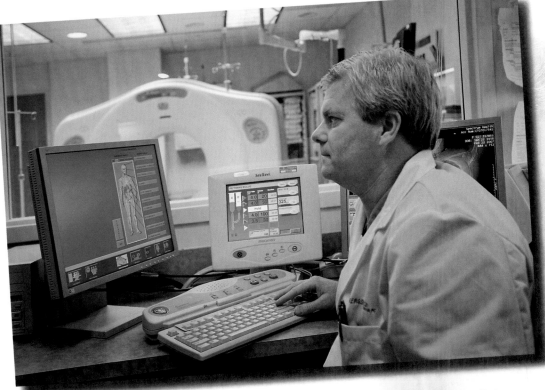

Bruce Murray, M.D., an emergency physician at Spectrum Health uses advanced technology to reviews images from a cardiac patient.

"Spectrum Health provides excellent health care value. Its hospitals are among the highest quality providers nationally. Its costs are in the lowest quartile compared with peers."

Heeding the Call for Better Health Care

Savvy consumers are always on the lookout for quality ratings on the products and services they wish to buy. But why is it easier to find performance reviews on electronics equipment than it is to learn about health care?

Six years ago, two enlightening reports were released by the Institute of Medicine. One was called "To Err Is Human" and cited medical errors as the cause of approximately 98,000 deaths annually. The other, entitled "Crossing the Quality Chasm," called attention to systems, processes and performances that were in dire need of an overhaul with increased accountability. This certainly shook up the health profession. As a result, Spectrum Health became one of the country's first health care organizations to voluntarily provide data to government and watchdog groups, such as The Joint Commission. While many hospitals track a handful of quality indicators, Spectrum Health goes far beyond the minimum requirements. Currently, it can report its performance on more than 50 clinical and surgical conditions that represent 70 percent of its volume. That is a claim very few health care organizations can make. In a move that initiated a welcome trend in the industry, Spectrum Health began issuing report cards with statistics concerning clinical quality of its services. Spectrum Health was the first health system in West Michigan to do this. Spectrum Health also published its first cardiovascular outcomes report in 2004 and began making public its average charges for 200 common procedures in 2006.

One of the earliest health plans to post quality metrics for consumers, Priority Health launched its rating system for physicians in October 2000. Members can check which primary care physicians have the most apples – a symbol of quality – before they choose a doctor.

An Impressive Reputation that Keeps Growing

Since its inception in 1997, Spectrum Health has worked to earn a place high atop the ranks of the nation's medical field. It has won more than 50 national awards and multiple recognitions for innovation and leadership locally, regionally and nationally. For example, Spectrum Health has been named one of the Solucient 100 Top Cardiovascular Hospitals® for seven years and Priority Health was recognized by the National Business Coalition on Health (NBCH) as the #1 health plan in the nation.

Spectrum Health is aptly named because it brings together an entire spectrum of health services. These include seven nationally accredited hospitals and many services that meet the health care needs of the region. Four key areas – heart, orthopaedic, cancer and pediatric care – are centers of excellence at Spectrum Health.

Centers of Excellence

In health care, a center of excellence is a program that has distinguished itself as a leader through quality of care, innovation, research, teaching, specialized services, cutting-edge technology, and highly-skilled multidisciplinary teams.

Heart. With a long history of innovation and firsts, Spectrum Health has been the cardiovascular leader in West Michigan for more than 50 years. Today, at the Fred and

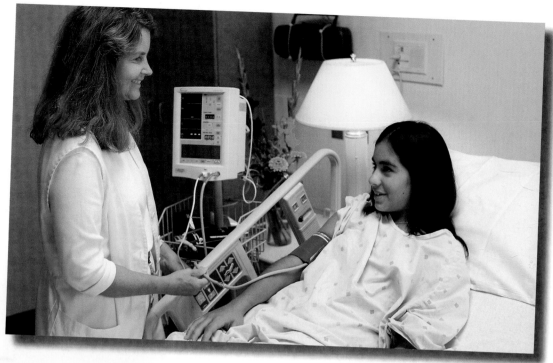

Lena Meijer Heart Center, nearly 60 specialists, including cardiologists, cardiac surgeons, pediatric cardiac surgeons, vascular surgeons, and interventional radiologists perform about 8,900 catheterization procedures and nearly 1,000 open heart surgeries each year.

Orthopaedics. Spectrum Health's excellence in orthopaedics dates back to advancements pioneered in the 1950s at Blodgett and Butterworth hospitals. Now one of the top 10 programs in the nation for volume of joint replacements, Spectrum Health's firsts in Michigan include new and effective minimally invasive hip replacement techniques and a new partial knee replacement procedure.

Today, Spectrum Health has a world-class multidisciplinary orthopaedics team that includes about 50 orthopaedic surgeons as well as dedicated orthopaedic nurses and rehabilitation specialists. They provide coordinated care from

patient education through surgery and rehabilitation.

Cancer. One of the largest accredited cancer services providers in the state, Spectrum Health has long been a cancer care leader. In fact, Spectrum Health annually diagnoses and treats the majority of all new cancer cases in Kent County and about 40 percent of all new cancer inpatients in its 13-county service area.

A destination for the most advanced clinical services available in the region, Spectrum Health operates four radiation therapy locations and offers a comprehensive array of

Excellence in patient care has earned Spectrum Health more than 50 national quality awards during the past 10 years.

"Since its inception in 1997, Spectrum Health has worked to earn a place high atop the ranks of the nation's medical field. It has won more than 50 national awards and multiple recognitions for innovation and leadership locally, regionally and nationally."

Spectrum Health employs more than 2,000 registered nurses who focus on providing exceptional experiences for patients and families.

therapeutic approaches. Spectrum Health's four multidisciplinary clinics provide an innovative

A $08 million renovation and expansion of Blodgett Hospital will result in 284 private rooms.

"Nurses are highly valued at Spectrum Health, which employs a large number of medical professionals, including more than 2,600 registered nurses."

option to patients facing treatment decisions for breast, gastrointestinal, lung, prostate or genitourinary cancers. The clinics bring together a team of medical specialists to coordinate patient evaluation and treatment planning. This saves time, lessens anxiety, speeds treatment, and ultimately may improve survival rates. The new Lemmen-Holton Cancer Pavilion, opening in 2008, will house outpatient sevices for the Spectrum Health cancer program.

Nurses are highly valued at Spectrum Health, which employs a large number of medical professionals, including more than 2,600 registered nurses. Using cutting-edge technology in state-of-the-art facilities, nurses are not only able to provide the highest quality of care for their patients, but they are also able to pursue their own personal

and professional goals. Flexible scheduling, career development opportunities, and scholarships for continued education all contribute to an environment that is as rewarding to the employee as it is to the patient.

Hospitals: A Community of Care

Blodgett Hospital has been actively serving the people of West Michigan for more than 150 years. It is known for its highly-regarded clinical programs and services, including the Center for Joint Replacement and digestive disease program as well as the regional burn center, which is the only one in West Michigan.

Spectrum Health is embarking on a $98 million plan for new construction and renovations at Blodgett Hospital in East Grand Rapids during the next three years. The project is intended to revitalize the facility as a leading community/teaching hospital and prepare for

anticipated increases in patient volumes in the coming years.

The plans call for a total of 284 private rooms along with many other improvements. A new 125,000-square-foot, five-story addition will include four patient care floors and one floor dedicated to mechanical equipment. The addition will house 120 private patient rooms along with new operating rooms.

Located in the center of downtown Grand Rapids, Butterworth Hospital is Spectrum Health's largest. It is classified as a Level 1 Trauma Center, which indicates that its staff and facilities are equipped to treat the most severe patient injuries and illnesses. Butterworth also has a busy Family Birthplace unit with nearly 8,000 babies delivered there each year.

Spectrum Health United Memorial has been a part of the system since 2003, and its legacy of care dates back to 1905. Through the United

Hospital in Greenville and Kelsey Hospital in Lakeview, community care is made very accessible to the residents of the Montcalm County area.

The new Hendrik & Gezina Meijer Surgery & Patient Care Center in Greenville was completed in 2006. The 55,000-square-foot surgery and patient care center was added onto the existing hospital and includes two surgery suites, a dedicated holding and recovery area, a fully equipped room in which physicians can perform less complex procedures, and a range of other technological and patient-care improvements.

Spectrum Health Reed City Hospital is a 25-bed acute care hospital. It received the 2006 and 2007 VHA Leadership Award for clinical excellence and the Total Benchmark Solution quality award for 2005. In addition, Reed City Hospital is a 10-star-rated Eden Alternative™ skilled nursing facility. It was the sixth

nursing home in Michigan to receive this special designation, which must be reviewed biannually to ensure continued accreditation.

hospice visits are made each year. Ongoing rehabilitation for patients who have sustained brain injury is a specialty of Spectrum Health Continuing Care.

Spectrum Health Reed City Hospital offers acute care services as well as an award winning nursing home.

Reed City Hospital also was the recipient of the 2006 Michigan Award of Excellence for improvement in quality measures. The facility was one of 31 nursing homes to receive this annual award of continued excellence and to be recognized by the state of Michigan, MPRO and Centers for Medicare & Medicaid Services (CMS).

The Kent Community Campus is the flagship location for Spectrum Health Continuing Care, which is the region's largest provider of long-term acute, rehabilitative, skilled nursing, residential and home care, serving more than 600 patients each day. More than 250,000 home care, rehabilitation, and

Kent Community Campus also houses the Spectrum Health Special Care Hospital, which is the only facility in Grand Rapids that specializes in long-term care for patients who are critically ill or injured. Patients receive high quality specialized care specific to their needs, which includes four to six hours of direct daily nursing care, as well as weekly meetings of the patients' team members so that the best approaches are always evaluated.

"Spectrum Health Reed City Hospital was the recipient of the 2006 Michigan Award of Excellence for improvement in quality measures."

Spectrum Health United Memorial recently opened its new 55,000-square-foot Hendrik & Gezina Meijer Surgery & Patient Care Center in Greenville.

205

The new Helen DeVos Children's Hospital will be completed in 2010.

"The goal of the children's hospital is to achieve leadership in comprehensive children's health care by establishing the highest standards in clinical effectiveness, operational efficiency, and personalized care for patients and their families."

A Commitment to Children's Health

Helen DeVos Children's Hospital, named for noted Michigan philanthropist Helen DeVos, was formed in 1993 and has since become a regional tertiary referral center at the forefront of the pediatric medical field. In addition to having top physicians and nurses, Helen DeVos Children's Hospital is also a teaching hospital, preparing medical students and residents for careers in caring for the health of children and their families.

Although its patients might be smaller than most, Helen DeVos Children's Hospital certainly has a big mission. As a referral center for 37 counties, Helen DeVos Children's Hospital admits more than 7,500 patients and receives over 150,000 outpatient visits each year, along with over 38,000 visits to the emergency department. Its radiology department—the only one for children in West Michigan— receives nearly 70,000 visits annually.

Helen DeVos Children's Hospital does not merely fulfill the region's need for specialized treatment for children, it also provides some of the best health care services on regional and national levels:

• The 95-bed neonatal intensive care unit is one of the largest neonatal centers in the U.S.

• Michigan's largest pediatric diabetes program

• One of the largest children's cancer and blood disorders programs in the Midwest

• The only bone marrow transplant program in West Michigan

At Helen DeVos Children's Hospital, 9,500 surgeries are performed each year because of the substantial number of specialists that work at the hospital.

Construction for the new Helen DeVos Children's Hospital began in 2006, with completion planned for 2010. The new Helen DeVos Children's Hospital will be the largest children's hospital in the region, and will bring services and specialists together under one roof. This facility will position Helen DeVos Children's Hospital to become one of the nation's leading children's hospitals. The goal of the hospital is to achieve leadership in comprehensive children's health care by establishing the highest standards in clinical effectiveness, operational efficiency, and personalized care for patients and their families.

Medical Education and Research

Medical education and research have always been priorities at Spectrum Health. Over the years, its hospitals have served as training grounds for countless medical students, resident physicians, nurse trainees and budding health professionals. Likewise, Spectrum Health's well-respected research department has offered clinical studies to thousands of patients for 30 years. Today, Spectrum Health is taking that commitment to a new level. Through several groundbreaking collaborations, Spectrum Health is helping to make Grand Rapids a national model for medical education and research development— with significant benefits to its patients.

West Michigan will soon have its own four-year

THE LEMMEN–HOLTON CANCER PAVILION & THE MICHIGAN STREET DEVELOPMENT

medical school thanks to the unique, multipartner collaboration with Michigan State University. Spectrum Health has pledged $55 million in building support for the project, plus $30 million toward research over the next decade.

Community Commitment

Spectrum Health is spending more each year on community benefit, which includes uncompensated Medicare and Medicaid reimbursement, as well as community outreach and health improvement programs. Spectrum Health provided $98.6 million in community benefit to West Michigan during its 2007 fiscal year. Uncompensated Medicaid and Medicare reimbursement constitutes the largest portion of Spectrum Health's community benefit dollars. In fiscal year 2007, uncompensated government care accounted for more than $74.3 million of the $98.6 million community benefit. In addition, $24.3 million went toward community outreach and health improvement programs. Spectrum Health dedicates $6 million of the $24.3 million to its Healthier Communities department, which annually serves more than 100,000 members of the community.

During the past 10 years, Healthier Communities has found ways to remove barriers to care to reach the underserved and at-risk members of our community.

In fact, in many ways, Healthier Communities is a catalyst for better health in West Michigan. The department has forged partnerships in multiple sectors of the community—other health care organizations, the government, police and fire departments, schools, not-for-profit agencies, religious organizations, neighborhood associations, Kent County Health Department, corporations, and private funders. The resulting relationships link people and programs to create a synergy of resources.

A lot goes into the successful completion of a building, and Siemens Building Technologies, Inc. is often a key player in the process. Part of Siemens, the 160-year-old German company, Siemens Building Technologies provides energy and environmental solutions, building control, fire safety, and security system solutions.

Siemens Building Technologies has 28,000 employees and operates from more than 500 locations in 51 countries. Headquartered in Buffalo Grove, Illinois, the United States division employs 7,200 people and has more than 100 locations across the country. One of those locations is in Wyoming, Michigan, where thirty-six engineers, technicians, sales people, and managers work at the West Michigan corporate branch office.

This office covers a broad area including Holland, Muskegon, Kalamazoo, parts of Lansing, and Traverse City. The local office staff is trained and certified for compliance, validation, and other programs, according to business development manager Michael J. Kirby, and personnel handle assessments of both existing facilities and new construction.

The division offers innovative facility management products and services for life science customers such as universities, the pharmaceutical industry, and research facilities including animal research, Kirby said. With such services, Siemens Building Technologies clients benefit from high quality environmental conditions in critical areas; minimized operational costs through monitoring and controlling environmental, equipment, and utility conditions; secure environments that protect staff, research integrity, product, and processes; and a safe and healthy work environment designed to minimize risk and liability. When it comes to meeting ever-changing regulations, reducing risk, and improving overall efficiency in the pharmaceutical and biotech fields, Siemens has a strong foundation to support its customers.

The global corporation Siemens has a long history of innovation, from transportation, industry, power, and automation to health care, communications, lighting, radio technology, and household appliances. The company is headquartered in Berlin and Munich and has some 475,000 employees worldwide. Customers can be found in more than 190 countries. And in 2006, the company had sales of €87.325 billion and a net income of €3.033 billion.

It all began in 1847 when inventor Werner Siemens and mechanical engineer Johann Georg Halske formed Telegraphen-Bauanstalt von Siemens & Halske in Germany to produce and market their patented pointer telegraph. From these early beginnings, the company went on to accrue more patents and supply telegraph lines across Germany, Great Britain, and Russia. In 1888, Siemens was raised to the nobility and became known as Werner von Siemens. The company weathered many storms over the years, from both World Wars, to the division of East and West Germany. Yet it continued to grow and strengthen, building a mighty corporation that stretches from Germany to Argentina, Saudi Arabia, Australia, and yes, Wyoming, Michigan.

"Siemens Building Technologies clients benefit from high quality environmental conditions in critical areas; minimized operational costs through monitoring and controlling environmental, equipment, and utility conditions; secure environments that protect staff, research integrity, product, and processes; and a safe and healthy work environment designed to minimize risk and liability."

Comerica Bank

A good bank offers more than financial services; it exceeds the customer's expectations with top-tier service.

"Comerica is a relationship bank that focuses on people and a complete understanding of an organization and its needs," said Joe Davio, regional president of Comerica Bank in West Michigan.

When it comes to working with businesses, "We make sure we understand the management team of a company, which includes their philosophy, business plan, strategies, and their hopes and dreams," Davio said. Additionally, "our consistent lending policies give us the ability to provide financing to companies in both strong and weak economic times. We have the ability to do that because of the depth and experience of our staff and our industry knowledge."

With more than 150 years of banking experience, Comerica Bank certainly knows its industry. The bank began in downtown Detroit, Michigan, in 1849 as the Detroit Savings Fund Institute. By the 1870s, it had more than $1 million in resources and was reorganized as the Detroit Savings Bank. As the company grew, branch offices opened throughout the city and suburban areas in southeast Michigan. In the early 1980s, the bank became Comerica, Inc. Michigan laws changed in 1985 to allow statewide branch banking, and Comerica offices spread across the state. West Michigan presence began in 1977 with the purchase of Kentwood National Bank, Kentwood, Michigan. In 1991, Comerica, Inc., merged with Manufacturers National Corporation to become one of the country's largest bank holding firms, with assets of $26.8 billion. Today, Comerica also has bank offices in California, Arizona, Texas, and Florida, as well as representative offices in several other states and internationally. Total assets at the end of 2006 were $58.0 billion.

A corporate headquarters move from Detroit to Dallas, Texas, which was announced in early 2007, will not change the Comerica focus. "Comerica is committed to Michigan for the long run," Davio said. "We employ over 7,000 people in the state, and we will continue to grow and to serve people, businesses, and our communities."

As part of Comerica's big picture, the West Michigan regional offices offer their customers all the banking services they could expect. "We provide first-tier service to businesses, business owners, and their employees. This means not only the traditional checking and savings accounts but also mortgages, student loans, consumer loans, and investment services," said Davio, who joined Comerica in 1985 and has more than 30 years of banking experience.

Comerica employs more than 360 people in West Michigan. "Our competitive advantage is the experience level of our people and their drive to service their clientele," Davio said. "Our people know our customers, and we receive excellent marks on various surveys. Customers are loyal to us, and we are loyal to them."

Amid the changing Michigan economy, Davio sees strength in West Michigan. "The economic health of the region is strong

Joe Davio, Regional Bank President

"We make sure we understand the management team of a company, which includes their philosophy, business plan, strategies, and their hopes and dreams."

Advisory Board of Directors, Grand Rapids/Holland Region

Comerica Bank Grand Rapids, Michigan

and continuing to adjust to more service and less manufacturing," he said. "However, manufacturing is also adjusting and will remain an important part of this economy, supporting the Michigan Medical Mile and other health, life science, and technology initiatives."

He continued, "West Michigan is a great place to do business because of the people that make up our communities. There is a can-do attitude present throughout the communities with a strong entrepreneurial spirit. The large number of family-owned businesses in this community makes the difference."

Davio also noted that the community is second in the nation philanthropically on a per capita basis. Comerica has contributed to that reputation, too, by supporting the arts, education, charitable

organizations, and business associations through cash contributions and its employees serving on boards of nonprofits and volunteering at various fund-raising events. These include United Way, the Grand Rapids Symphony, area Chambers of Commerce, the Grand Rapids Public Schools, and many more.

Comerica supports employee volunteerism through volunteer leadership grants, a Volunteer-of-the-Year program, and by matching employee donations to various organizations, including God's Kitchen and Baxter Community Center in Grand Rapids.

The Comerica advisory board for the West Michigan region is comprised of individuals with strong local connections and plenty of board experience, too. As of

2007, the board consisted of Micki Benz, vice president of Community Development for Saint Mary's Health Care; John D. Bouwer, a local independent business consultant; Harvey Gainey, chairman, president, and principal owner of Gainey Corporation; Brian Harris, the majority owner and CEO of H & H Metal Source; Richard Postma, chairman and chief executive officer of US Signal Company, L.L.C.; Rob Sligh, Jr., chairman, CEO, and majority owner of Sligh Furniture Company; and Norma Van Kuiken, a member of the Grand Rapids Ballet advisory board and co-chair of the Ballet's capital campaign.

In the end, Davio said, "Our mission: 'We are in Business to Help People be Successful' and our slogan: 'We Listen. We Understand. We Make It Work' say it all.

"Our mission: 'We are in Business to Help People be Successful' and our slogan: 'We Listen. We Understand. We Make It Work' say it all."

Davenport University is known for preparing

Davenport University's main campus opened in Caledonia Township in September 2005.

"Students who are serious about practical education and career goals choose Davenport University."

graduates for in-demand careers in business, technology, and health professions. With a mission of educating individuals to excel in the knowledge-driven environment of the 21st century, Davenport continues to introduce degree programs that are among the first of their kind in the state and nation.

Academic Leadership

With a dedication to academic excellence at its core, Davenport University aggressively develops leading edge degrees. Davenport was among the first universities in the country to offer degrees in network and biometric security. Addressing the economic shift from manufacturing to services, Davenport was the first university in Michigan to offer a degree in services management and marketing. Other degrees or specialties that prepare students for the hottest emerging careers include computer gaming and simulation, forensic accounting, and health information management. Students attend Davenport University to prepare for careers, and Davenport prides itself on preparing students to hit the ground running in the real world.

Start. Stay. Succeed

Davenport's approach to serving students with quality can be summed up with "Start. Stay. Succeed."SM To ensure students get the best start, the university admits only those students whose academic records demonstrate their potential to prosper in higher learning. Davenport helps students stay through graduation with a learning environment that features individual attention from staff and faculty, a focus on career goals, financial assistance, and various

activities from clubs to sports that help students connect outside the classroom. The ultimate measure of success is for students to graduate and go on to rewarding careers.

Davenport University President Randolph K. Flechsig.

Accomplished Students

Students who are serious about practical education and career goals choose Davenport University. Members of student organizations such

as Business Professionals of America and Delta Epsilon Chi International consistently take home first-place trophies from state, national, and international competitions. Many of our student athletes are academic all-stars.

Building on a Rich Tradition

The Lady Panthers basketball team won their league championship in 2007 and in 2000 scored the highest combined GPA of any team in their national athletic association.

Davenport University has pioneered a rich tradition of practical education that spans more than 140 years. Davenport continues to

build on that tradition, today offering more than 70 degrees in business, technology and health professions, an MBA and a Master of Science degree. Appointed president in 2000, Randolph Flechsig has

provided a distinct vision and innovative leadership. Davenport University is accredited by the Higher Learning Commission, North Central Association of Colleges and Schools.

New Main Campus

Davenport University serves thousands of students at its main campus, the W.A. Lettinga Campus in Caledonia Township. The campus includes the Richard DeVos and Jay Van Andel Academic Center, Peter and Pat Cook Residence Hall and Sneden Library Information Commons. The campus is environmentally efficient, and the modern buildings are filled with natural light

and open space. Buildings feature the latest technology, a corporate environment, and a design that encourages interaction among students and faculty. A student center and field house will open in fall 2008.

Today's Davenport University

Today's Davenport University is a destination of choice for bright, career-minded students. The University is focused on the growth and continuing quality of academic programs that make it an extraordinary value in private education. Davenport University Online also serves a growing number of students from across the country and around the world. Some 13,000 students are enrolled at the main campus in Grand Rapids and at locations throughout Michigan and in northern Indiana.

Recreational and social activities are an important part of campus life and the learning experience at Davenport's main campus.

"The University is focused on the growth and continuing quality of academic programs that make it an extraordinary value in private education."

Huntington Bank has a way of making customers feel truly at home, not like they are just an account number. Each banking office evokes a small-bank feeling, although in actuality, your friendly neighborhood office

West Michigan headquarters building at 50 Monroe in Grand Rapids.

was opened in Columbus, Ohio by P.W. Huntington and his staff in 1866. In 1905 it was incorporated as The Huntington National Bank of Columbus. Over the next century, Huntington grew steadily in Ohio, merging with and acquiring

Huntington Bancshares extends selective services nationally, including Dealer Sales offices in Arizona, Florida, Georgia, Nevada, New Jersey, New York, North Carolina, Pennsylvania, South Carolina, and Tennessee; Mortgage Banking in Maryland and New Jersey; and Private Financial Group offices in Florida. Huntington operates over 100 banking offices in Michigan, with 69 in West Michigan alone.

From 2002 through 2006, Huntington Bank in West Michigan has seen a steady increase in both loans and deposits. A 34 percent increase in total loans plus a 15 percent increase in total deposits represent an overall growth of $1 billion during this five-year period alone. As a result, shareholders also reap the profit of the improvement in business performance, with a 56 percent increase in Huntington dividends.

is part of a much larger corporation with over 140 years of customer service. But don't let the $55 billion in total assets fool you; the local Huntington Bank that you've known for years is still small enough to care, but has the national resources to really take care of you.

A Local Bank with National Resources

Although Huntington Bank has been a financial fixture in West Michigan since the 1990s, its first office

other banks and eventually spreading into other states, including Indiana, Kentucky, West Virginia, and Michigan.

Today, Huntington Bancshares Incorporated is a regional bank holding company with $55 billion in total assets. It operates more than 700 regional banking offices throughout Indiana, Kentucky, West Virginia, Pennsylvania, Ohio, and Michigan, in addition to offering financial services via the Internet, a 24-hour telephone bank, and its network of over 1,400 ATMs.

A Great Place to Bank and an Even Better Place to Work

Despite its impressive assets and nation-wide service network, Huntington Bank is very much a local bank. Superior customer service is at the very center of the bank's philosophy, which is upheld by the values of teamwork, communication,

The new banking office prototype, now open at Bayberry Plaza in Byron Center.

accountability, service, diversity, and passion. These six values have proven to be the right combination for success judging by the annual awards Huntington has received from Greenwich Associates, who recognize excellence in business. Huntington was given the National and Regional Awards for Overall Customer Satisfaction and the National Award for Branch Service Performance. The team at Huntington Bank is especially proud of these awards, since they directly represent customers' opinions of its services.

Many Huntington employees find that working to make customers happy also creates a desirable work environment. For three years running, Huntington Bank has been recognized by the Michigan Business & Professional Association (MBPA) as one of the "101 Best and Brightest Companies to Work for" in West Michigan. Additionally in 2005, Huntington was singled out by the MBPA as an Elite Award Winner for its superior work in corporate and associate communications. This special recognition proves that not only does Huntington Bank form strong relationships with its customers, but it does so with its employees as well. Employee retention rates have seen a steady increase since 1999, reaching higher than 81 percent associate retention in recent years.

Stepping Outside the Office and into the Community

When people talk of a bank's assets, they are usually referring to things like stocks, bonds, and money market accounts. But if you are talking about Huntington Bank, there is another important asset to add to the list: people. Through its Community Partners program, Huntington Bank is able to reach out to the West Michigan community by contributing to and volunteering for some of the region's worthiest causes.

Since 2001, Huntington Bank has invested over $5 million in its Community Partners initiatives. Dozens of West Michigan organizations have benefited from a portion of these funds. From arts and culture to education and healthcare, Huntington has proven its varied interests in serving the community (see sidebar).

Although monetary investments are certainly a major facet of Huntington's community programs, banking office employees have also been known to donate their spare time as volunteers. Huntington employees volunteer to help with many programs throughout the community including donning work boots and tool belts to pitch-in with Habitat for Humanity to build homes for low-income families in Kent County.

Huntington Bank employees are well on their way to making West Michigan a better place to live, but if they ever needed inspiration, they need only look to Jim Dunlap, president of the West Michigan region of the bank. He is chairman of the board for Heart of West Michigan United Way, The Right Place, Inc., and the YMCA. He is also a board member of Meijer Gardens and Sculpture Park, West Michigan Strategic Alliance, Grand Rapids Convention and Visitors Bureau, Grand Rapids Symphony, and

"Many Huntington employees find that working to make customers happy also creates a desirable work environment. For three years running, Huntington Bank has been recognized by the Michigan Business & Professional Association (MBPA) as one of the "101 Best and Brightest Companies to Work for" in West Michigan."

Being active in the communities that you serve defines Huntington's local bank mission.

Grand Rapids Chamber of Commerce Regional Issues Committee.

Investing in the Future of West Michigan

West Michigan enjoys a strong economy thanks to businesses like Huntington Bank. In order to maintain this prosperity, it is necessary to embark on initiatives that will secure West Michigan both as a regional and national business competitor. Health care remains a special interest of Huntington Bank, as seen by one of its most recent initiatives, the "City on the Hill" project. City on the Hill is a $120 million healthcare complex that is being constructed on Michigan Street in Grand Rapids. Because of its expertise in commercial real estate as well as the health care sector, Huntington was chosen to be a financial partner in this endeavor. In the last decade, West Michigan has truly put itself on the map when it comes to serving the health care industry.

Another special interest of Huntington is to provide business development opportunities for women. Huntington Bank's Women's Initiative began in 2003 as a way to allow businesswomen to network and form key relationships that would enhance women-owned businesses in the community. In 2004, Huntington was recognized with the Women's Resource Center Employer Recognition Award, which is given to West Michigan-region companies that strive to improve the workplace and offer advancement opportunities for working women.

Whether your next trip to Huntington Bank is to sign for a mortgage loan or to grab some cash from the ATM for a night out, rest assured that you will receive the same excellent customer service that has been a part of P.W. Huntington's legacy for more than a century.

Since 2001, Huntington Bank has invested $5 million with its Community Partners, proving that it has many diverse interests when it comes to sustaining the city of Grand Rapids. These Community Partners include:

American Cancer Society
Aquinas College
Calvin College
DeVos Children's Hospital
Dwelling Place
Economic Club of West Michigan
Ferris State University
Grand Rapids Area Chamber of Commerce
Grand Rapids Ballet
Grand Rapids Community College
Grand Rapids Opera
Grand Rapids Symphony
Grand Valley State University
Grandville Arts Academy
Guiding Light Mission
Hope Network
John Ball Zoo
Junior Achievement
Metro Health
Michigan Women's Foundation
Neighborhood Ventures
Spectrum Health
St. Cecilia
St. John's Home
St. Mary's Hospice
United Way
Van Andel Institute
Van Andel Public Museum
Van Singel Performing Arts
Western Michigan University
Women's Resource Center
WOOD TV8—Commitment to Community
YMCA
YWCA

The YMCA of Greater Grand Rapids has become a social centerpiece for the communities it

The vision of the YMCA of Greater Grand Rapids is to be the community leader in building strong kids, strong families, and strong

confidence. Its core values of Respect, Responsibility, Honesty, and Caring are found in every soccer game, swimming lesson, or after school program. The YMCA of Greater Grand Rapids builds strong kids, one at a time, and has had impressive success with its programs in giving kids the tools they need to make positive choices. For example, 94 percent of teens involved in YMCA programs have chosen not to smoke cigarettes and 97 percent of teens involved in YMCA programs have chosen to stay away from drugs.

With the opening of two, state-of-the-art facilities—the David D. Hunting YMCA and the Wolverine World Wide Family YMCA—and the introduction of cutting-edge, non-traditional YMCA program offerings, such as arts and humanities, music lessons, dance, mentoring, and ESL (English as a Second Language) classes, the YMCA of Greater Grand Rapids increased its membership from 22,000 to 46,000 in 2006.

The 150,000 square foot David D. Hunting YMCA is one of the largest urban YMCAs in the USA, and the first-ever L.E.E.D.-certified YMCA for its environmental efficiency.
Photo Credit: Justin Maconochie

"The vision and goal of the YMCA of Greater Grand Rapids is to be the community leader in building strong kids, strong families, and strong communities."

The David D. Hunting YMCA features two, family-friendly aquatic facilities – a family fun pool and a competitive lap pool, suited for members of all ages.
Photo Credit: Mark Thomas

serves by providing family-friendly opportunities and programs for people of all ages. Founded in 1866, the mission of the YMCA of Greater Grand Rapids is to put Christian principles into practice through programs that build healthy spirit, mind, and body for all. Its mission is thoroughly inclusive—no one is ever turned away because of inability to pay. Through the Strong Kids Campaign, Heart of West Michigan United Way, grants, and donations, the YMCA provided over $4 million in 2006 to financially assist individuals and families with memberships, programs, and child care.

communities. Through various programs offered at its seven branches and a year-round camping facility, the YMCA promotes the development of character, with a special focus on youth.

YMCA programs focus on building teamwork, self-esteem, and self-

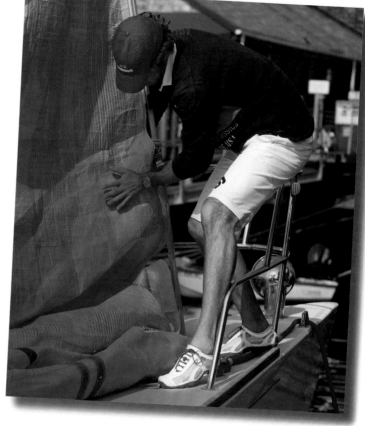

against a softening in one or two footwear segments.

Bates, for example, is a leading supplier of footwear to the U.S. military and private sector companies, while Harley Davidson offers bold, sexy—and functional—footwear to a very different market. Hush Puppies remains Wolverine's most international brand with its iconic Bassett Hound residing in the closets of consumers in 135 markets around the world. Sebago is a leading supplier of marine footwear, while Merrell covers a range of high-performance shoes, for hiking on the trail or in the city.

In spring 2007, Wolverine released the first Patagonia-branded footwear to complement the well-known line of eco-friendly outdoor wear. Another new strategic direction is the development of apparel collections to add to selected footwear lines. The

Wolverine brand has a line of "rugged casual, performance-oriented" apparel targeted to its market. In autumn 2007, Merrell apparel will reach the market place combining the brands unique blend of performance and style.

New Global Strategy

Moving into its third century, Wolverine has the same dynamism and progressive outlook that launched the company in 1883. Its vision now reaches beyond footwear and beyond borders and is expressed in its vision statement, which reads "to excite consumers around the world with innovative footwear and apparel that bring style to purpose."

In 2006, Wolverine launched Project 2.0, which is meant to guide the company to the next level—past the $2 billion mark in revenue. This growth will be fueled by continued focus and development of its core footwear brands, by building on the momentum created by its new initiatives—Merrell apparel and Patagonia footwear, by increasing operational efficiencies, and finally, by actively enhancing its global retail presence. Wolverine now owns eighty-two stores around the world, along with a growing Internet business. With its retail partners, Wolverine brands are showcased in 2,300 shop-in-shops and 400 concept stores internationally.

That presence translates into a global operation that employs some 4,500 workers with sales of 47 million pairs of shoes in some 180 countries, creating 1.142 billion in revenue.

While pondering whether to go into the business back in 1883, Wolverine's founder, G.A. Krause, is purported to have said: "There is some opportunity here." Even he could not have anticipated that opportunity would lead the company he began.

"There is some opportunity here." Even he could not have anticipated that opportunity would lead the company he began.

Ever since its founding in 1884, Ferris State University has been known as a school that equips its students for success

University founder, Michigan governor and U.S. Senator Woodbridge N. Ferris started his educational institution with an initial class of 15 students in 1884.

"No requirements were demanded for admission except a willingness to work early and late."

Ferris State University today enrolls more than 12,000 students system-wide.

in the real world. From its inception, the school attracted "lumberjacks, miners, farmers' sons and daughters, and girls who worked in Michigan factories." Its first classes, taught by Woodbridge Ferris and his wife, Helen, were in English and bookkeeping.

Although Ferris envisioned a school in which "education should involve the training of the head, the heart, and the hand," he understood that the students who came to him needed a practical education they could use to improve their lives. And, since this private school also needed to attract students in order to remain in business, Ferris

Industrial School targeted its curriculum to appeal to those nontraditional students.

"In due time men and women who, for some cause had missed getting even an elementary education, discovered that they could satisfy their ambition at a school organized primarily for their benefit," writes Ferris in his autobiography. "No requirements were demanded for admission except a willingness to work early and late."

Thus, in addition to an ongoing emphasis on preparing teachers, the first programs added to the curriculum were stenography and pharmacy. In fact, Ferris taught his first pharmacy student from a state handbook. Today, Ferris State University still has the largest pharmacy program in Michigan.

"Our heritage is

about creating access and opportunity," says David L. Eisler, president. "These have been our core values since our very beginning."

Trials and Setbacks

Ferris Institute survived, albeit not without struggle, through political and economic turbulence as well as through local upheavals. In 1949, the State of Michigan finally decided to assume governance of the private school. The bill was signed by Governor G. Mennen Williams with the formal takeover set to occur the following year.

Unfortunately, tragedy struck early that year. On the evening of February 21, 1950, a fire broke out in an air shaft in Old Main, one of the school's original buildings. The fire quickly spread to the old Pharmacy building, and before the night was over, the institute was virtually destroyed. The newer Alumni building was the only major facility left standing.

Despite the uncertainty as to the future of the

institute, students and teachers immediately began cleanup efforts, converting student dormitories into classrooms; friends of the institute donated supplies, laboratory equipment, books. Within a week, 600 students returned to classes that had resumed in every nook and cranny of the school. On July 1, 1950, the State of Michigan quietly assumed control of one of Michigan's oldest colleges.

At the time, Ferris was primarily a vocational school that also provided a high school education to nontraditional students. Under the guidance of its new president, Victor Spathelf, Ferris State College began to expand.

In 1959, the college was accredited by the North Central Association of Colleges and Schools, which established its credibility as an academic institution and facilitated the acceptance of its credits at other institutions. In 1987, Ferris State College officially became Ferris State University.

Continuing the Heritage

Today, Ferris continues its heritage of preparing students for successful careers. "It does students no good to give them degrees they can't use," says Eisler.

And in fact, 98 percent of students who graduate from Ferris find work in their field. "That's an extraordinary statistic," says Eisler.

Contributing to that success are the close links Ferris maintains with leaders in business and industry throughout the state. Advisory committees of business leaders oversee the development of Ferris programs, and Ferris graduates are found in business and industry throughout the state.

Ferris' College of Allied Health Sciences, for example, staffs hospitals, not only with nurses, but also with radiologists, respiratory therapists, and healthcare

administrators, among other specialties. And its College of Business offers degrees in golf management, tennis management and hospitality management. A student can get a four-year degree in welding technology or in heating and refrigeration. The university also has the largest criminal justice program in the state. It

offers two doctoral degree programs in pharmacy and optometry.

So, while the college provides a well-rounded liberal arts education, its emphasis remains firmly on professional degree programs. In addition to the traditional four-year bachelor degree, Ferris also offers two-year associate

The Granger Center for Construction and HVACR is a state-of-the-art learning center for students in the College of Technology.

"It does students no good to give them degrees they can't use," says Eisler.

More than 120 years after its founding, Ferris State University continues to have a student-to-faculty ratio of about 15:1.

Ferris' main campus in Big Rapids today occupies more than 880 acres.

Ferris' College of Allied Health Sciences is preparing the next generation of health professionals.

Ferris' athletic teams, the Bulldogs, compete in a wide range of sports, including football, soccer, men's and women's basketball, golf, tennis, volleyball and NCAA Division-I ice hockey.

degrees that can "ladder" into four-year programs.

State Networks

In recent years, Ferris has brought its unique degree programs to satellite campuses throughout the state. So, not only do traditional students come from every county in the state to attend Ferris at its main campus in Big Rapids, but the university has also expanded its outreach to remote locations as well.

By partnering with community colleges, Ferris offers many of its four-year degree programs in various locations across the state, from Escanaba to Dearborn to online classes as well. A student can get an associate degree from a local community college and continue on to earn a bachelor's degree from Ferris at the same institution. Ferris coordinates with the community college on the transfer of credits, and it uses the college's facilities to bring its specialized expertise to more than twenty locations across the state.

"With the unique degrees we offer, it's easy to see why there is a need for what we do," says Eisler. "These programs are cost-efficient and help students who are place-bound." In this way, a student from Dowagiac can earn a master's degree in education or a student from Traverse City can get a bachelor's degree in accountancy right at his or her local community college.

"We really serve two distinct clientele," says Eisler. "The average age on our Big Rapids campus is 23, while the average age of students at our satellite locations is 32." Ferris addresses the needs of both populations because it also offers two-year degree programs at the Big Rapids campus. In addition, 43 percent of new students enter Ferris with associate

degrees. So, the university understands well the needs of community colleges and the students who attend them and is adept at seamlessly integrating its degree programs with those of community colleges around the state.

And a City Campus

In addition to its satellite locations, Ferris serves an urban student population at its second campus in downtown Grand Rapids. Ferris has expanded its close partnership with Grand Rapids Community College to create a full-fledged city campus complete with student housing and Ferris' unique degree offerings.

Enhancing its presence in Grand Rapids is the university's merger with Kendall College of Art and Design. "Kendall is the preeminent furniture design program in the country as well as having strong programs in graphic and industrial design and the fine arts," says Eisler. "Now we have a school for working artists in Grand Rapids."

Main Campus

Yet, Ferris State University's anchor and focus remains its main campus in Big Rapids. Every fall approximately 10,000 students enroll in programs on the main campus from all quadrants of Michigan— about one-third from the Grand Rapids area, another third from the Detroit Metropolitan area and the final third from every county in the state. They come for a traditional residential college experience. "It's a welcoming, safe environment that helps

connect students with success," says Eisler. In addition, more than 2,000 students enroll in off-campus programs, bringing Ferris' total enrollment to its highest level in history at 12,575 students during the fall of 2006. To that end, Ferris offers these students a quality education with lots of faculty oversight—classes are small (averaging about 15 students) and are taught by professional faculty, not graduate assistants. The university offers a full palette of degrees—more than 170 programs at all levels, from two-year associate degrees to a variety of post-graduate programs.

The signature building on campus is the Ferris Library for Information, Technology and Education, a $40 million, state-of-the-art facility. FLITE, which opened in 2001, bridges the old-school library model with stacks of books and periodicals with the wired and digital library of the future. Architecturally, the building creates a campus focal point. It represents a repository of knowledge that is both extensive and dynamic. Beyond housing traditional print materials, the library is meant to create open, flexible space for a variety of uses. It is comfortable and welcoming for users, providing spaces for studying, meeting and learning.

In addition to FLITE, the Granger Center for

Construction and HVACR is Ferris' newest building. Dedicated in 2004, the 45,000 square foot addition to the Construction Technology Center expands and provides room for the state-of-the-art heating and cooling systems that give students a hands-on education in geothermal and other systems.

Looking Ahead

Woodbridge Ferris would hardly recognize the modest private school he struggled to maintain in a remote corner of Michigan. But he would surely appreciate his school's effort to retain the educational approach he believed in.

More than a century later, Ferris State University continues to satisfy the ambition of students at every stage of life by equipping them for success.

Dedicated in 2001, the Ferris Library for Information, Technology and Education houses special archival collections, banks of computers for student use and also is a patent and trademark depository library.

Woodbridge N. Ferris remains a constant presence on the Big Rapids campus.

Many Graphic Design students at Ferris take on work for corporate and nonprofit clients – including Grand Rapids' 5/3 River Bank Run – during their senior year.

Located in the heart of Grand Rapids, Ferris State University's "second campus" has its finger on the pulse of west Michigan and its eye on

In 2004, Ferris State University opened new apartments for students in downtown Grand Rapids.

FSU-GR's Digital Animation and Game Design program has been a huge success with students and employers alike.

the future. It serves the needs of working adults as well as traditional students with strong programs in established fields such as construction management and healthcare, while staying agile and entrepreneurial enough to respond quickly to academic and marketplace needs.

"We're really focused on practical applications that would meet the needs of the labor market," says Vice Chancellor Don Green. "And we're also developing programs for the next generation in the labor market."

That next generation of employers might be looking for the imaging skills of graduates from Ferris-Grand Rapids' popular Digital Animation and Game Design program, for example. Ferris is the only university in the state to offer this program. Employers might also be

Operated in conjunction with Grand Rapids Community College, the Applied Technology Center is a convenient location for busy professionals pursuing degrees to advance their careers.

looking for well-rounded, technically competent graduates—like those in the Industrial Technology and Management program.

Through its partnership with Grand Rapids Community College (GRCC) and by drawing on the resources at Spectrum Health and St. Mary's Hospital, Ferris-Grand Rapids offers bachelor's degrees in several forward-looking healthcare programs. These include information management ("Someone has to manage patient records and billing," says Green. "That is a huge program for us."), respiratory therapy and nuclear medicine.

Partnering for Education

In addition to developing practical and applicable degree programs, Ferris-Grand Rapids also represents a solid partnership with GRCC. While Ferris-Grand Rapids maintains an identity as a city campus with the ability to serve both traditional and working students with a variety of classes, it is co-located with GRCC in the Applied Technology Center. Ferris-Grand Rapids works closely

with GRCC to offer students a variety of options for earning a degree at the most affordable price.

The university offers 2+2 and 3+1 options whereby a student attends GRCC for two or three years (at community college prices) and finishes his or her degree at Ferris-Grand Rapids at the same location with a no-hassle, seamless transfer of credits. "We work very hard to build degree programs that allow for as much transferability from GRCC as we can," says Green. "If you can get your coursework from a community college, you cut the cost of a degree program dramatically."

And while most students at Ferris-Grand Rapids commute to school, the campus is creating a culture for the traditional, residential student as well. To that end, comfortable, roomy student apartments are available near campus and in the heart of downtown Grand Rapids.

Whether a student is finishing a bachelor's degree in the middle of a career or looking for a full-fledged residential campus experience, Ferris-Grand Rapids offers the best of both worlds.

Kendall College of Art and Design of Ferris State University

For over 75 years, Kendall College of Art and Design has been preparing students to become working artists. "The Kendall mission has always been very simple: We prepare our students for professional lives as artists and designers," says Oliver Evans, president. Indeed, the college has fulfilled its mission so successfully, and its programs are so respected that 90 percent of its graduates find just such work.

The David Wolcott Kendall School of Art opened its doors to its first 35 students in 1931. Named in honor of the renowned designer and "Dean of American Furniture," Kendall's two-year art fundamentals program became so popular that the most serious challenge the school has encountered over the years has been lack of space for its burgeoning student population.

In 1981, Kendall College of Design became an accredited, degree-granting institution, offering four-year Bachelor of Fine Arts programs. After years of outgrowing facilities, Kendall College moved to its present location in downtown Grand Rapids in 1984, where it has graced the area with a touch of class and vitality.

A Union of Two Institutions

As the century waned, it became obvious that the college needed access to more academic resources and expanded student services in order to retain its preeminence among design schools. At that point, Ferris State University was also seeking to expand its 25-year presence in Grand Rapids. A union of the two institutions seemed to enhance the capabilities of both.

Ferris brought educational programs and operational efficiencies to Kendall. Art students at Kendall now have access to a much broader choice of degree programs, such as art education. And Kendall brings unique resources to Ferris as well, such as adding classes in design to its two-year architecture program.

In addition, the similarity of their missions blended well. "It was a good marriage because the two institutions complement and add value to each other," says Evans. "We both have an overriding sense of mission in preparing people for professional lives."

Into the Future…

Ongoing innovation, such as the interface of technology and design, provides opportunity for future generations of Kendall students, as does the continual need for good design in many industries. As it has in the past, Kendall maintains its close ties with business and industry, and continues to adapt its programs to the realities of the working world its students enter.

"The focus at Kendall has always been on responding to the world and paying attention to what that world is expecting," says Evans.

Ferris' Kendall College of Art and Design, named for David Wolcott Kendall, the "Dean of American Furniture Designers," was made possible through the generosity of his widow, Helen Kendall.

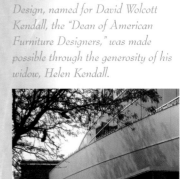

Kendall College of Art and Design is one of Ferris' fastest-growing colleges.

Kendall expanded its academic offerings to include Master's of Fine Arts degrees in 2003.

American Seating has been providing seats internationally for

American Seating's first product innovation, the combination student-desk, has been in classrooms for over a century.

"American Seating's strength lies in the skills and experience of our people and in the design and manufacture of our products," said Ed Clark, Chairman of American Seating.

schools, baseball parks, churches, historic theaters, modern auditoriums, and city buses for more than a century. The Grand Rapids corporation began as Grand Rapids School Furniture Company in 1886, but it soon diversified beyond student desk-chair sets. In 1889, the company entered the entertainment industry. By 1892, the company was manufacturing the most seating products in the world. In 1926, it became the American Seating Company.

The company has made a tradition out of being on the forefront of the

industry. "American Seating's strength lies in the skills and experience of our people and in the design and manufacture of our products," said Ed Clark, Chairman of American Seating.

Today, American Seating's offerings fit into two areas: Architectural Environments, including seats for stadiums, auditoriums, classrooms, and contract office furniture and, since the 1950s, transportation seating on buses, motor coaches, and railway cars across the United States and Canada.

The Architectural Environments products, too, are seating folks regionally and internationally. Just a few of the locations are the Radio City Music Hall in New York, the U.S. Senate, numerous locations at Yale University and stadiums and ballparks including Wrigley Field, Comerica Park in Detroit, Dodger's Stadium in Los Angeles, and the new, 42,500-seat Busch Stadium in St. Louis. Internationally there are the Venetian Macao in Macau, Japan, and Parque O'Higgins in Santiago, Chile who also offer quality seating to their guests.

Baseball fans have been filling American Seating stadium seats since 1912 when the company first supplied chairs to Fenway Park, home of the Boston Red Sox. Chicago White

Sox fans have been rooting for their team in American Seating chairs quite a while, too – beginning at Comiskey Park in 1916 and then at the 36,000-seat U.S. Cellular Field. And American Seating was also involved in Hurricane Katrina cleanup efforts in New Orleans, when it helped to restore seating at the New Orleans Superdome, where American Seating had originally furnished seats when the structure opened in 1975.

Since it introduced the first tilt-back opera chair in 1893, the company has developed numerous products to stay at the forefront of the industry. "In good and tough economic times, the folks of West Michigan continue to show resilience and the ability to look forward to the future," Tom Bush, President of American Seating, said. "The region is struggling in certain manufacturing sectors, and also evolving. To survive, companies must continue to lead through innovation, solid strategic planning, and creativity."

American Seating product innovations include the first three-quarter safety fold stadium seat, blow-molded plastic seats, Visually Redirected Seating, waterproof aisle lights, and the first heated outdoor stadium seat. With one of its newest products, the patent-pending InSight™ public transit seat, American Seating provides the industry's largest personal sitting area as well as increased legroom and back height, and advanced ergonomics.

Staying ahead of industry trends has kept this now privately owned company healthy for more than 120 years. It has survived many challenges over the years, from the Great Depression to wartime, the post-WWII boom to the oil crisis of the 1970s. Still based at its longtime headquarters northwest of downtown Grand Rapids, American Seating employs some 500 workers.

"As a longtime resident of the Grand Rapids manufacturing community, we have, and will continue to benefit from, a highly stable and solid workforce that is also able to adapt to changing market demands," Clark said.

Although the production of all kinds of chairs and seating has been the company's mainstay, during World War II, it also manufactured aircraft wings for airplane trainers. Other wartime products included pilot ejection seats, tank and combat vehicle seats, and a

daily output of 10,000 folding chairs.

In addition to adapting to market conditions, the company has always lived within its community. "Being a good corporate citizen is very important to our company, and that includes community service. Beyond the practical benefits to us as an employer, it is simply the right thing to do. Our continued investment in improvements to our west side location is indicative of our long term commitment to the community," Clark said.

That commitment includes caring for the natural environment. The company has been working on reducing the use of solvent-based adhesives and has eliminated the use of solvent-based paints and coatings. All scrap metal, stainless steel, and used oil is reclaimed or recycled, and when possible, plastic seating materials from stadium re-construction projects is reclaimed, melted down, and made into usable materials.

American Seating Corporate Headquarters, Grand Rapids, Michigan.

The company works on its impact in the region in other ways, too. "American Seating employees continue to volunteer, conduct fund raising, and look for ways to give back to the community," Clark said. "Many of our employees grew up in Grand Rapids, and on the west side. Whether it is working with Student of the Month programs at Eastern Elementary School, Grand Rapids Junior Achievement, or holiday sponsorships, our employees show a sustained interest in helping. We are proud of them!"

After some 120 years, the company has certainly earned the right to be proud of itself, too, in its steady, positive presence in the Grand Rapids community and in the seating industry.

"As a longtime resident of the Grand Rapids manufacturing community, we have, and will continue to benefit from, a highly stable and solid workforce that is also able to adapt to changing market demands," Clark said.

American Seating's first InSight installation took place in Chicago Transit Authority's buses.

229

I t's not on a corner, but for 120 years, the law firm of Varnum, Riddering, Schmidt

record of service as a trusted advisor remains steady—a significant factor in the firm's longevity.

West Michigan.

"West Michigan is unusually entrepreneurial," said Lawrence. "In the history of the area, so many industries have come and gone. But there's something about this area that encourages entrepreneurs, and that's good for our entire community."

Reflecting that entrepreneurial spirit is the recent development of new industries in West Michigan. While the furniture and automotive industries that once dominated area economics continue to be active, Varnum also serves clients in the financial services, energy, alternative energy and life sciences industries.

Varnum attorneys Peter Roth, Mary Kay Shaver and Christopher Fowler.

"We are relentless in keeping our eye on what's best for the client," said Bill Lawrence, the firm's executive partner. "We work hard to provide a high level of legal expertise while keeping a focus on client service."

& Howlett has been a cornerstone of the West Michigan community. The turn of the 21st century saw the firm at 160+ attorneys in six locations throughout Michigan, including its iconic presence in the Grand Rapids skyline.

The firm has a long history of serving clients at some of the most respected businesses in the region, and through these relationships, has had a front row seat to many of the exciting changes in and around West Michigan. Recent changes include population growth and urban development as well as the maturation and evolution of various industry segments. Regardless of the changes, the firm's long

"We are relentless in keeping our eye on what's best for the client," said Bill Lawrence, the firm's executive partner. "We work hard to provide a high level of legal expertise while keeping a focus on client service."

Adds Mike Wooldridge, chairperson of the firm's Policy Committee: "Our client focus has resulted in great relationships with our clients over the years, and that makes the practice of law exciting and enjoyable."

Also contributing to the firm's success is the nimbleness with which it approaches the evolving business community—a must in an entrepreneurial community like

And of course, some areas of law will always be in demand: business, trial services and labor law are essential regardless of the industry, and tax specialties will be important as long as there are taxes. Varnum's strong reputation of excellence in all these areas often makes it a first choice for entrepreneurs.

Another hallmark of the firm is its commitment to community. The firm places a high value on participation in the civic, arts, social service, and economic development organizations that serve the area.

"Service to community has always been a part of the firm," Lawrence said. "Of all the major nonprofits around town, you'd be hard pressed to find one whose board has not been served by a Varnum attorney. As a firm, we value that involvement and we are privileged to work with the many organizations that play such an important role in defining our community."

The firm's attorneys serve as board members and leaders of literally hundreds of these organizations, from the Grand Rapids Community Foundation, Habitat for Humanity and St. John's Home to the Civic Theatre and John Ball Zoo.

The quality of work culture too, is important at Varnum. For one thing, it is an important factor in attracting and keeping the best people—a business imperative today.

"I think we, as a law firm, are very much in a talent business, and we have a lot of very talented, unselfish, committed people here - staff and attorneys alike," Lawrence said.

With over 300 people in the Grand Rapids office alone, Varnum is a community unto itself and offers its staff a congenial atmosphere with company picnics, anniversary and holiday celebrations, and general enjoyment of working together.

"We will celebrate just about anything here," Wooldridge noted, "be it holidays, birthdays, transitions, or client successes." Recently, the entire Grand Rapids office celebrated a successful trial outcome with an impromptu celebratory picnic—complete with a champagne toast—on the firm's 17th floor deck overlooking the city.

That culture of teamwork may be part of the reason Varnum associates recently rated the firm extremely well in a national publication's survey of quality of life at law firms, (*The American Lawyer Magazine*, August 2007) and why the firm is consistently rated one of the "101 Best and Brightest Companies to Work For." (Michigan Business and Professional Association.)

Enjoyment of work and work culture at Varnum holds true across the board.

"I look forward to coming to work every day," said Wooldridge. "I think that's a reflection of the people I work with - the attorneys, staff and clients. It's a reflection of West Michigan generally and the quality of people we work with. It's all about relationships."

Bill Lawrence, executive partner, with Mike Wooldridge, chairperson of the firm's Policy Committee.

"Service to community has always been a part of the firm," Lawrence said. "Of all the major non-profits around town, you'd be hard pressed to find one whose board has not been served by a Varnum attorney."

231

Melody is one of the children that Mark Thomson, executive director of St. John's Home, particularly remembers. "She came to us from a psychiatric hospital. We were told she was hopelessly disturbed and that we should just prepare her for life in an institution."

Today, Melody is a police officer and emergency medical technician in Pennsylvania. "She's not locked up in an institution; in fact, she's saving people's lives," says Thomson.

"When you tell kids that you'll pay for college, that tells them, 'We think you're a winner,'" says Thomson.

"We regard these children as our own," says Thomson. "I ask myself every day if this would be good enough for my own children."

Meeting the Needs of Children

Kids like Melody come to St. John's Home when they have nowhere else to go—when other placements have failed. And while her story is dramatic, it's not unusual. St. John's Home is known for exceptionally high success rates with some of the most troubled kids in West Michigan. About 80 percent of these children move on to less restrictive settings, such as foster homes, within a year. And they continue to succeed in those placements. By contrast, the state average for successful placement hovers around 55 percent.

St. John's is a residential home for children ages six through seventeen. In reality, it is more like a neighborhood with homey residences set on a park-like 25 acres in the middle of Grand Rapids. Long before the cozy homes were constructed on its present site, St. John's Home was a Roman Catholic orphanage on Leonard Street. While today its focus is to serve emotionally impaired children as a non-denominational, non-profit organization, the original mission of caring for needy children still animates the environment.

High Expectations and Lots of Love

But the reason miracles like Melody occur fairly regularly at St. John's Home is due to three fundamental principles, the first of which is love. "We regard these children as our own," says Thomson. "I ask myself every day if this would be good enough for my own children."

The second principle is that children live up to the expectations set for them. Staff at St. John's Home believes in the potential of its kids, so much so that the home has established a scholarship program that guarantees a college education for any child who has lived there. "When you tell kids that you'll pay for college, that tells them, 'We think you're a winner,'" says Thomson. The home usually has a handful of kids attending college every year.

Third, children at St. John's Home are busy. They visit museums and amusement parks; they tour Washington, D.C., and visit black colleges in Atlanta, Georgia. Their days are filled with purposeful activity that enriches lives that have too often been bleak and difficult.

Not surprisingly, St. John's Home has found a fertile community in which to flourish. "People in Grand Rapids are remarkably generous," says Thomson. "I'm not sure we could continue to exist elsewhere."

Each patient receives an individualized treatment plan created by a multidisciplinary team. Some patients may use specialized equipment, such as the Giger MD, as they work toward reaching their rehab goals.

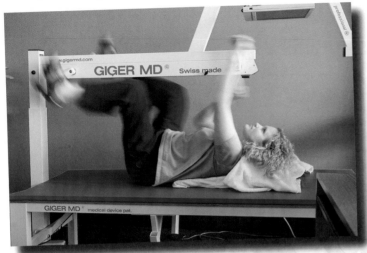

"They know that the son or the daughter that they're helping – the mother, the father they're helping – could very well be their own son, daughter, mother, or father," said Mary Free Bed president Bill Blessing.

Each year thousands of children are cared for by experts specializing in pediatric rehabilitation. Mary Free Bed offers individual treatment rooms specifically designed for children and teens, as well as child-sized therapy equipment.

Mary Free Bed Rehabilitation Hospital offers many unique services for people with disabilities. Our Orthotics & Prosthetics department features an on-site lab where experienced technicians prepare the patient's orthosis or prosthesis through custom fabrication.

West Michigan has a long history of compassion, and it's on display daily at Mary Free Bed Rehabilitation Hospital. This institution with the unique name provides an array of rehabilitation services to those who have been disabled by injury or disease.

A staff of more than 650 committed professionals works hard to achieve the hospital's mission "to restore independence, hope, and freedom."

"They know that the son or the daughter that they're helping – the mother, the father they're helping – could very well be their own son, daughter, mother, or father," said Mary Free Bed president Bill Blessing.

The free-standing, 80-bed rehabilitation hospital is owned and operated by the Mary Free Bed Guild of Grand Rapids, a women's organization begun in 1891. The hospital name is based on the intent of a small group of women who decided to raise funds to provide one "free bed" in a local hospital for patients who couldn't pay for their own hospitalization – and to seek donations from women named Mary. As both need and support increased, that original free bed evolved into a self-sufficient, free-standing institution that today helps some 1,200 patients annually in its inpatient services alone.

Mary Free Bed Rehabilitation Hospital provides inpatient and outpatient care for adults, children, and infants who have suffered spinal or brain injuries, amputation, strokes, or just about any other physical condition that limits their mobility. Located in downtown Grand Rapids, Mary Free Bed works with patients from Petoskey to Battle Creek, St. Joseph to Saginaw, and beyond. While numerous physical therapy facilities exist across the country, less than fifty stand-alone rehabilitation hospitals provide both inpatient and outpatient services.

In addition to superior physical therapy clinics and specialty medical treatment services, the hospital supports its patients with exceptional programs, products, and services. The lab at the Mary Ives Hunting Center designs prosthetics, orthotics, powered wheelchairs, communication devices, and other adaptive technologies. The Rehab Technology Center staff sets up a patient's hospital room, home, or even office with technological tools to help patients regain control over their environments. Two on-site apartments help patients choose the tools that will best accommodate their disabilities and support their activities. A driver rehabilitation program allows patients to drive a full-size practice vehicle on site. And therapists take patients on field trips to local attractions to help them adjust to normal activities.

Mary Free Bed reaches beyond its walls to support community programs, as well, contributing more than $1 million annually to area non-profit events and programs. Within the institution and throughout its community, the hospital supports advocacy in the areas of diversity, women's issues, and, of course, disabilities.

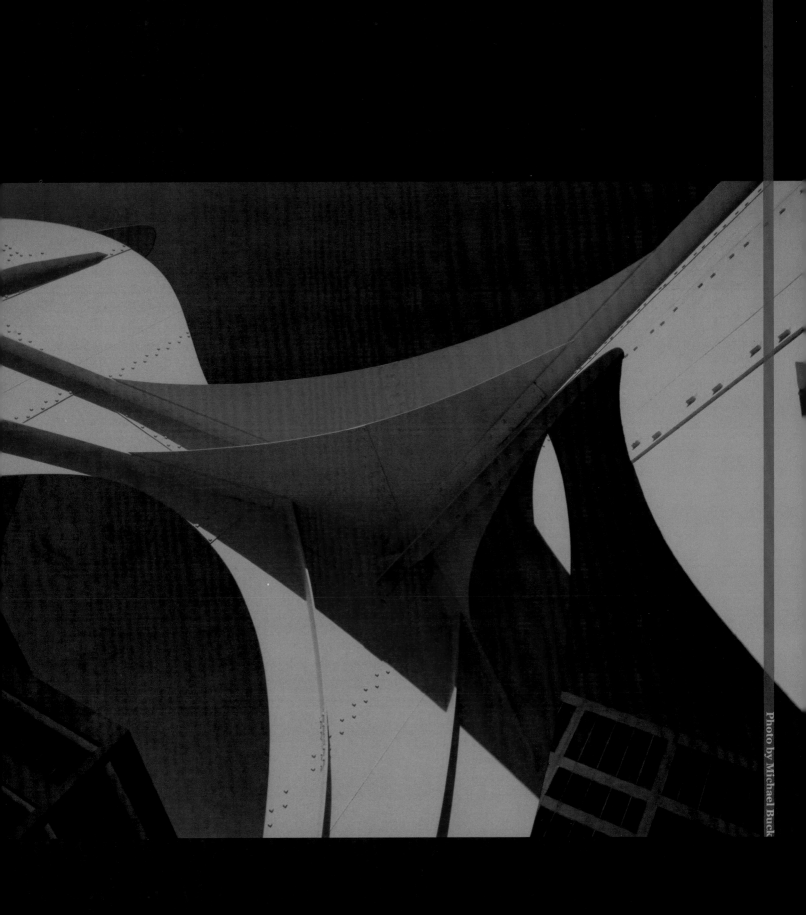

Owen-Ames-Kimball Co.

Owen-Ames-Kimball Co. Co.

Building since 1891, Owen-Ames-Kimball Co. has created the

Originally built as the Majestic Theatre in 1903, Owen-Ames-Kimball Co. has developed a valuable relationship with the Grand Rapids Civic Theatre over the last 3 decades, performing the theatre's first renovation in 1979 and completing a major historic restoration in 2000. Photo by Laszlo Regos Photography©

"We're one of the few construction companies in Michigan who have received ISO-9001 certification," says Schoonveld. "We know that exceptional quality is in the details, so our staff includes talented craftspeople who are highly skilled in carpentry and concrete work, and we insist on the very best subcontractors."

landmark buildings of Grand Rapids for over a century. The skyline of the city is a testament to the company's enduring traditions of excellence and innovation, from historical treasures that include McKay Tower, the Welsh Auditorium, Ryerson Library and the Masonic Temple to inspiring contemporary designs, such as the Van Andel Museum Center, Kent County Courthouse, the conservatory at Frederik Meijer Gardens and the Gerald R. Ford Presidential Museum.

Today, the firm continues to build West Michigan, offering general contracting, construction management and design/build services to a broad variety of clients, large and small. It pursues its original mission – to provide the finest professional construction services to meet clients' needs – by continually adapting its business strategies to

changes in the industry. "We have a clearly defined process, a right way to do things," says Bill Schoonveld, president, "and through that process, we're able to stay at the leading edge of our industry, driving the latest trends."

Building Trust Through Quality and Communication

Owen-Ames-Kimball Co. is a client-centered company that provides effective solutions to the specific financial, environmental and scheduling challenges presented by its clients' projects. A key factor in the firm's success is its focus on an open dialog with its customers. "Effective communication is one of the principles we live by," says Schoonveld. "We involve the client from day one, offer frequent progress reports and are always available to answer questions. By providing timely information about every aspect of the project, including project costs, we empower the client to make informed decisions and we build trust." For every project, the client has a single, accountable point of contact, responsible for on time and within budget delivery.

Trust is the reason clients keep coming back to Owen-Ames-Kimball Co. Long-term clients include area giants such as Herman Miller, Steelcase and Amway. The firm has

also been entrusted with the renovation of significant buildings that it originally built many years ago, including Ryerson Library and the Meijer Majestic Theater.

Owen-Ames-Kimball Co. also builds trust through attention to detail, offering all-encompassing constructability reviews and post-construction certification reviews. "We're one of the few construction companies in Michigan who have received ISO-9001 certification," says Schoonveld. "We know that exceptional quality is in the details, so our staff includes talented craftspeople who are highly skilled in carpentry and concrete work, and we insist on the very best subcontractors."

Loyalty and Accountability

While strong client relationships and an unparalleled reputation for quality account for the firm's longevity, its growth and continuing potential are tied to dedicated, fully engaged employees. "We hire the best people and we create a work environment where they can build a rewarding career," says Schoonveld. "People say that this business is losing the skilled masters in carpentry, plaster and stone to old age, but we believe that the 20-year-old we hire today will become a master over a long career with us and that at the middle of the

21st century, he or she will have passed on those same valuable skills to the next generation."

The longevity of the company's employees speaks volumes. In an industry known for high turnover rates, field superintendents and project managers average more than 16 years with the firm. Schoonveld, an employee since 1978, is only the seventh president that Owen-Ames-Kimball Co. has had in its 116-year history. By the same token, the company fosters long-term relationships with its subcontractors.

Owen-Ames-Kimball Co. has been employee-owned for more than fifty years. Today more than 90 percent of its project managers and field superintendents are shareholders. Every owner is an employee and no one owns more than 10 percent of the company. As shareholders, employee-owners are personally invested in the success of each project. "As an owner, I have tremendous commitment to the job," says Brad McAvoy, P.E., LEED AP, Director of Engineering Services. "Not only is the company's reputation at stake, so is mine."

As a leader in the construction industry, Owen-Ames-Kimball Co. has consistently promoted the diversity of its workforce. The firm actively recruits new staff members through traditional and nontraditional sources to employ men and women who reflect the diverse demographics of the surrounding community. It

was the first construction firm to hire a female project superintendent, is a strong supporter of the West Michigan Minority Contractors Association and the National Association of Women in Construction and is proud of its status as an equal opportunity employer.

The company has the foresight to recognize that its continuing success is directly tied to the abilities of its workforce. For this reason Owen-Ames-Kimball Co. has an ongoing employee training program that emphasizes job skills, safety, quality, integrity and willingness to step up to responsibility. "By investing in our employees, we're investing in our future and the future of our clients," says Schoonveld.

Technology and Sustainability

Committed to employing the best people using the best tools, Owen-Ames-Kimball Co. embraces technology. At every job site, field supervisors and other key employees use laptops and BlackBerrys to speed communication, check specs and keep the project on time and within budget. "We're exploring new materials that are lighter, stronger, more affordable and easier to work with, and are keeping a close eye on new developments in time-saving construction processes and equipment," says Schoonveld. No matter what the future of construction holds, the firm will remain at the cutting edge.

The company has been at the forefront of

environmentally sustainable design for decades, having played an integral role in some of the most prominent "green" building projects in the country, including the award-winning Herman Miller "GreenHouse" project and the Steelcase Wood Plant, the first LEED-Silver certified manufacturing facility in the country. A member of the US Green Building Council, the firm currently has 21 LEED-Accredited Professionals on staff, and has worked extensively with the LEED rating system. "We're committed to sustainable design for many reasons," says McAvoy, "most notably because it just makes sense: the economic benefits are every bit as important as the environmental benefits, and it's clearly the wave of the future."

Strategic Growth

Building on a foundation of success as a full-service construction firm with a wide range of project experience, Owen-Ames-Kimball Co. created two wholly owned subsidiaries: Owen-Ames-Kimball Company in Fort Myers, Florida in 1982 and Muskegon Construction Company in Muskegon, Michigan in 1929. The company's headquarters remains in the heart of Grand Rapids.

Superb craftsmanship and strong client partnerships have made Owen-Ames-Kimball Co. an industry leader for over a century. Trust, technology and employee commitment ensure that it will be building West Michigan for many years to come.

A 14-foot, cascading waterfall; five stories of glass windows; and 22-foot, concrete, treelike supports were included in the construction of the 15,000-square-foot Frederik Meijer Gardens conservatory, which showcases 16,000 exotic plants and trees.

Owen-Ames-Kimball Co. built the Gerald R. Ford Presidential Museum in 1981, giving Grand Rapids yet another notable landmark that has drawn national attention and thousands of visitors yearly.

Located in downtown Grand Rapids on the banks of the Grand River, the Van Andel Museum Center posed the challenge of building part of the structure over the water.

This state-of-the-art construction provides enhanced training facilities. The ballistics range is used by many area police departments and is very useful in the post 9/11 era.

Saint Mary's Health Care is dedicated to providing patient-focused

"Supported by the Catholic faith and a tradition of service to the community, Saint Mary's Health Care is an institution which cares for more than 25 percent of the Grand Rapids-area population."

care based on its on five core values—respect, social justice, compassion, care of the poor and underserved, and excellence—which guide its staff members to provide the highest level of care with a focus on clinical and service outcomes.

Saint Mary's is a member organization of Trinity Health, a corporation formed through the merger of Holy Cross Health System and Mercy Health Services, two entities that carried their own legacy of the Catholic service tradition. Saint Mary's has long been known in the community for excellent primary care and family medicine; more recently, its specialty areas include oncology, neuroscience, and orthopedics, as well. The Lacks Cancer Center is the premier cancer-dedicated facility in West Michigan.

The hospital combines state-of-the-art technology with highly personalized service to each patient. Saint Mary's also sets itself apart from other health care programs with its epilepsy program, which provides comprehensive treatment services, from diagnosis to life-changing surgery, for this disorder. It is the first and only dedicated adult and adolescent program of its kind, bringing first-rate care directly to the Grand Rapids area.

In February 2007, Saint Mary's opened its Southwest campus, which houses primary care physicians, an Urgent Care facility, an ambulatory surgery center, a pharmacy, laboratory, and radiology services, among others, under one roof conveniently located in the fast-growing southwest quadrant of Grand Rapids.

In addition to providing cutting-edge care to its communities, St. Mary's also looks to reach out to underserved segments of the population. Clinica Santa Maria is at the forefront of this mission, providing primary care to the poor, Hispanic, and homeless of West Michigan's Hispanic community. Staffed by volunteer doctors and a bilingual staff, Clinica Santa Maria offers a full range of health services, including dental services, comprehensive pregnancy and post-natal care, as well

as providing care for patients with chronic conditions, such as diabetes and arthritis.

Already at the forefront of medicine in West Michigan, Saint Mary's Health Care has plans to expand its leadership role. Currently under construction, the $60 million, 145,000 square foot Hauenstein Center will open early in 2009 to provide both inpatient and outpatient neurological services for conditions such as Parkinson's disease, Alzheimer's and other memory disorders, epilepsy, stroke, and sleep disorders all under one roof.

Supported by the Catholic faith and a tradition of service to the community, Saint Mary's Health Care is an institution which cares for more than 25 percent of the Grand Rapids-area population.

Zeeland Community Hospital

The Rapid Central Station Interurban Transit Partnership.

"Building lasting relationships, honoring all commitments with integrity, always innovating, having passion for one's work… these simple values really do form the foundation on which our business – and success – is built."

Michigan Street Development team members (L to R) Gary Shannon, senior superintendent; Brian Crissman, senior project manager; and Dan LaMore, vice president.

A familiar sight on the many black and white construction signs dotting West Michigan, The Christman Company name has become synonymous with significant economic growth and development throughout the region. The firm has been recognized as a newsmaker and an innovator leading the construction services industry in the latest practices and technology. Yet to hear Dan LaMore, vice president and principal in charge of West Michigan operations, describe the company, a lot hasn't changed in the 113 years that Christman has been in business.

"We were founded by H.G. Christman in 1894 with a set of fundamental business principles," said LaMore. "Building lasting relationships, honoring all commitments with integrity, always innovating, having passion for one's work…these simple values really do form the foundation on which our business – and success – is built."

Yet there's nothing simple about the structures that Christman has put in place in recent years, particularly the Michigan Street Development, which is slated for completion in 2010. This unique public/private project will include a medical office and research facility consisting of three quarters of a billion square feet in four buildings with a 2,300-space, four-story parking deck. Owned by Michigan Street Development LLC, a partnership of The Christman Company and the DeVos family, the Christman-led project also incorporates nonprofit organizations Spectrum Health and Van Andel Research Institute, as well as the City of Grand Rapids. Located on the Michigan Street hill between Division Avenue and Coit Street, the project is a strategic economic growth project for the City of Grand Rapids and its emerging "Medical Mile" Life Science Corridor.

The $150 million first phase consists of the parking structure, the 280,000 square foot Lemmen-Holton Cancer Pavilion for Spectrum Health and a seven-story medical building planned to contain a hotel on the upper floors. A second phase will include "The Secchia Center," the new home of the Michigan State University College of Human Medicine, with the fourth building to be completed in a third and final phase.

Plans for the other buildings include office, laboratory, research, technology, and academic space. The massive project will ultimately be valued at more than $250 million. The project was recognized in 2007 by Grand Rapids Business Journal with its "Newsmaker of the Year" award, which cited the growth of not only construction jobs, but also thousands of permanent health care jobs that the project will help secure.

There is also nothing simple about the full range of professional services the firm offers. One example is the construction management planning that helped result in The Rapid Central station, a project of the Interurban Transit Partnership in Grand Rapids, becoming the first public transit facility in the nation to receive U.S. Green Building Council LEED® (Leadership in Energy and Environmental Design) certification. Another is construction of the Michigan Street pedestrian tunnel for Spectrum Health which utilized the New Austrian Tunneling Method excavation and support technique, something never before used in the United

States. Yet another example is participation in the first-ever West Michigan safety partnership agreement with the Michigan Department of Labor and Economic Growth, the Michigan Occupational Safety and Health Administration, and more than fifty employers and supporting organizations in support of safety and health promotion on the Michigan Street Development project.

The Christman Company has 400 employees in locations in Grand Rapids, Lansing, Traverse City, Ann Arbor, and Alexandria, Virginia, and provides a full range of professional services including construction management, general contracting, design/build, program management, real estate development, facilities planning, and consulting. Markets served range from health care, education, office, sports and recreation, religious, and historic preservation, to research and high technology facilities, industrial, government and public, retail and hospitality sectors.

Consistently ranked by Modern Healthcare magazine as one of the country's top construction management firms, Christman was ranked at 149 in the 2007 Engineering News-Record "ENR 400" list of the top 400 contractors nationally, making the firm not only the top constructor in West Michigan but also Michigan's third-largest building contractor and the state's largest non-Detroit-based construction services firm. Other awards include the MIOSHA Gold Safety Award for the unprecedented achievement of 2.1 million hours without a lost-time accident, the first-ever "Policyholder of the Year" award from Accident Fund Insurance Company of America for an exemplary claims record among 45,000 policyholders, and numerous local, state, and national recognitions for nearly every construction excellence award, including being the first-ever Michigan recipient of the Marvin M. Black National Excellence in Partnering Award from the Associated General Contractors of America.

"The Christman Company has 400 employees in locations in Grand Rapids, Lansing, Traverse City, Ann Arbor, and Alexandria, Virginia, and provides a full range of professional services including construction management, general contracting, design/build, program management, real estate development, facilities planning, and consulting."

Historians are still unsure how ice cream originated. Was it Charles I of England who was looking for a new royal dessert to serve his guests? Or was it Marco

Polo who brought back the recipe from China? In any case, West Michiganders know for certain the source of their first scoop. It all began in 1895 with a group of local dairy farmers who formed a co-op on Chicago Drive in Hudsonville, Michigan, to better market their dairy products. More than a century and millions of gallons of cream later, Hudsonville Ice Cream continues to tempt the taste buds of many an ice cream aficionado in West Michigan.

The Hudsonville Creamery was operating successfully for more than 30 years before the dairy farmers decided to introduce ice cream to their product line. In the summer of 1926, the co-op churned out six ice cream flavors: vanilla,

chocolate, strawberry, butter pecan, orange pineapple, and tootie fruitie. This happened to be the same year that inventor Clarence Vogt introduced his continuous freezer, which allowed for the mass production of ice cream and other frosty treats.

In 1930, co-op member Dick Hoezee came on board. In 1946 he bought controlling interest and moved the company in 1948 to Burnips to allow for the widening of Chicago Drive. In 1949, Hoezee purchased Vogt's freezer, allowing ice cream to become a more accessible, year-round treat.

Over the next 20 years, Hoezee worked to update the churning and manufacturing process of ice cream, as well as adding new flavors to the original six. The recipes of the original ice cream were never altered. In 1972, Hoezee's sons Dell, Jack, Rich, and Phil bought the company and continued their father's entrepreneurial spirit, expanding the ice cream line to include fifty scrumptious flavors. Today, Hudsonville Creamery & Ice Cream manufactures ice cream, frozen yogurt, sorbet, and sherbet. Dip

shops sell individual servings from 3 gallon tubs, while convenience stores, local and regional grocery stores sell pints, half-gallons, and gallon containers of our "oh so creamy" ice cream.

The Hoezee brothers continued Hudsonville Ice Cream's operations until 2003, when they sold it to another West Michigan family. Dell Hoezee still serves as a consultant to the company.

One of the sweetest notes in Hudsonville's legacy is not the ice cream recipes, but the people who are churning out the treats. The average team member has been at Hudsonville Ice Cream for 18 years. This is a testament not only to company loyalty, but also to the employees' ability to learn and grow within the dynamic environment.

Whether you are in the mood for a single-scoop cone or a gallon container to keep in your freezer at home, Hudsonville Ice Cream can fulfill your craving. What was at first simply a better way for dairy farmers to market their product has blossomed into what continues to be a mouth-watering treat for generations of Michiganders.

The cornerstone of a good community is its infrastructure, from its local government to its health care and emergency services.

Mercy General Health Partners

The Muskegon area has a solid foundation, thanks in part to Mercy General Health Partners.

Formed in 1998 when Mercy Hospital and Muskegon General Hospital merged, the comprehensive medical organization offers services ranging from inpatient, outpatient, and emergency room treatment, to gastric bypass surgery, and oncology and cardiac care.

The hospital's reach extends from Mason County in the north to Ottawa County in the south. As a specialty referral hospital, Mercy General works with other hospitals in the area to provide services that are not available at other locations.

"We partner locally with several community organizations for health care access and treatment and to ensure we are meeting the needs of this community," said President and CEO Roger Spoelman.

Mercy General Health Partners is a member of Trinity Health, the fourth largest health care organization in the United States. As a faith-based and mission-driven organization, Trinity Health supports Mercy General's active participation in the community.

"Unlike any other industry, health care provides medical treatment services to anyone who walks through the doors, regardless of their ability to pay,"

President and CEO, Roger Spoelman

Spoelman said. "It is the mission of our organization to heal the body, mind, and spirit and to improve the health of our communities. Mercy General Health Partners is here to do just that, whenever the need arises."

The care provided by Mercy General Health Partners has been recognized by several healthcare quality organizations; from HealthGrades®, as a Distinguished Hospital for Clinical Excellence; to one of West Michigan's 101 Best and Brightest Places to Work For; to being named a Solucient Top 100 Hospital in the nation.

"Many of the services Mercy General offers this community are top notch," Spoelman noted. "We are the sole provider of cardiac services along the lakeshore with designations from Priority Health and Blue Cross and Blue Shield as a Cardiac Center of Excellence. Our bariatric surgery program has assisted over 1,200 people in achieving their weight loss goal. This

"It is the mission of our organization to heal the body, mind, and spirit and to improve the health of our communities. Mercy General Health Partners is here to do just that, whenever the need arises."

program is accredited by the American Society for Bariatric Surgeons and is the third largest program in Michigan. Additionally, orthopedic and spine services, emergency services, nephrology, and a solid Primary Care Network of physicians has the reputation within this community for excellent patient care and treatment."

Mercy General delivers more than 1,500 baby deliveries, 8,700 outpatient surgeries, and 4,600 inpatient surgeries annually. It also logs more than 62,000 emergency and MediCenter visits each year, with door-to-physician-time often under 20 minutes.

The hospital is increasing its services, too, as the new Johnson Family Center for Cancer Care at Mercy General Health Partners reaches the final stages of construction, with completion expected in spring 2008. Prior to the opening of the center, some 12,000 patients received treatment at Mercy General each year for their medical

oncology needs. While the hospital has provided medical oncology services for more than 15 years, it will now offer radiation oncology.

Through a partnership between Mercy General and Cancer & Hematology Centers of Western Michigan, the new center will include treatment and examination rooms, a resource library, conference rooms, private family meeting rooms, a specialty boutique, and healing garden.

A member of Trinity Health, Mercy General's mission reflects a long and rich tradition of faith and healing. Catherine McAuley founded the Sisters of Mercy religious community in 1831 in Ireland. Trinity Health is a merger between Holy Cross Health System and Mercy Health Services in 2000.

Keeping pace with advancements in technology, Mercy General hosts state-of-the-art services, including the Emergency Center and the only open MRI equipment in the region. Other centers of excellence include the

Center for Sleep Disorders, the Special Delivery Birth Center, and the Center for Weight Management. Mercy General is also a teaching hospital for physicians and hosts numerous osteopathic residents and interns each year. Approximately 2,000 dedicated employees and 200 volunteers work at Mercy General.

"It gives me great satisfaction to work along side some of the best physicians and people in medicine and know our patients receive excellent care when they walk in our doors," Spoelman said.

Looking at the bigger picture, he added, "West Michigan offers a lifestyle hard to beat anywhere else in the nation. There is a wonderful synergy being created in this community, which bodes well for our future, and Mercy General Health partners is dedicated to providing the very best healthcare services for the lakeshore region for years to come."

Muskegon General Campus

For more than a century, URS has been in the business of designing buildings, many of which have become familiar landmarks in Grand Rapids: Fifth Third Bank,

Steelcase Inc. LEED Certified Wood Furniture Manufacturing Facility.
Photo: Justin Maconochie

East Grand Rapids Performing Arts Center, East Grand Rapids Public Schools.
Photo: Chuck Heiney

The Fred and Lena Meijer Heart Center, Spectrum Health – Butterworth Campus.
Photo: Justin Maconochie

the Calder Plaza Building, and the Ledyard Building. Yet, while still firmly rooted in West Michigan, URS possesses offices worldwide. As a regional headquarters and a "Center of Excellence" for one of the largest architectural and engineering design firms in the world, URS combines commitment to the community with world-class resources and expertise.

Mail-order Houses to the Medical Mile

The company began in 1903 as J.H. Daverman & Son and expanded its base later by designing mail-order house plans. A plan for a gracious Victorian home sold for $10, and many still grace city streets throughout the Midwest.

Over the years, Daverman became a well-known and trusted local architectural firm. The company built a base of loyal clients who still remember the old Daverman firm. "We have employees who have been here for 35 or 40 years,

and many of our clients have been with us for 30 or more years," states Ronald R. Henry, AIA, vice president and managing principal.

Beginning in the 1980s, Daverman undertook a series of acquisitions and mergers that thrust the local firm onto a global playing field. Today, the firm with humble beginnings in Grand Rapids, is part of one of the largest engineering design firms in the world, with more than 28,900 professionals in a variety of disciplines. And now, because of its size and global reach, the Grand Rapids location has access to specialized expertise and resources. "Someplace in our company, we have a world-class expert in anything you can imagine, from design to the environment," states Henry.

With almost 300 employees, URS in Grand Rapids, is the largest of its four Michigan locations. It is also known as a "Center of Excellence" with specialized expertise in designing health care and K-12 educational facilities. Additional services include surface and air transportation; retail, commercial, and industrial design; environmental, water, and wastewater resources; and pipeline design.

URS has designed school facilities for more than a hundred districts throughout the state of Michigan, including East Grand Rapids, Forest Hills, Rockford,

Farmington, and Lake Orion school districts. URS has also made its mark on the Michigan Street Corridor "Medical Mile." Projects of note include: Michigan State University's Secchia Center - College of Human Medicine, the Fred & Lena Meijer Heart Center, and the Lemmen-Holton Cancer Pavilion.

Giving Back...

Despite its global reach, URS remains fully invested in the Grand Rapids community. As a 100 + year-old company, URS supports local health care, education, and the arts—three areas that are directly linked to its fields of endeavor. It also encourages its employees to volunteer locally within the community. In addition to supporting charities like the Children's Miracle Network, a national telethon that benefits the local DeVos Children's Hospital, employees also answer phones during the telethon, organize fundraisers, and volunteer at the Renucci Hospitality House where families stay when their loved ones are in the hospital.

As URS in Grand Rapids looks toward a second century, the process of creation continues to be a vital and compelling endeavor to those engaged in it. "It's incredibly rewarding to see a project you've been involved in, a vision you've had with your client and all the user groups, become a reality," says Henry. "It's an extraordinary feeling."

"A person can now find these various racks at virtually every grade school, high school, and college in the U.S. and Canada."

Founded in Grand Rapids by Elvah O. Bulman, dispenser manufacturer Bulman Products, Inc. has been making it easier for folks to wrap, pack, and ship products and gifts since 1905.

It all began when the enterprising Bulman entered the workforce at age 16, earning $2.50 per week nailing bed slats at a local furniture factory. Soon he

to pursue his interest in machinery. No slouch when it came to design and engineering, he received a dozen patents during this time.

In 1905, it was time to take a bold step, and Bulman started his company in a small barn behind his home on Eastern Avenue. His first product was a small twine dispenser, the forerunner of a complete line of

dispenser has remained its mainstay over the years.

Orville Bulman, E.O.'s son, joined his father in the business after spending a year in Chicago working as a newspaper cartoonist. This artistic young man eventually became president of the firm and led it for decades, yet a simultaneous career as a painter brought him a different kind of satisfaction. He sold more than 2,000 paintings during his lifetime and had more than 40 one-person exhibits. He and his paintings were featured in issues of both *Newsweek* and *Life* magazines in the 1950s, and some of his paintings found homes with the Duchess of Windsor, Robert F. Kennedy, former U.S. President Gerald R. Ford, and Marjorie Merriweather Post. In later years, the Grand Rapids Art Museum received a generous gift from Orville and his wife Jean that enabled the museum to acquire a painting by Picasso.

In 1970, the Bulmans sold the Bulman Manufacturing Company to Rospatch Corporation. Ten years later, Rospatch asked Jack Kirkwood to head the division as general manager. Kirkwood did so, and obviously liked what he saw, because a year later, he purchased the company. Currently, Kirkwood and his son, Jim Kirkwood, share ownership in the business, serving as president

Original Bulman Factory, 1905

was working in the machine department, where he gained skills and knowledge that would help him in his future career. Although he spent the next 12 years working first in a grocery store and next in the circulation department of the Grand Rapids Herald, young E.O. continued

dispensers that the company today provides to schools, manufacturing companies, and retail businesses such as supermarkets, department stores, and any others that handle packing, wrapping, and shipping products. While the company once dealt in light fixtures and steel shelving, the indispensable

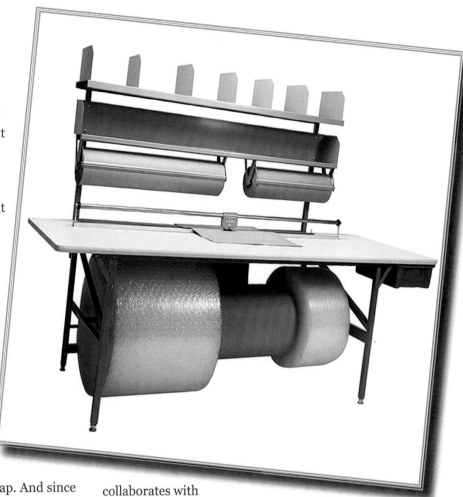

/CEO and vice president, respectively.

The dispenser manufacturer always has developed and changed products to better serve customer needs. The original paper dispensers and cutters were made of cast iron and wood tops, which did the job but certainly weren't easy to move. More mechanisms were patented over the years and, not coincidently, the dispensers became more user-friendly. Spring-loaded housing assemblies were connected to smaller, lighter blades. Heavy cast iron was replaced with light and medium gauge steel. Yet ultimately, E.O. Bulman's initial ideas continue to drive the company's offerings.

"These cutters, with a few minor alterations, continue to be at the heart of what we do here," said Jim Kirkwood, who got to know the business as a college student spending his summers running drill presses and spot welding. Today, products include steel

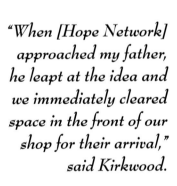

tube racks that hold up to eight rolls of paper. "A person can now find these various racks at virtually every grade school, high school, and college in the U.S. and Canada," he added.

Bulman Products also offers slide cutters to cut packing materials like foam and bubble wrap. And since about 2001, Bulman packing tables and shipping stations have been popular items. With its roll cutters and slide cutters, these complementary products add up to a full-service packing station.

"Because we serve what some may call a niche market, our business remains consistent with small growth each year," Kirkwood said. "We're certainly not recession-proof, but even over the last five or six years, when many businesses in this area were forced to lay off large numbers of very capable individuals, we did not lay off a single person and were actually able to offer plenty of overtime and year-end bonuses to everyone who works here."

In addition to its own employees, Bulman Products collaborates with Hope Network, a nonprofit organization, to provide a workplace for individuals with disabilities to assemble cutter housings and pack hardware and assembly instructions.

"When [Hope Network] approached my father, he leapt at the idea and we immediately cleared space in the front of our shop for their arrival," said Kirkwood. "Since that time, Hope's stay here has been nothing but positive. Hope has their own in-house supervisor who we coordinate with, and he spreads the work out to Hope's members here. Given that arrangement, Bulman employees actually only need to interact with Hope's on a voluntary basis. There is a lot of that interaction, and there was from day one."

"When [Hope Network] approached my father, he leapt at the idea and we immediately cleared space in the front of our shop for their arrival," said Kirkwood.

An integral part of the Grand Rapids landscape today, the Grand Rapids

Nearly all WMU students in Grand Rapids are older adults completing graduate degrees on a part-time basis. Classes, meetings with faculty, and student advising sessions are scheduled in the evenings or at other convenient times.

WMU offers the only CACREP accredited Counseling program in the region. Students gain extensive, supervised counseling experiences with real clients in Grand Rapids' only campus-based Counseling Clinic featuring one-way glass interaction observation rooms.

"One of the nation's top 100 public universities, WMU has always provided high quality academic programs and services through its experienced, talented faculty and staff."

WMU provides exceptional facilities and services for both small outdoor and large indoor wedding receptions. A full-time wedding planner is on staff to assist with all the details.

Campus of Western Michigan University (WMU) came close to being the university's founding location. At the turn of the last century, several local politicians and business leaders worked to establish Western State

Normal School in Grand Rapids. However, due to "much political wrangling," the institution first began in Kalamazoo in 1903, said Dr. James Schultz, director of the Grand Rapids campus. It didn't take long before the school came to Grand Rapids, though. Teachers began taking advanced education courses there just six years later.

One of the nation's top

100 public universities, WMU has always provided high quality academic programs and services through its experienced, talented faculty and staff. The Grand Rapids campus, designated as a Graduate Center, has helped thousands of educators and business professionals earn advanced degrees in programs as diverse as Educational Leadership (MA & PhD), Counselor Education and Counseling Psychology (MA), and Engineering Management (MS). Many of these programs have been offered for decades. The Master of Business Administration program came to Grand Rapids in 1964, and the Master of Social Work program started there in 1979. Today, more than 2,000 students are enrolled in more than twenty-five fields of study.

As its offerings expanded over the years, so, too, did the university's facilities. Originally housed in numerous rented locations throughout Grand Rapids, WMU purchased and moved all operations to 2333 East Beltline Ave. SE in 1990. Ten years later, WMU renovated a facility at 200 Ionia Ave. SW in downtown Grand Rapids, creating a much needed second location.

The Beltline campus, a 40,000 square foot facility, is located in a lovely wooded setting just north of a thriving shopping area. The downtown campus, a

77,000 square foot facility, is in a renovated building in the energetic urban district south of the Van Andel Arena. Both locations are also sophisticated conference centers where area professionals meet for symposiums and other business and social events.

A short time after opening its downtown campus, WMU welcomed Cooley Law School to its facility, the first law school in Grand Rapids. At the same time, the Center for Counseling and Psychological Services also opened there. "It has served over 1,500 clients while providing clinical experience for masters and doctoral students," Schultz said. In 2006, the center received a grant to expand into career counseling and related fields.

As the Grand Rapids Campus of WMU continues working with its students to best meet their educational needs, it maintains its tradition of service to the community—something it began almost 100 years ago.

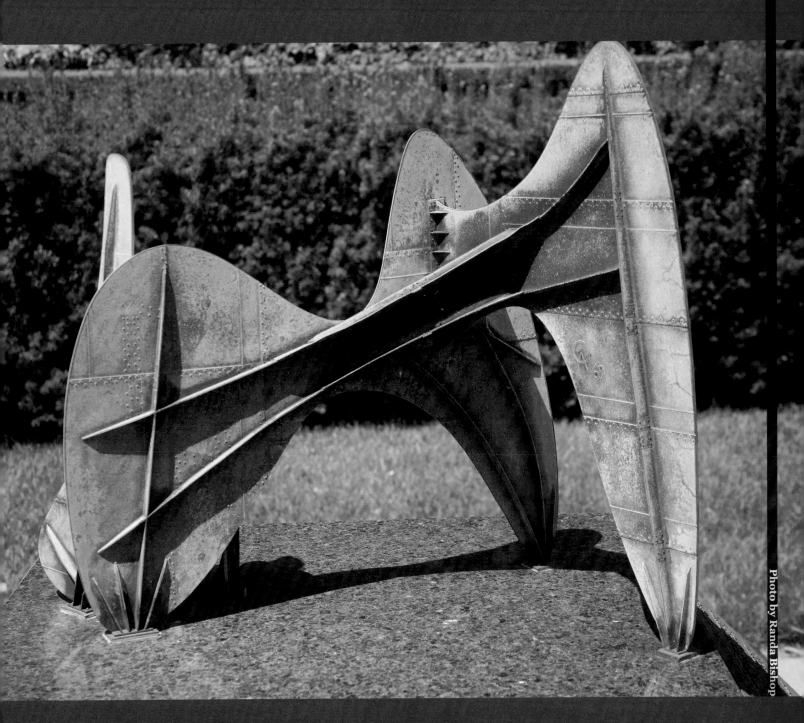

Steelcase Inc.

Steelcase Inc. is much more than just an office furniture company. Today's global organization,

and safes. Two years later, Metal Office begins diversifying with a new product, the Victor fireproof steel wastebasket. And in

in Toronto, Ontario. During the 1970s, it formed joint ventures, purchased new manufacturing plants, and started international dealer distribution organizations both within the United States and abroad, as far away as Japan, the Middle East, and Europe.

The global corporate headquarters on 44th Street in Grand Rapids opened for business in 1983. That same year, Steelcase won a national award from the President's Council on Environmental Quality for a new manufacturing process that reduces pollutants in the painting process.

The company strives to help its customers do their work better, faster, and more effectively through integrated workplace solutions. It also strives to do right by the environment, and has innovated numerous products and materials over the years to reduce its footprint. In 1993, Steelcase reached "label-free" status by eliminating specific ozone-depleting substances from its products. Ten years later,

Steelcase office environments facilitate collaboration, increasing communications and work effectiveness.

with more than 1,400 patented ideas, 13,000 employees and 800 dealers worldwide, offers some 500 product lines in the areas of architecture, furniture, and technology, and it is considered a thought leader in the ways people work. From its original steel desks to today's extraordinarily modular office systems, the offerings of the company have diversified and broadened to accommodate the evolving workplace.

Begun in 1912 when Peter M. Wege, Sr., Walter Idema, David Hunting, and ten other stockholders started the Metal Office Furniture Company in Grand Rapids, the company specialized in filing cabinets

"Interestingly, the surrender documents that ended World War II in 1945 were signed by General Douglas MacArthur and Japanese officials on a Steelcase table."

Right: Steelcase Inc. Global Headquarters, Grand Rapids, Michigan.

1915, it got into the business of desks: 200 fireproof steel desks were sold to Boston's first skyscraper, the Customs House Tower. The next year, Metal Office's first dealer opened its doors in St. Louis, Missouri. In 1921, Metal Office officially registered the Steelcase name as a trademark, but did not rename the company until 1954. Interestingly, the surrender documents that ended World War II in 1945 were signed by General Douglas MacArthur and Japanese officials on a Steelcase table.

The same year the corporation was renamed Steelcase, it launched international operations with a 15,000 square-foot plant

Steelcase had eliminated the emission of almost all volatile organic compounds (VOCs) from its metal finishing operations in Michigan.

In 1989, the corporation also built the Corporate Development Center, at the time the largest office building in West Michigan, in the middle of a pasture in Gaines Township, where its pyramidal shape can be seen from airplanes flying to and from the Gerald R. Ford International Airport. Situated on one of the Midwest's few prairies, building employees and visitors are likely to see grazing deer, a few geese or ducks paddling in the wetlands, some really lovely wildflowers and native plants, and other harbingers of nature.

In 2002, Steelcase opened a new wood furniture plant in Grand Rapids, which is the first manufacturing facility in the world to achieve certification under the LEED (Leadership in Energy and Environmental Design) program from the U.S. Green Buildings Council. Steelcase continues its commitment to the environment, having joined the U.S. Environmental Protection Agency's

Climate Leaders program, an industry-government partnership dedicated to reducing greenhouse gas emissions, in 2006.

The company also takes care of the aesthetic environment, too. In 1987 Steelcase opened the historic Meyer May House in the Heritage Hill district of Grand Rapids after a complete restoration of the Frank Lloyd Wright-designed house. Used for special corporate functions, it is also open to the public for tours.

Steelcase has won numerous awards over the years, including a 2006 IDEA gold award (Industrial Design Excellence Award) for Furniture and Fixtures for its Think® chair, the top award from the Industrial Designers Society of America. The company was also awarded three gold and three silver Best of NeoCon® awards at the 2007 NeoCon World's Trade Fair, the largest annual contract furniture industry trade show in the U.S. The company has designed and engineered many innovative products, of course, including the Leap® chair, which was specifically created to address back pain issues; the award-winning Think® chair, an environmentally

sustainable chair; and the Pathways® product portfolio, which integrates furniture, work tools, technology, and interior architecture products.

In addition, the company itself has been honored in various ways. In 2000, Steelcase was named one of the 100 best-managed companies in the world by IndustryWeek magazine. In 2005 the company was awarded a Shingo Prize for manufacturing excellence and the Hong Kong Design Centre awarded the Think chair the Design for Asia Award. In 2007 Steelcase was ranked seventeenth on CRO's (Corporate Responsibility Officer) list of top 100 corporate citizens.

Steelcase was founded by individuals who were committed to their community as well as to solid work ethics. The principles the founders brought to the company have become stated core values interwoven within the company's operations: act with integrity, tell the truth, keep commitments, treat people with dignity and respect, promote positive relationships, protect the environment, and, quite simply, excel.

Steelcase provides a complete line of wood products.

Steelcase provides products that fully integrate architecture, furniture and technology products, including full height, demountable glass walls.

"The company also takes care of the aesthetic environment, too. In 1987 Steelcase opened the historic Meyer May House in the Heritage Hill district of Grand Rapids after a complete restoration of the Frank Lloyd Wright-designed house. Used for special corporate functions, it is also open to the public for tours."

253

Spartan Stores is the largest publicly traded grocery retailer and

independent grocers formed a buying cooperative—the Grand Rapids Wholesale Grocery Company—on December 27, 1917. Its first purchase was a boxcar of sugar.

Over the years, the cooperative weathered the economic and political upheavals of the Depression, the Second World War and finally entered the relative calm of the 1950s. Not only did the cooperative grow 120 percent in the five years between 1952 and 1957, but it also began distributing its own products under the Spartan label. In 1957, the company changed its name to Spartan Stores, Inc.

A Household Name

Over the years Spartan, through its private label brand and its green logo, became a familiar sight on store shelves throughout the state. New distribution centers opened in Grand Rapids and in Plymouth, Michigan, giving Spartan a larger footprint in the state to supply thousands of products to its independent retailers.

Strategy for a new millennium

In the 1990s, Spartan set out in a broader direction as part of its long term plan to support the independent grocery retailer and to grow its own retail business, While distributing some 40,000 nationally branded products and 1,800 corporate brands to independently owned stores, Spartan began acquiring stores as well. By the end of the decade, Spartan had acquired five

"Spartan Stores is the largest publicly traded grocery retailer and distributor headquartered in West Michigan, employing more than 9,100 associates. Spartan Store operates eighty-eight supermarkets, fourteen drug stores, and twelve fuel and convenience centers throughout Michigan and northwest Ohio and distributes groceries to nearly 400 independent retailers in Michigan, Indiana and Ohio."

distributor headquartered in West Michigan, employing more than 9,100 associates. Spartan Store operates eighty-eight supermarkets, fourteen drug stores, and twelve fuel and convenience centers throughout Michigan and northwest Ohio and distributes groceries to nearly 400 independent retailers in Michigan, Indiana and Ohio, quite a contrast from its roots as a grocery buying cooperative in 1917.

The grocery business was as challenging and competitive in the early 1900s as it is today. Even then, larger stores were encroaching on the turf of the traditional Mom-and-Pop corner grocery. In order to strengthen their purchasing power, forty-three

independent grocery chains throughout western and northern Michigan, building its retail chain supermarkets.

In August 2000, Spartan Stores went public, trading on the NASDAQ under the symbol SPTN.

With a new vision and a significant new investment in bricks and mortar, Spartan Stores sharpened its focus and its strategy—to continue to grow its grocery distribution business and build its retail supermarket presence.

Beginning in 2003, the company began to reposition and refresh its brand. The clean new Spartan logo on its private label products has resonated well with customers as has the introduction of several new labels, such as Full Circle, a line of natural and organic products.

The company also began an ambitious program to remodel and refresh its stores, creating bright, pleasant places to shop with the conveniences customers appreciate. Spartan's strategy is to create a "neighborhood market", which emphasizes personal service, convenience, and quality, and which differentiates Spartan-owned stores from its big-box competitors. Spartan also articulated a "consumer-centric" focus, which seeks to identify the needs and preferences of its customers—both those who shop at its stores as well as the distribution customers who buy Spartan-branded products for their own stores. This consumer-centric approach might mean providing services, such as pharmacies and gas stations, at its grocery stores, or it might mean partnering more closely with its distribution customers in order to offer "value-added" service. In 2006, Spartan Stores significantly strengthened its retail market position and competitive stance by acquiring D&W Fresh Markets. The following year, the acquisition of Felpausch Food Centers, a previous 50-year distribution customer, gave Spartan Stores retail presence in new communities and aligned with its business strategy to grow its retail business. New distribution customers also contributed to the company's growth and considerably increased Spartan's distribution presence Michigan and Indiana.

The result of years of intensive effort is profitability and a strong position in the marketplace. Clearly articulated strategies, streamlined efficiencies, and a laser focus on consumer centric merchandising and marketing have created several consecutive years of growth and positive earnings. In 2007, Spartan Stores owns and operates retail stores in Michigan and Ohio and is the leading grocery distributor in Michigan. In a challenging business environment, Spartan is well-positioned to remain a force to be reckoned with in the regional grocery business.

"Clearly articulated strategies, streamlined efficiencies, and a laser focus on consumer centric merchandising and marketing have created several consecutive years of growth and positive earnings."

"90 Years of Client Centered Construction."

Triangle Associates, "a client-centered construction company," offers

Triangle Associates Inc. corporate headquarters.

Datema & Son's construction truck in the early 1900s.

Cross installation at Saint Mary's Lacks Cancer Center.

construction management, general contracting, and design/build services. Founded as George Datema & Sons in 1918, Triangle has been providing construction services designed to meet the specific needs of its clients. Rooted in a tradition of solid work ethics, pride in craftsmanship, and an honest approach in dealing with people, the company has blended those qualities with today's technologies.

Projects include educational, medical and housing facilities; commercial, retail, hospitality and entertainment projects; manufacturing and industrial plants; civic and government buildings; wastewater and water treatment plants; and historic renovations. Notable projects are Calvin College Prince Conference Center and Lodge, Terrazzo Fine Shops and Daniel's, Cook Valley Estates, Avenue for the Arts - Downtown Revitalization, and the Spectrum Health Helen DeVos Women & Children's Center.

Grand Rapids is per capita, at the fore front of sustainable building in North America and has been recognized as such by the USGBC. About 30 percent of Triangle's projects involve LEED (Leadership in Energy and Environmental Design), a sustainable building certification under the auspices of the US Green Building Council. With more LEED projects completed or underway than any other area contractor, Triangle is a leader in sustainability and green building.

Triangle's LEED projects, include Herman Miller, Forest Hills Fine Arts Center and Goodwillie Environmental School, East Grand Rapids Community Center, Saint Mary's Lacks Cancer Center and American Cancer Society's Hope Lodge in Grand Rapids.

"The Lacks Cancer Center was the second hospital in the U.S. and the first in Michigan to earn LEED certification," said President and CEO Craig Datema, AIA. "We have worked on a number of LEED buildings, but this one has architecture that garnered national attention." The Cancer Center is attached to the existing hospital and includes a cupola with a large cross atop it. That cross was blessed by Pope John Paul II. Getting the cross to the Vatican and then safely returned was an unusual task for Triangle personnel; they succeeded, and the cross returned in time for a special ceremony.

Headquartered in Grand Rapids and employing more than 180 people, Triangle has been a long-time community supporter through philanthropic work and diverse employee programs.

"We invest in our employees," said Datema, who is a fourth-generation company leader. "Triangle's key objectives are aligned with individual employee development goals such as development courses, State Builder Licensing, LEED Certification and Building Accreditations."

Triangle actively participates in diversity career fairs, and supports the Institute for Healing Racism, West Michigan Hispanic Chamber, West Michigan Minority Contractors Association, and Michigan Works.

"While our state transitions through a challenging economy, Triangle pursues new opportunities for growth and diversification. As the marketplace improves, we are confident Triangle will be positioned to play a major role in Michigan's evolving economy."

Celebrating its 90th Anniversary, Triangle Associates is geared for continued success. The company's mission statement is clear, "Triangle builds...exceptional facilities, great people, and strong communities."

A lot has changed since 1928, but Hoekstra Truck Equipment is still outfitting and changing vehicles to

create vocationally specific products. It all began when John F. Hoekstra saw a need for snow plows and graders to be attached to motorized vehicles and to be motorized themselves. While the company still handles such trucking needs, it's grown and evolved to include much more.

"As a company, we've never been afraid to change or innovate," said John F. Hoekstra, nephew of the founder and the president of the firm. Hoekstra and his two sons, Tom Hoekstra and Mark Hoekstra, continue in the tradition of their great uncle by meeting challenges and adapting to the changes in business of the ever evolving truck market.

Back in 1915, John F. Hoekstra's interest in automobiles led him to a job as a truck driver when he was just 15 years old. After that experience, he worked in various capacities in the automotive industry, often involving the Ford Motor Company.

In 1928, he bought equipment from the bankruptcy sale of the William Ford Company, a tractor equipment business where he had worked for a short time for Henry Ford's brother. With that initial investment, Hoekstra Truck Equipment began. It wasn't an easy beginning for the company, since the stock market crashed just a year later. But Hoekstra persevered and diversified as he saw fit, a tradition his nephew has continued.

In the 1930s, John Hoekstra got into the school bus business, and in 1941, his brother Alfred Hoekstra was hired as a salesman. During the 1940s, World War Two effectively stopped all automotive manufacturing in the United States and drove the company to focus on repair work. The brothers survived that time, and the two worked together for another 20 years. In 1962, Alfred purchased the firm from his brother. His son John Hoekstra, the current president, joined the company in 1971 and bought it from his father in 1977.

The company was located for years at Ottawa Avenue and Sixth Street in downtown Grand Rapids, where the William Ford Company was based. But by

> *"As a company, we've never been afraid to change or innovate," said John F. Hoekstra, nephew of the founder and the president of the firm. Hoekstra and his two sons, Tom Hoekstra and Mark Hoekstra, continue in the tradition of their great uncle by meeting challenges and adapting to the changes in business of the ever evolving truck market.*

1972, the growing Hoekstra Truck Equipment moved to its current location on 36th Street SE.

In the 1980s, Hoekstra separated the business into two entities, Hoekstra Truck Equipment and Hoekstra Transportation, to reflect the company changes. In 1981, Hoekstra acquired the dealership for Thomas Built Buses for the state of Michigan. Thomas Built Buses, based in North Carolina, is a subsidiary of Freightliner Corporation, a DaimlerChrysler company.

"1981 was really a significant time for us. It entirely changed the business," Hoekstra said. "We doubled the size of the company."

As the company continued to grow and diversify, it opened a branch in Troy, Michigan in 1991 and in 1999 moved Hoekstra Transportation—the school bus division—to a new facility on Roger B. Chaffee Boulevard SE, just around the corner from the 36th Street address.

Tom Hoekstra and Mark Hoekstra, who joined the company in 1995 and 1998, respectively, handle operations and sales for the bus division.

"We strive to be actively involved with the schools, from parts and service to full support and maintenance

for smaller school districts," Hoekstra said. That began in the early 1990s. A full-service bus dealership at both the Grand Rapids and Troy locations, Hoekstra Transportation handles bus leasing, new and used sales, reconditioning, and maintenance programs—"really whatever the customer needs," he added. "Budgets for schools are continually tightening, so equipment is expected to last longer and perform better than ever."

In addition to providing equipment to the educational system, Hoekstra Transportation has been involved with various safety initiatives through the Michigan Association of Pupil Transportation (MAPT) and other school organizations. (Hoekstra is an active member of both the MAPT and Michigan School Business Officials). As an equipment dealer, Hoekstra works with federal, state, and manufacturer groups regarding equipment changes including lighting, the "stop arm," and going to an eight-light system from a four-light one, for example.

Hoekstra Transportation has received numerous award and recognitions from Thomas Built Buses over the years, and the company named Hoekstra Transportation the nation's top dealer of the year in 1984 and 2000.

Today, seventy-five employees work at Hoekstra's three locations. Hoekstra Transportation is a certified dealer for equipment companies including CAT, Carrier, the Braun Corporation, and

Cummins. All of the factory-trained technicians are ASE certified by the National Institute for Automotive Service Excellence.

Hoekstra Transportation supplies the RAPID and DASH buses to the City of Grand Rapids, airport shuttles, and demand response buses like the popular "dial-a-ride" systems in smaller cities. Through its Hoekstra Specialty Vehicles division, which began in 2001 and is Michigan's first and largest commercial Sprinter van dealer, the company sells, leases, and services Freightliner Sprinter vans and trucks, which are those tall, thin vehicles that can get up to 27 miles per gallon. Hoekstra said he's looking to expand in this specialty vehicle area, and expects to open another facility.

Looking at the company's past, present, and future, Hoekstra sees a solid foundation. "We are a core business providing basic services," he said. "Snow needs to be plowed, trucks break down and need repair, and public transportation is necessary for many small communities." The good work of Hoekstra Truck Equipment never ends.

"We are a core business providing basic services," he said. "Snow needs to be plowed, trucks break down and need repair, and public transportation is necessary for many small communities." The good work of Hoekstra Truck Equipment never ends.

Douglas E. Wagner is the Managing Partner of Warner Norcross, which has more than 190 lawyers in five offices across Michigan.

From its modest beginning more than 75 years ago, Warner Norcross & Judd LLP has grown to be the largest and most respected law firm in West Michigan.

The founders quickly expanded their legal service offerings to include real estate, manufacturing, trucking and banking. Several of the firm's first clients grew alongside Warner Norcross and are still 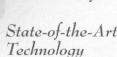 clients today, including Old Kent Bank (now Fifth Third Bank) and Wolverine World Wide.

to assisting with current clients. As a result, within a few years the firm was double the size of the next largest firm in Grand Rapids. "The assumption was that if you have good people, you bring them in, and they'll build their own work," says Charles McCallum, partner.

Today, Warner Norcross is a full-service law firm with five offices around the state serving a broad range of clients from multinational organizations to small, privately held companies to individuals. The firm's 190 attorneys practice in a wide variety of specialties and are supported by more than 200 professionals and staff. The firm currently has offices in Grand Rapids, Holland, Lansing, Muskegon and Southfield. Warner Norcross is proud to have celebrated its 75th anniversary in 2006 with a series of events for attorneys, staff, alumni and community.

"Warner Norcross & Judd is a full-service law firm with five offices around the state serving a broad range of clients from multinational organizations to small, privately held companies to individuals."

The firm got its start in 1931 when George Norcross and Siegel Judd, both lawyers and stockbrokers at the time, interrupted a dinner party at the Chicago home of attorney David Warner to ask him to join them in the founding of a law firm in Grand Rapids. Norcross had experience in bankruptcy, while both Warner and Judd had worked extensively with corporations, so the trio focused their legal services on bankruptcy and corporate reorganizations – both high-demand areas after the 1929 stock market crash.

Growth to a Full-Service Law Firm

By the late 1950s, the firm represented a growing list of West Michigan's most prominent corporations, and soon began expanding to serve clients across Michigan – and across the country. To accommodate the growth, Warner Norcross began aggressively recruiting top law students from the best national schools, encouraging them to develop their own clients in addition

State-of-the-Art Technology

Whether communicating with a client across the world or a partner across the state, seamless communication and efficient document management are key resources. Warner Norcross believes that state-of-the-art technology helps it deliver the best service to clients, regardless of their location. Since the first mimeograph machine was installed in the late 1940s, the firm has stayed at the technological forefront of its industry.

Warner Norcross has been named as one of the most "tech-savvy" law firms in the country. Use of cutting-edge tools such as extranets, video conferencing and portable technology demonstrates how Warner Norcross uses technology to serve clients. As technology continues to evolve, Warner Norcross is committed to utilizing the most current technology resulting in the highest efficiencies and responsive communication—just as it has for the past 75 years.

Commitment to an Inclusive, Enjoyable Workplace

Warner Norcross staff and attorneys are encouraged to be involved in the communities in which they live and work. The firm as a whole is committed to creating a diverse workforce and to encouraging inclusiveness within the community. This effort goes far beyond mere words and guides the direction and governance of the firm at core levels. The firm is working aggressively to foster a workplace culture based on three fundemental principles of diversity: respect, inclusion and teamwork.

A Diversity Committee, led by a dedicated Diversity Partner and in conjunction with the firm's Management Committee, is charged with fostering a more inclusive work place, expanding recruiting efforts and promoting education and awareness. The firm

Warner Norcross celebrated its 75th anniversary in 2006 with a year-long series of community events and activities.

publishes and distributes an Annual Diversity Report, which highlights recent activities and confirms the firm's ongoing commitment. "Our firm's leadership is committed to diversity and has a sense of urgency. These factors have allowed us to make rapid progress this year," says Rodney Martin, Diversity Chair.

"We've made this commitment in the firm that we will do everything we can to promote an environment that is welcoming and that is capable of sustaining both minority attorneys as well as minority staff," says Valerie Simmons, of counsel.

Excellent work and responsive service keep Warner Norcross among the top firms in the country—and one of only two in Michigan and 115 throughout the country to be listed in *America's Greatest Places to Work With a Law Degree.* "People expect more when they hear you're with Warner Norcross & Judd, and you don't want to disappoint them," says Stephen Waterbury, partner.

"Our firm's leadership is committed to diversity and has a sense of urgency. These factors have allowed us to make rapid progress this year," says Rodney Martin, Diversity Chair.

"The number of women and their roles within the Firm certainly has changed." says Susie Meyers, partner and the third woman to serve on the Firm's Management Committee. For the first time, women outnumbered men in the fall 2006 class of associates joining Warner Norcross.

April 15, 1931   MICHIGAN TRADESMAN

NEW COMMERCIAL LAW FIRM
Warner, Norcross & Judd Join Hands May One.

David Warner, Vice-President in charge of the Chicago office of R.H. Rollins & Co. for the past two years, has resigned his position with that house to return to Grand Rapids and reengage in the commercial law business with two Grand Rapids attorneys, Geo. S. Norcross and Siegel Judd. Mr. Norcross has been engaged in the practice of the law for several years. He is at present associated with others under the style of Corwin, Norcross & Cook. Mr. Judd succeeded Mr. Warner as corporate attorney for the former firm of Travis, Merrick, Warner & Johnson. Later he retired from the law firm to succeed Mr. Warner as local manager for R.H. Rollins & Co.

The three have had long and varied experience in the work they have conducted so successfully under former conditions and will undoubtedly achieve a still larger degree of prominence and success under the new regime.

It is a matter of congratulations that a man so thoroughly versed in the intricacies of commercial and corporation law is to return to Grand Rapids and that he will be associated with other men who have made their mark in their particular lines.

David Warner

Geo S. Norcross

Siegel Judd

Original press announcement on the founding of Warner Norcross appeared in the Michigan Tradesman.

With roots going back to the 1930s, the Paul Goebel Group, an independent insurance agency, has been helping individuals and businesses for decades with their insurance needs. The Paul Goebel Group designs, markets, and administers a wide range of plans for life, disability, accident and health, property and casualty, and professional liability insurance. The company also acts as the administrator for endorsed association group insurance programs for some 50,000 attorneys, certified public accountants, engineers, and other professionals throughout Michigan.

Over the years, Paul Goebel Group has become a premier agency for association, commercial, and personal lines of insurance in West Michigan. Through its association programs, it provides insurance to sole proprietors and firms of all sizes that belong to such professional organizations as the State Bar of Michigan, the Michigan Association of Certified Public Accountants, the Michigan Society of Professional Engineers, and the Michigan Optometric Association.

"We find programs that will directly benefit association members. We look for insurance companies that not only understand association group insurance, but can also underwrite the policies," said company president and owner Margaret (Meg) Goebel. Our associations designate the Paul Goebel Group as the exclusive administrator of their endorsed insurance programs, and their members can receive special rates and benefits."

Celebrating its 75th year in 2007, Paul Goebel Group first began as the Heines-Kesler Company. As leadership changed over the years, so, too, did the company name. In 1962, Paul Goebel Jr. joined the agency. Just a year later, his name became part of the company name, and in 1983, the agency became Paul Goebel Group. His daughter started working for the agency in 1976. Today, she is the sole owner of the 30-employee company, which has been located in the Waters Building in downtown Grand Rapids for more than 45 years.

"People have asked why I don't change the agency name to the Meg Goebel Group," said Meg. "I feel it's important to continue my father's legacy. It's perpetuating a tradition and being a part of the Grand Rapids community."

Community has always been important to the Goebels. Meg's grandfather, Paul Goebel Sr., owned a local sporting goods store and served three terms as the mayor of Grand Rapids during the 1950s and 1960s. Paul Goebel Jr. was also politically involved in the community, serving as a county commissioner while running his agency.

His daughter juggles quite a few responsibilities and interests herself. The *Grand Rapids Business Journal* named Meg one

From left: Paul Goebel Group staff members Sherry Gorman, CPA and controller; Jeff Elble, vice-president of sales; Meg Goebel, president and owner.

"We find programs that will directly benefit association members. We look for insurance companies that not only understand association group insurance, but can also underwrite the policies."

Meg Goebel, president and owner, Paul Goebel Group.

of the 50 Most Influential Women in West Michigan in 2006 and 2003. In addition, she is on the board of the Grand Rapids Area Chamber of Commerce, the Michigan Chamber of Commerce, the Economic Club of Grand Rapids, the Broadway Theatre Guild, and has previously served on the board of the YWCA, the Grand Rapids Art Museum, and numerous other associations.

As a board member of the Alliance for Health, Goebel said she feels it's important to stay involved with healthcare as well as health insurance issues. "This industry changes so dramatically over time," she added.

This is why she strongly values her membership in the American Institute of Professional Association Group Insurance Administrators (AIPAGIA). Goebel was the second female president in the organization's history. Formed of insurance agencies from across the nation that are similar to Paul Goebel Group, AIPAGIA is an association that enables its members to share ideas and discuss industry trends.

The staff of Paul Goebel Group also keeps involved in the industry and community, but Goebel doesn't monitor that activity. "I encourage them to be involved in their community, but I also respect their privacy," she said. "In the end, I'm a big advocate of personal and professional growth."

Meg has experienced growth of her own over the years, going from being the boss's daughter to the boss. It wasn't always an easy career path. "Being female has presented its challenges," she said with a laugh. "I did things my own way for the most part and reaped the benefits of working hard."

While her father was an important mentor and supporter for her in her early years, she still had to prove herself to the rest of the world. "As a female I had to work twice as hard as anyone else, and as a daughter, I had to work ten times as hard."

The success of the agency speaks well of her hard work. With life, auto, accident, homeowners, health, professional liability and disability insurance plans for individuals, groups and association members, Paul Goebel Group continues a strong tradition of finding the right insurance programs to meet the diverse needs of its clients.

Lake Michigan Credit Union Corporate Office

Sandra Jelinski, Chief Executive Officer

"Over the years, Lake Michigan Credit Union leaders have been attentive to customers' financial needs as well as changes in the ever-evolving financial services industry."

With assets exceeding $1 billion, Lake Michigan Credit Union is the largest credit union in West Michigan. Founded in 1933 by Grand Rapids schoolteacher Lloyd F. Hutt, Grand Rapids Teachers Credit Union, as it was then called, has grown mightily. Today, Lake Michigan Credit Union (LMCU) is a full-service financial institution with 125,000 members, 21 branch locations, and more than 65 ATMs.

The credit union, which could be called a healthy response to the Great Depression, was started by thirteen teachers who pooled their resources in an attempt to take control of their financial well-being. Based on the continued growth and success of the credit union, it looks like they made a sound decision.

Today, Lake Michigan Credit Union is a community credit union serving folks who live, work, worship, or attend school in Kent, Ottawa, Muskegon, and Allegan counties. Its offerings range from basic checking and savings accounts to debit cards and online services, personalized mortgage services, auto loans, and investment services. In addition, the Lake Michigan Auto Center in Hudsonville offers a variety of previously leased vehicles for sale, and the Lake Michigan Insurance Agency provides home, auto, life insurance, as well as a full line of commercial protection. The credit union also provides great rates and numerous services with no or low fees.

Over the years, Lake Michigan Credit Union leaders have been attentive to customers' financial needs as well as changes in the ever-evolving financial services industry. That focus is reflected in the different ways the credit union has developed. In the last five years, LMCU has opened nine new branch locations providing its customers with twenty-one convenient branches throughout West Michigan. The credit union has also greatly expanded its product offerings. Here are just a few examples: LMCU diversified its checking products to include not only free checking, but two options for interest-bearing checking accounts; it added a suite of VISA® Platinum credit cards, which gives users a choice of cash back, rewards points, or a low rate; LMCU launched a new mortgage division that

offers some of the best rates and mortgage products in the marketplace; LMCU enhanced its online services by expanding its Web site with improved functionality giving members more options, convenience, and security when managing their accounts online; and LMCU now offers Health Savings Accounts. All of this was done to ensure member satisfaction. All of this was done so LMCU customers can take care of all their financial needs in one place, with people they trust, at their convenience.

Members are the number one priority for Lake Michigan Credit Union, and staff focuses on and stays committed to providing the best customer service. One way this is addressed is through the very friendly "Five Star Service Promise," which includes a promise to "Greet You With a Smile, Call You By Name, Excel in Service, Respond the Same Day, Thank You Kindly."

Although originally a teacher's credit union, the organization underwent significant changes over the years through acquisitions and increased membership. In 1959, the teacher's credit union had more than 1,000 members and more than $1 million in assets. With such growth, it was time to move operations from Lloyd Hutt's home to a business office, which was located at 2424 South Division Street in Grand Rapids. It stayed educator-focused for the next decade or so. By 1971, assets had increased to more than $10 million and Grand Rapids Teachers Credit Union opened its Michigan

Street office and began to manage three other credit unions, Food Marketers, Health Care and Saint Mary's Hospital.

Two decades later, in 1992, Grand Rapids Teachers Credit Union assets passed $120 million with membership at approximately 33,000. Assets for the managed credit unions passed $40 million, and the institution acquired Aquinas College Credit Union and began serving college students as well as educators. Through the 1990s, advancements in technology allowed the credit union to introduce Internet Home Banking, Online Bill Pay, and Debit Cards, which broadened both the services and reach of the credit union. Growth continued as the credit union acquired Blodgett Hospital Credit Union and relocated its home base to the Credit Union Corporate Center.

In 2001, all of the managed credit unions, called the CU Financial Group, were consolidated into one credit union, the Grand Rapids Teachers Credit Union. Less than a year later, the Lake Michigan Credit Union name and logo were adopted. In 2003, LMCU acquired Grand

Shore Credit Union in Grand Haven.

While growing within the community, LMCU stays very active in its community, too. It sponsors the CaddyAm golf tournament that benefits the ALS Association West Michigan Chapter. Staff members put together teams to walk at the National MS Walk. LMCU is very involved in supporting education, offering classes on important financial issues at almost 40 area schools through its Money Matters program. And in memory of Lloyd Hutt, the credit union awards ten $1,500 college scholarships to area high school seniors in its annual Hutt Scholarship program.

While the credit union's charter changed so everyone in the four-county community can join Lake Michigan Credit Union, both teachers and heath care workers continue to be an important part of LMCU membership. Looking forward, the credit union will provide enhanced convenience to health care workers as it plans to open a new branch on the 'medical mile' in downtown Grand Rapids. Mr. Hutt and the twelve teachers who founded the initial teachers' credit union would be proud.

Hudsonville Branch

"Five Star Service Promise,"
which includes a promise to
• Greet You With a Smile
• Call You By Name
• Excel in Service
• Respond the Same Day
• Thank You Kindly

Lloyd. F. Hutt, Founder

265

In 1933, Earl Beckering Sr. founded his own business and called it Beckering

GVSU Cook DeVos Center for Health Sciences.

Construction Company. Originally from the Netherlands, Beckering had worked his way over to the United States as a carpenter on a ship, and finally settled in Grand Rapids. From the very start of his business, Beckering established a reputation for a strong work ethic, personal service, quality craftsmanship, and a hands-on management approach, and through the years these qualities have continued to be his company's trademark. In

"Our people have done more for the reputation and growth of this company than anything else," he says. "Because of that, along with the trust we've built with our customers through the years, Pioneer has been a very successful company."

GVSU Richard M. DeVos Center.

1962, under the leadership of Beckering's son, Earl Beckering Jr., the company's name was changed to Pioneer Construction, reflecting the innovative attitude and expanding services of the rapidly growing firm.

In 1975, Earl's son, Thomas Earl Beckering took over as president of the company. Tom grew the company into what it is today, one of the largest full-service general contracting firms in Michigan. According to Tom, Pioneer owes its growth and success to its employees, who are some of the finest skilled tradesmen in the industry today. "Our people have done more for the reputation and growth of this company than anything else," he says. "Because of that, along with the trust we've built with our customers through the years, Pioneer has been a very successful company." Beckering joined the firm in 1971, when sales were slightly more than $5 million annually. In 1975, he became president, and in 1979, he purchased the company from his father. Under Tom's leadership, Pioneer's sales have grown beyond $100 million annually. Pioneer has a workforce of nearly 300 employees many of whom have worked with the company more than 15 years.

In 2005 Pioneer entered its fourth generation of continuous family ownership when the company was purchased by Tom's daughter

Barbie and his son in law Tim Schowalter. Tim joined Pioneer in 1995 and became president in 2004.

A Complete Line of Services

Pioneer entered the 21st century as a leader in the industry, offering a broad range of services from construction management to full service general contracting as well as maintaining crews and equipment for steel erection, concrete construction and all manner of general trades.

"Our clients vary from large universities to emerging small businesses with very limited resources, and we try to maintain flexibility in the services we provide. The key to success is to never change our philosophy of quality and efficiency in dealing with either large or small projects."

Tailored Building Systems, a division of Pioneer, addresses the needs of small businesses requiring post frame and metal building construction. Tailored specializes in design/build projects that are custom designed for the specific needs and budgets of each unique client.

Pioneer's Construction Management teams provide the highest level of professional services that are demanded in today's marketplace. They provide pre-construction budgeting, value engineering, budgeting and market trend analysis, and then are able to deliver projects with efficiency and quality, on time and on budget. To maintain its high standards, Pioneer seeks out and retains some of the top project managers and superintendents in the industry, and has assembled an administrative staff of experienced, knowledgeable, and fully qualified professionals.

"We have made a conscious effort to develop and hire true builders; managers and professionals who not only understand the process of construction management," says Schowalter, "but who understand the plans, construction details, and the building itself."

Community Visibility

In 2008 Pioneer will celebrate it's 75th birthday. The legacy of Pioneer Construction is built into the West Michigan landscape. Buildings such as the Richard M. DeVos Center at the GVSU Pew Campus, Bridgewater Place, GVSU Cook DeVos Center for Health Professions, as well as many other major projects for companies and institutions such as Skytron, Huntington Bank, Spectrum Health, Grand Rapids Community College, Cascade Engineering, National City Bank, Amway Hotel Corp, Porter Hills Retirement Community, and Lacks Enterprises, just to name a few.

Beginning in the 1970s, the company established a relationship with Foremost Insurance Company, and handled millions of square feet of construction in

Resurrection Life Church.

Foremost Industrial Park, including the current Crowne Plaza Hotel and the IBM building. In addition, Pioneer also constructed one of the most elegant buildings in West Michigan: the new Foremost Insurance world headquarters, located in a wooded setting in Caledonia.

Pioneer has also become a leader in the revitalization of the downtown area, renovating several major historical buildings for condominiums and businesses. But with all the growth of the company and the evolution of the industry, Pioneer strives to maintain its roots. "We are a company built on people and values," says Schowalter, "I think that is why we have maintained our own crews and do our own work in so many trades. I think Barbie's great grandfather would have been proud to see this tradition of craftsmanship continue today."

Pioneer has become a strong member of the Grand Rapids community. "We recognize our responsibilities as a leader in our industry and are continually challenging ourselves in areas of community service as well as by setting an example of professional integrity in our business relationships." Says Schowalter, "Our

Tanaz Salon and Day Spa.

employees represent what is the very foundation of our community; from managers and professionals to skilled tradesmen we take pride in our work ethic and in the quality of what we build."

Pioneer Steel Erection Crews working in Downtown Grand Rapids.

"We have made a conscious effort to develop and hire true builders; managers and professionals who not only understand the process of construction management," says Schowalter, "but who understand the plans, construction details, and the building itself."

267

While they might not recognize the name Haviland Enterprises, Inc., people across the globe have benefited from its products

for decades. A chemical blender, packager and distributor, the firm sells a huge variety of products to both industrial and consumer markets.

With core values that include both achieving profitable long-term growth and having fun, the company has been able to smoothly blend more than chemicals over the course of its history.

Headquartered in Grand Rapids, Haviland Enterprises, Inc. is the parent company of two entities. Haviland Products Company, a distributor and blender of chemicals for markets across the United States and beyond, serves a wide variety of commercial and manufacturing industries, from the automotive industry to the food and beverage industry (which receives deliveries from

the company's food grade FDA-registered facilities). Haviland Consumer Products manufactures, packages, and sells more than seventy-five swimming pool and spa chemicals and manufactures and markets extruded, spiral-wound and blow-molded plastic hose. Haviland handles more than 2,500 chemicals and processes.

The company's board of directors reflects its focus on attaining good chemistry: It has eight members, with two family members (President E. Bernard Haviland and Corporate Secretary-Marie Haviland), Chief Executive Officer Thomas J. Simmons, and five individuals outside the organization.

Bernie Haviland and Marie Haviland are two of twelve children born to chemical engineer J. B. Haviland, who founded the company as a laboratory and chemical supply firm in Grand Rapids in 1934. A number of the siblings attended local Aquinas College, and the Havilands have supported the private college for years, particularly

in the sciences. Haviland Enterprises was incorporated in 1976 and has become one of the largest privately owned chemical blending/distribution companies in the United States.

Haviland's 160 employees, many with advanced scientific degrees, are also company owners. An employee stock ownership plan began in 1997, with approximately 40 percent of the stock now owned by employees.

"I think having business success and sharing with employee-owners is a significant resource for Haviland—it's a win-win situation. Our job is to achieve value for all our stakeholders – shareholders, customers, suppliers and employee-owners," said Simmons, who has been with Haviland since 1992.

"Teamwork is a big deal for us," he continued. "Everyone works together with a common goal; everyone pulls together." That effort goes outside company walls, too. In 2006, Haviland employee-

"I think having business success and sharing with employee-owners is a significant resource for Haviland."

owners organized a local effort to build a house in Grand Rapids for Habitat for Humanity, and the company surveys its people to log their community involvement and to help fund their efforts.

Haviland Products Company is International Organization for Standardization (ISO) 9000: 2001 certified and a founding member of the National Association of Chemical Distributors (NACD). As a participant in the NACD Responsible Distribution program, it has pledged to maintain the highest standards in handling, shipping, and using chemicals.

Considered an industry leader in personal and environmental safety, Haviland has a lending library of more than a hundred safety videos available to customers and the community. It maintains a good relationship with local fire departments, which tour its facilities to "get a sense of exposure to chemicals in general," Simmons said, so they are better prepared to deal with chemicals in any number of situations. "We're highly aware of our responsibility and we want to do everything we can and

more to protect the environment."

Haviland has 500,000 square feet of manufacturing and warehouse space at three locations, one in Kalamazoo and two in Grand Rapids, and it ships more than 300 million pounds of chemicals and compounds annually. Customers range from individuals looking for swimming pool treatments to specialty and industrial chemical companies, to Fortune 100 companies and original equipment manufacturers (OEMs).

Both Haviland divisions are supported by a state-of-the-art testing and formulation laboratory that also provides technical consulting for its customers. Technical expertise includes—but certainly isn't limited to—chemical formulation, electroplating and electroless plating, waste water treatment, corrosion control, solvent blending and stripping, electropolishing, and plastic extrusion. Value-added services include field technical service, vendor managed and consignment inventories, supply chain management and logistics, tank telemetry, toll blending and contract manufacturing, custom packaging and private labeling, and safety and compliance training.

"Our chemical contract blending capability or 'dedicated processes' have become strategically more vital and more significant to our business over the past several years," Simmons said. "This has resulted from our success in transforming the business from an historical distribution model

into a more value-added products and processes model. In addition, we have assumed a greater role in blending our own specialty chemical products through vertical integration in our manufacturing operations."

"We have made a conscious and successful effort to diversify away from the domestic automotive industry," Simmons added. "For example, we've always had a presence in the pharmaceutical industry, but it's been relatively new for us to focus more on that and on the food industry."

The success of Haviland continues thanks to good work both inside and outside the company. "Grand Rapids is just the right size," Simmons said. "My experience is that the city is very business-oriented, and the local government and government agencies are very pro-business." As a member of The Right Place and its Manufacturing Council, Simmons knows how local governments and agencies help businesses help each other and themselves.

Once again, when it comes to excellence, it comes down to having all the right elements that add up to good chemistry.

"Grand Rapids is just the right size," Simmons said. "My experience is that the city is very business-oriented, and the local government and government agencies are very pro-business."

While some siblings can barely share a room, the week in cavernous washing machines that can handle the 225,000 napkins and 15,000 tablecloths its customers soil

Jeff, Greg and Tim Jeltema

"Valley City Linen serves restaurants, nursing homes, hotels, health care facilities, and dental clinics throughout the state, laundering some 400,000 pounds of dirty linen every week in cavernous washing machines that can handle the 225,000 napkins and 15,000 tablecloths its customers soil every day."

Trucks from the early days.

Jeltema brothers see nothing unusual in the fact that the three of them amicably run the business that their grandfather began in 1935. In fact, these brothers have been involved with the family laundry business all their lives. "The business has been good. We have different areas of responsibility, so we stay pretty happy," says Greg.

"Tim takes care of the office and finances. I do sales and distribution; Greg does operations," adds Jeff.

Valley City Linen serves restaurants, nursing homes, hotels, health care facilities, and dental clinics throughout the state, laundering some 400,000 pounds of dirty linen every

every day.

And those 3,000 or so customers comprise a Who's Who of household names, such as Olive Garden, Marriott Hotels, Cascade Country Club, Chili's, the Gilmore Collection restaurants, and Cobo Hall in Detroit.

Decades of Struggle and Growth

Paul Sr. and Maude Jeltema began their company in 1935, calling it Valley City Coat and Apron Company. The business washed personal laundry for customers as well as aprons and linens for butcher's shops and grocery stores. Twelve years later, in the midst of a busy life and a growing business, Paul Jeltema died suddenly, and Maude was left with the laundry and five young sons. The business became a family affair with all five sons eventually working in the laundry.

Six decades later, the next generation of Jeltema brothers remember working with their father, Paul, and their uncles, riding in the delivery truck and watching grandma mend linens. "I remember when she sewed through her finger," says Jeff.

And they all remember the fire. Ten days before Christmas in 1972, a fire destroyed one-third of the plant. The family pulled together, working non-stop

for three days. Competitors from as far away as Petoskey and Lansing, most of them also family-run laundry services, offered to help wash laundry. Valley City Linen was open for business on Monday morning. Still, "every now and then, I get a whiff of something burning and it brings back that memory," says Tim, who was a child at the time.

In the late 1970s, tragedy struck again when two of the uncles died, leaving a gap that Greg, then just graduated from college, was the right age to fill. Jeff, who "always wanted to work in the business," joined him after earning a degree in business from Davenport. Tim returned to the family business after earning a degree in naval architecture and marine engineering.

A Statewide Footprint

After years of slow but steady growth, the company began to expand quickly in the 1990s. For one thing, their father, who eventually bought out his brothers, had always insisted on reinvesting in good technology and new-model machines. In the 1970s, for example, Valley City Linen was one of the first laundries to computerize its office processes. "This is a very capital-intensive industry," says Jeff, "but you have to invest to stay ahead of the curve."

In 1994, Valley City Linen opened a distribution center in the Detroit area in order to serve restaurant chains that tend to enter the state through the southeast market. So, while the company controls a large market share in West Michigan, its biggest growth market is in the Detroit area.

Distribution centers are now located in, Oak Park and Traverse City, giving the company the ability to serve customers statewide.

The business has grown steadily since Paul Jeltema Jr. and his sons took control of the company in 1988.

Into the Future...

As one of the few privately owned laundries, Valley City Linen has acquired strong regional presence and a national reputation in the textile laundering industry.

Greg is slated to serve as chairman of the national board of the Textile Rental Services Association, a global trade organization that primarily engages in lobbying, training, and education. "Big Chief Muckety-Muck," jibes Tim. Jeff will chair the regional board of another trade organization of 160 independent laundries that operates as a buying group

and that has organized to offer national customers consistent programs and pricing through its nationwide network of members.

As a family, the Jeltemas have always been active members in their church (East Leonard Christian Reformed) and strong contributors to Christian schools. "We are people of faith, and God has been good to our family," says Tim.

"We are also fifth generation Grand Rapidians," adds Greg, "and the third generation in this business. We have very deep roots in this community."

"Valley City Linen opened a distribution center in the Detroit area in order to serve restaurant chains that tend to enter the state through the southeast market. So, while the company controls a large market share in West Michigan, its biggest growth market is in the Detroit area."

"As a family, the Jeltemas have always been active members in their church (East Leonard Christian Reformed) and strong contributors to Christian schools. 'We are people of faith, and God has been good to our family,'" says Tim.

When we pick up a box of cereal from our local supermarket or a ream of paper at the office supply store, we typically don't think much about how the company's major strengths. We take great pride in what we do and that shows," said John Baysore, Dematic's president and CEO.

The company celebrates its 70th year in 2009, having started in 1939 as the Rapids-

Renamed Rapistan in 1966, the company stayed that way until 1992, when it became Mannesman Dematic, Siemens Dematic in 2001, and finally Dematic Corp. in 2006. Today, the company employs more than 1,300 individuals at its North American headquarters, located on the northeast side of Grand Rapids.

"The strong value set and hard work ethic prevalent in the people of West Michigan makes this area a great place to run a business," Baysore said.

"As a long-standing employer of high-quality jobs, the company has provided employment for thousands of people during its long history," Baysore added. "The community has also benefited from our long-standing tradition of helping to make our community better. From our days as the Rapistan Employee Association until today, our employees have contributed, participated, and rolled up their sleeves to make our community better. Dematic employees have stepped up to help organizations such as Habitat to Humanity, First Robotics, Toys for Tots, and the Juvenile Diabetes Research Foundation, among others."

Giving back is an employee tradition. From passing a hat to collect money when a coworker had a house fire, to having money deducted from paychecks to support nonprofit

In addition to a strong local presence, Dematic also has a large global presence.

> *"The strong value set and hard work ethic prevalent in the people of West Michigan makes this area a great place to run a business," Baysore said.*

goods got where we need them to be. Thanks to the technologies and engineering of companies like Dematic, the products we need can be found in the right place at the right time, again and again, so we don't have to think about it.

"Dematic brings almost 70 years of experience as a provider of quality supply chain automation solutions for warehousing and distribution. Our ability as a company to get the job done—no matter what the level of manual vs. automation, or simple vs. sophisticated—is one of the

Standard Company, which itself was created when the Grand Rapids-based Standard Caster Company and Rapids Manufacturing Company merged.

In those early days, Rapids-Standard produced casters and wheel conveyors. Some of its first products included equipment for distributing military supplies. As the years passed, the company's offerings moved from gravity conveyors to motorized, belted conveyors, and then to today's more complex computer-controlled conveyor systems.

The Dematic schoolhouse has long-been a symbol of the material handling education that the company has offered since its days as Rapistan.

community that attracts top talent to our area."

He continued, "Our ability to have a quality, hard working, and dedicated workforce is a key component for us. We need a vibrant and economically strong community to attract and retain top talent."

The world's leading supplier of automated material handling systems for manufacturing, production, warehousing, and distribution, Dematic serves a broad customer base in the areas of mail-order, grocery, hardware, apparel, chemicals and pharmaceuticals, office supply, and general merchandise. Really, any industry that transports, sorts, stores, and stocks

"Our ability to have a quality, hard working, and dedicated workforce is a key component for us. We need a vibrant and economically strong community to attract and retain top talent."

organizations, to organizing fund-raisers like bake sales, silent auctions, and motorcycle rallies, the people of Dematic have shown themselves to be community supporters in a variety of ways.

The company also supports development and education in its trades, too. For example, Dematic sponsored the area's first robotics teams at the local high school level and has an engineering internship program to help to promote its innovative, technological field.

"We are more than just a manufacturer; we also provide material handling solutions. This requires a high level of technical competency," Baysore said. "Strong engineering programs at area colleges and universities build the foundation for our future success."

Baysore appreciates the diverse skills and talents available in the community. "This strong West Michigan

engineering community, with the mechanical controls and software engineering skills, will be able to meet the challenges of our customers

for years to come," he said. "That's why I have reinstated our engineering co-op program. These relationships with the engineering schools and technical institutes create an attractive

products needs logistics services, and Dematic can deliver. Part of the Dematic GmbH & Co. KG company of Offenbach, Germany, the company had sales of nearly $1 billion in 2006.

Dematic's innovative products, like the C-L100 conveyor, are setting the standard in the industry.

Dematic's S-L300 sorter allows customers to sort a higher volume of products at a slower speed.

Half of the worldwide sales from Dematic global comes from Dematic's North American headquarters in Grand Rapids.

The company Web site states, "We are the industry's only OEM providing complete resources for supply chain and material flow analysis, systems concepting and engineering, project management, controlled quality manufacturing, installation, and comprehensive life-cycle support." More than 10,000 of its systems have been installed worldwide, serving customers large and small.

Offerings by the ISO-certified manufacturer include medium and heavy duty gravity and powered transportation and accumulation conveyors and accessories, sorting equipment, order fulfillment systems, automated guided vehicle systems, automated storage and retrieval systems, automated electrified suspension monorails, trailer loading systems, controls, software, design services, project management, installation, and system integration.

Maintenance and customer service are not only important, but considered a competitive advantage for Dematic. After all, what company wants to deal with costly downtime due to a system problem? Supporting all manufacturers' systems, Dematic also services its own wares 24 x 7, including conveyor systems installed in the 1960s that are still up and running. In addition, the company is ready to help its customers with emergency

At Dematic's Technology Center, products are tested and demonstrated for customers.

situations and offers longer term assistance as needed with permanent, on-site staff. And Dematic offers a variety of training programs, both on- and off-site as well as via the Internet, in the areas of operations, maintenance, and information technology. All training integrates a five-step process involving analysis, design, development, implementation, and evaluation that was created to support the alignment of learning and business outcomes.

On top of all that, Dematic is recognized as a thought leader in the industry. A number of employees have patents on their inventions, with a total of more than 250 patents currently in active use. In celebration of its employees' innovation, the company has held award ceremonies to honor its employee inventors. In 2006, some twenty inventors were honored for twelve granted patents and sixteen filed patent applications.

Engineering and product testing and development labs support and facilitate innovation. Lab features include a customer load test lab, an order fulfillment test module, software development and software integration labs, a controls emulation lab, product development prototyping, and product lifecycle testing.

While Dematic is a world leader in a very complex, logistical industry, the company also realizes that a knowledgeable customer can make better, more informed decisions. The company's little red schoolhouse, an old renovated school building located on the corner of Michigan and Plymouth NE in Grand Rapids, has been hosting training sessions since 1963. Many professionals in the logistics and material handling have been trained at this facility.

For decades, Dematic Corporation has been helping companies—and their customers—find the right products at the right place at the right time. For that, consumers everywhere can be grateful.

Kuyper College is a Christian-leadership college that educates and trains men

At Kuyper, low student-to-professor ratio promotes lively classroom discussion.

Below Right: The Zondervan Library is one of only two repositories for all books published since 1930 by the Zondervan Publishing House.

"Kuyper provides students who desire a well-rounded biblical and academic college experience with the opportunity to see, understand, and live all of life through the filter of Scripture."

and women for ministry and service. According to College president Nick Kroeze, Kuyper accomplishes this objective through the integration of a high-quality academic curriculum and a Reformed worldview. "Kuyper provides students who desire a well-rounded biblical and academic college experience with the opportunity to see, understand, and live all of life through the filter of Scripture. This is instrumental in guiding students through the process of discovering God's glory, communicating this truth to others, and honoring the Lordship of Jesus Christ," said Kroeze. "Furthermore," he continued, "Kuyper provides students an

educational experience that is not only life-changing, but world-changing. Through their professional

endeavors and service to Christ, our graduates are making a difference in the lives of people in the United States, Canada and in more than fifty other countries throughout the world."

Kuyper College's history began in 1939 when it was founded as the Reformed Bible Institute. In 1970, after a five-year redesign of curriculum and programs,

it changed its name to Reformed Bible College—as it began to confer four-year Bachelor degrees. "Today, while the College has grown in enrollment and academic offerings, the mission is the same as it was in 1939," said Kroeze. "The College seeks to place students in ministry and professional areas of leadership around the world to meet the spiritual and social challenges facing people today. This is the essence of our purpose, the essence of our identity—to bring God's grace into today's culture."

Kuyper College's curriculum combining faith and learning is just one of seven foundational elements that the College calls *TheKee—The Kuyper Education Experience*. These components have been designed to have a synergistic relationship to help prepare students to be Christian leaders. The first element—*Integration of Faith and Learning*—is paramount. Every Kuyper graduate completes two majors—one in his or her chosen field

and one in Bible and Theology. "This convergence of high-quality academics and Christian perspective develops graduates who understand how their beliefs and vocational pursuits complement each other," said Kroeze.

Other elements of TheKee include: *Spiritual Formation,* which helps students discern their spiritual gifts and grow in the understanding of who they are in Christ; *Field Education and Career Development Internships* featuring hands-on experience in real-world situations; a *Study-Service Abroad* program that provides students with the opportunities to learn and serve in several locations throughout the world; a

Christian colleges.

Kuyper College currently offers professional degree programs in twenty-one areas of study. While many of their programs prepare

Free University in Amsterdam, a Christian university founded on Reformed worldview principles. "There is great affinity," said Kroeze, "between the life's work of Abraham Kuyper and the historical mission of the College—to promote the practical application of God's Word into the everyday lives of all people."

Kuyper College sits on beautiful rolling woodlands about 15 minutes from downtown Grand Rapids. Completely wireless, the campus also houses the Zondervan Library—one of two repositories for the complete catalog of Bibles, books, and media produced by the Christian publishing company Zondervan.

Accredited by the Association for Biblical Higher Education, North Central Association of Colleges and Schools, Kuyper also offers a social work degree program that is accredited by the Council on Social Work Education.

In-between classes, students catch up on the latest news.

Left: Students from Nigeria, Nepal and Korea are representative of the many international students at Kuyper College

The Kuyper College campus, although close to downtown, features beautiful rolling landscapes.

Multi-Cultural and Diversity program designed to ensure an ethnically balanced student body, is also inclusive of over twenty-five different denominations; and a *Faculty-Student Ratio* of 15 to 1 which results in highly personalized and customized instruction from a committed faculty. The last element of TheKee is a *Cost-Reduction* program, which ensures that tuition and room and board fees are approximately 30 percent less than comparable

students specifically for ministry, others offer a wide range of degree programs that train students for careers in business, social work, communication, information technology, education, nursing and other professions.

The College is named after Abraham Kuyper (1837-1920). Prime minister of the Netherlands from 1901 to 1905, Kuyper also founded the first Christian Democratic Party, and the

Saint Mary's Southwest - A 2-story LEED Certified healthcare facility with a variety of services including an ambulatory surgery center, an urgent care center, diagnostic center, and primary/specialty physician offices.

"The company prides itself on being very customer focused," VanderZyden said, **"and applying its four core values—integrity, enjoyment, quality, and improvement— in everything it does."**

Left: River House Condominiums - Construction of a new, 32-floor condominium building with some commercial space on the lower levels is underway.

Middle: Advance Packaging - Construction of a large, corrugated paper manufacturing plant with more than 400,000 square feet. One special feature was the installation of imbedded steel rail in the floor to assist in automatic movement of the finished product throughout different areas of the plant.

Wolverine Building Group, which is comprised of Wolverine Building, Inc., Wolverine Construction Management, Wolverine North America, and Fryling Construction, continues to grow and expand, making its presence well known.

The company has grown since it was founded in 1939 by Peter Bouwman as Wolverine Tile Company, specializing in tile installation. As one of the Midwest's leading installers of porcelain panels for automobile service stations and fast food restaurants, Wolverine Tile Company grew quickly and eventually began constructing complete gas stations. When Peter Bouwman's son James joined the company in the fifties, Wolverine became one of the first companies in West Michigan to use pre-engineered steel in its construction.

In 1957, Wolverine Tile Company became Wolverine Building Products, Inc., to better reflect its broader services. Then in the seventies, Wolverine developed its design/build capabilities (making the company a pioneer in this field) and soon expanded into general contracting. By the 1980's, the company became simply Wolverine Building, Inc., and project managers Stan Cheff and Jeff Ridings became the new owners

Wolverine Construction Management was developed in 1993 to offer construction management services to institutional clients in West and Central Michigan. Wolverine Construction Management now sets an industry benchmark in health care and educational facility planning and construction, as well as other institutional planning and construction management.

During this same time, Fryling Construction Co., founded in 1945 by Nicholas Fryling, was building its own niche as the premier multi-unit and commercial retail builder in West Michigan. In 1995, as a means of diversification Wolverine acquired Fryling Construction. In 1998, Wolverine Building Group was formed to combine all three divisions in new corporate headquarters in Kentwood.

Today's leadership entered the firm in the 1980's when new Ferris State University graduate, Michael Kelly, was hired to head up Wolverine's drafting department and Richard VanderZyden joined the team as project manager. Kelly and VanderZyden

assumed company ownership in 2001.

Today's four divisions were developed with a conscious intent to diversify the company. Wolverine Building, Inc. continues with its focus on design/build contracting. Wolverine Construction Management provides construction management services to the healthcare, education, and institutional markets. Fryling Construction adds its reputation as one of the premier multi-unit housing and commercial retail builders in West Michigan. Wolverine North America, the most recent division was formed in 2006 in response to client requests and provides program management and construction services across the nation.

"We're building the facilities that people are going to be working in," states VanderZyden, "growing businesses and institutions." The company focuses on three areas: health care facilities, multi-family structures, and commercial and industrial facilities.

"The company prides itself on being very customer focused," VanderZyden said, "and applying its four core values—integrity, enjoyment,

quality, and improvement—in everything it does."

"We really try to continually get better in what we do," he said. The company looks for better ways to build, hire and recruit, apply cutting-edge technologies, and manage projects. "We're very proactive in everything, and we take pride in that. Our goal is to be better, not just to grow and diversify. Servicing our clients is what causes us to grow."

The company mission is "To Build Great Things," which means building solid customer relationships as well as quality buildings.

Proof of the company's endurance is evident across West Michigan, from Fifth Third Ballpark in Comstock Park and Spectrum Health Fred and Lena Meijer Heart Center downtown Grand Rapids to the Calvin College pedestrian crossing over the East Beltline, to name just a few projects. And proof of Wolverine's healthy customer relationships is evident in the fact that Robert Grooters Development Company has been working with the company for 20 years and called on the company to construct what will be the tallest building in Grand Rapids when it's completed in 2008 – River House Condominiums.

Giving back is important to the firm, too. "Wolverine Building Group believes that community involvement is vital in facilitating the growth of our local community," states the company Web site. In that spirit, the firm sponsors a number of community teams and events and encourages employees to be active in community service

programs and projects.

The company also hosts students from area high schools for career days. It's a great opportunity to catch the interest of teens who might want to pursue a career in the construction field.

VanderZyden said the industry has changed over the years, and as projects are getting bigger and taller, the construction professionals are getting more educated. "More and more, college graduates are getting to be the norm in the field," he noted. Wolverine is hiring more degreed civil engineers and construction managers, for example.

"We see a bright future for our firm and West Michigan," VanderZyden said. "We're very committed to West Michigan and the community – and we love being a part of it here."

Spectrum Health Fred & Lena Meijer Heart Center - A 10-story, 332,000 square foot, world-class cardiac care facility for Spectrum Health, in downtown Grand Rapids, MI. A challenging construction project; work was performed while maintaining uninterrupted hospital services.

"We see a bright future for our firm and West Michigan," VanderZyden said. "We're very committed to West Michigan and the community – and we love being a part of it here."

Wolverine Building Group Presidents – Richard VanderZyden (left) and Michael Kelly (right).

Grand Rapids Theological Seminary "provides inexhaustible opportunities to learn and grow" said

lives through continuing education in biblical studies.

The seminary offers Master of Divinity degree programs including Adult Ministries, Chaplaincy

Grand Rapids, which is home to many Christian institutions, has been a great place for the seminary, Fagerstrom noted. "Its rich Christian ministries and heritage of healthy churches set us apart from most metropolitan communities where there are theological schools."

Students receive their education at a 13:1 student-teacher ratio. "I believe our greatest strength is our faculty! A seminary is its faculty and GRTS has some of the best professors in the nation." Fagerstrom said.

The seminary began quite informally in 1941 as an evening Bible institute at Wealthy Street Baptist Church. In 1944, the seminary became the Grand Rapids Bible Institute and Theological Seminary. Its first graduating class had two graduates in 1949. The institute became a state-approved degree-granting Bible college in 1963 and then a Christian liberal arts college in 1972.

"Our students gain a rich experience from the classroom to the Christian ministry workplace during their entire seminary training."

Douglas Fagerstrom, seminary president. Opportunities for master's level students come through both the classroom and local ministry contexts, such as churches and other parachurch ministries to help students connect biblical teaching and theory with everyday life.

Located next door to its parent institution, Cornerstone University, the seminary has a student base that includes about fourteen different denominations. Recent enrollment is more than 250 students, and Fagerstrom said that number is increasing. Students range from those seeking to enter the ministry and those who want to enhance their

Ministries, Church Planting, Counseling Ministries, Intercultural Studies, Pastoral Ministries, Women's Ministries, and Youth Ministries. Master of Theology programs include Old and New Testament, Historical Theology, Systematic Theology, Historical Theology, and Systematic Theology. Master of Arts degree programs include Counseling Ministries, Educational Ministries, Historical Theology, New Testament, Old Testament, and Intercultural and Interdisciplinary Studies. The school's objective is "to fully engage men and women for a lifetime of learning, serving, and leading."

The core curriculum involves spiritual formation, preaching and teaching, pastoral care, counseling, cross-cultural ministry, church planting, leadership development, and more – all designed to help students connect classroom learning with the realities of actual community engagement. That involvement has translated to in-depth community service throughout the world.

Graduates are living and serving in areas as diverse as Asia, Liberia, Romania, Pennsylvania and, of course, West Michigan.

Grand Rapids Theological Seminary offers three learning centers in addition to traditional classrooms. The Lifelong Learning Center, which provides resources, events, and consulting services, helps seminary alumni and constituent ministry leaders to continue growing as leaders. The Global Learning Center reaches beyond the region to embrace its mantra of "One world. One story. One church. Many cultures." The Contextual Learning Center, which is part of most degree program requirements, places students, called "Residents," within the Grand Rapids community to serve mentors and ministry leaders of local churches and parachurch ministries. Fagerstrom said the opportunities of the CLC are often a primary attraction to prospective students.

"All of our students are fully engaged is serving area churches, ministries, and counseling centers," he said. "Our students gain a rich experience from the classroom to the Christian ministry workplace during their entire seminary training." Resident seminarians serve area churches including Ada Bible Church, Calvary Church, Blythefield Hills Baptist Church, and many more as well as outreach programs including International Aid and Mel Trotter Ministries.

The seminary offers "rolling admissions" so

new students can begin their coursework during any semester (except international students), and features Preview Days and individual campus tours for prospective students to experience the seminary life. Financial aid programs include academic, vocational interest, and need-based aid. More and more area business people and medical professionals are taking courses at GRTS.

Importantly, Grand Rapids Theological Seminary is accredited by the Association of Theological Schools and the Higher Learning Commission of the North Central Association of Colleges and Schools. In addition to going into education and ministry service, graduates of the seminary also have the opportunity to become military chaplains, because the United States Army, Navy, and Air Force all accept its master's degree graduates as chaplaincy candidates.

At the end of the day, Fagerstrom said he delights in "hearing from our

graduates [from] all over the world and the United States who are effectively serving God in churches and other Christian ministries. Our students are graduating and impacting the world with the message of the gospel of Christ. Men and women are going into our cities, our nation, and the world to help people make a difference in building God's kingdom. "

"All of our students are fully engaged is serving area churches, ministries, and counseling centers."

Kaydon Corporation Bearings Division is the forerunner of the $400 million Kaydon Corporation, located in Ann Arbor, Michigan. Kaydon Bearings is the largest division of the Corporation

Kaydon Bearings Division headquartered in Muskegon, Michigan.

Kaydon Bearings Division produces many different sizes of bearings for a wide variety of applications and several different product lines.

and is the undisputed world-wide industry leader in high precision, thin section bearing design and manufacturing.

Headquartered in Muskegon, Kaydon Bearings was founded in 1941 as Kaydon Engineering by A. Harold Frauenthal who named the company after his children, Kay and Don. The company began as a machine tool builder but, due to the impending threat of U.S. involvement in World War II, it soon shifted its focus to meet the U.S. Navy's critical need for large precision gun-mount bearings for its battleships.

Despite severe wartime shortages of equipment, material, and labor, Mr. Frauenthal's vision, ingenuity, and energy quickly moved Kaydon Bearings into full production. By December 1941, the company had grown to 130 employees and was supplying bearings to the Navy before the attack on Pearl Harbor.

Kaydon Bearings' performance for the Navy was so impressive that in February 1942 the company received the Army-Navy "E" award for its outstanding contributions to the war effort. The Army-Navy "E" award is the highest honor a company can receive and Kaydon's continued excellence in production garnered additional awards before the war ended.

When the war ended in 1946, Kaydon Bearings developed its plans for peacetime success that included proprietary techniques for manufacturing precise, large bearings for the machine tool, automobile production equipment, construction machinery, and glass and paper making machinery.

With over 60 years of experience, Kaydon Bearings has developed unique processes and techniques that enable it to produce high precision custom bearings that its competitors simply can not or will not attempt to make—a fact that everyone at Kaydon is extremely proud of. To this day, their competitors find it hard to overcome the challenges of manufacturing the delicate thin section bearings that

Kaydon specializes in. They established this market over 60 years ago and remain the global leader.

Today, Kaydon Bearings designs and manufactures some of the largest and smallest, most precise turntable and custom bearings in the world. Kaydon's large, turntable bearings are ideal for wind turbines, cranes, excavators, aerial work platforms, gun turrets, radar pedestals, forestry equipment, surveillance equipment, scanner equipment, and material handling equipment. Kaydon's Reali-Slim® bearings are ideal for applications in aviation, aerospace, robotics, machine tools, semiconductor manufacturing, lab instrumentation and medical equipment, and any application where a lighter, thinner bearing is required.

So, whether it's a large, 80" bore diameter bearing weighing 3,500 lbs. for a wind turbine, or a lightweight, 1" bore diameter bearing for an aviation, aerospace or robotics application, Kaydon designs and manufactures truly unique bearings that provide long operating life under the most demanding environmental conditions.

Over the years, Kaydon Bearings has amassed an impressive library of proven bearing designs, applications and advanced manufacturing techniques. All bearing design and development is done in Muskegon and many of the company's most complex components are built there. The Muskegon plant is Kaydon Bearings' most

sophisticated manufacturing facility and specializes in supplying performance-critical bearings for the military/aerospace and semi-conductor industries.

The Kaydon Bearings Division headquarters in Muskegon oversees three manufacturing facilities in the Carolinas and two in Mexico, which supply a wide variety of specialty bearings for the semiconductor, wind energy, medical, and heavy equipment industries.

Kaydon Bearings employs approximately 800 people with over 200 employees in Muskegon and plans to add more employees as sales have almost doubled over the past 2-3 years. To meet this growth, Kaydon Corporation has made significant investments in the Muskegon plant and has more planned.

Kaydon Bearings Division is a great place to work. Besides enjoying opportunity for advancement, competitive benefits, wages, and retirement programs offered in a safe working environment and located in a great community, Kaydon employees enjoy taking part in local activities and company-sponsored sporting events.

All members of the Kaydon Bearings Division family take great pride in knowing that they engineer and manufacture the best and most complex bearings in the world. Great attention to detail must be, and is, delivered on a daily basis to produce bearings used in flight-sensitive equipment such as airplanes and helicopters. Tolerances

measured in microns are common place.

Kaydon Bearings is also an asset to the Muskegon community. It actively sponsors the Frauenthal Center for the Performing Arts located in downtown Muskegon, which is named for its founder, and it plays an active role in supporting a multitude of charitable organizations and programs from the Red Cross and the United Way to the Boy Scouts and Girl Scouts.

Kaydon Bearings is proud of their heritage and more importantly looking forward to a bright future. Their highly engineered products applied to many of the most demanding, technically advanced applications in industry, provide them with limitless opportunities to grow and prosper.

An aerial view of the Muskegon Plant in relation to Muskegon Lake and Lake Michigan.

"Kaydon Bearings employs approximately 800 people with over 200 employees in Muskegon and plans to add more employees as sales have almost doubled over the past 2-3 years."

Kaydon is a world-wide leader in high precision thin section, close tolerance bearing design and manufacturing.

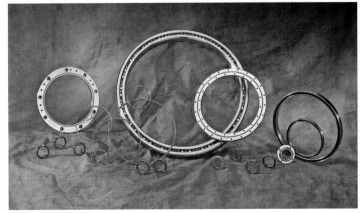

The award-winning WOOD TV8 has an impressive history of firsts when it comes to West Michigan television. Not only was it as weather updates and school closings, the Web site also has been developing its blogging section to better reflect and cover the community and its events.

first joined the WOOD TV8 staff in 1974 and is the niece of former White House correspondent Helen Thomas; investigative reporter Henry Erb, who joined 24 Hour News 8 in 1970 and received a Lifetime Achievement Award from the Associated Press in 2006; and chief meteorologist Craig James, who came to the station in 1985 and has won the Michigan Association of Broadcasters Award for Broadcast Excellence three times.

WOOD TV's Studio.

the first television station in Grand Rapids, but it was also the first to offer color, the first to broadcast its audio in stereo, the first to offer close-captioning in its newscasts, the first to bring 24-hour news coverage to West Michigan, and the first to use satellite news gathering broadcasts and to broadcast in HDTV.

The NBC affiliate, broadcasting on channel 8, also has the number one Web site in West Michigan, according to president and general manager Diane Kniowski. In addition to up-to-the-minute news reports and useful information such

The site premiered in 1996.

TV station faces familiar to viewers include news anchor Suzanne Geha, who

Over the years, WOOD TV8 has racked up a number of awards itself, including various Emmy Awards for its news programming. Recent awards include Station of the Year, which WOOD TV8 received at the annual Michigan Association of Broadcasters awards for the fifth consecutive year in 2007. Other awards the station has received include the Associated Press Awards,

> *"Over the years, WOOD TV8 has racked up a number of awards itself, including various Emmy Awards for its news programming."*

Storm Team 8 Meteorologists, Craig James and Bill Steffen.

the School Bell Award from the Michigan Education Association, and the Gracie Allen Award from the American Women in Radio and Television.

The station began more than 50 years ago when radio station owner Leonard A. Versluis debuted the area's first television station as WLAV TV on August 15, 1949. Broadcasting from what is now the McKay Tower in downtown Grand Rapids, the TV station offered news, game shows, variety entertainment, and sports events.

Purchased in 1951 by Grandwood Broadcasting, the owner of WOOD radio, the young television station became WOOD TV. (The WLAV call letters have lived on through a popular local radio station.) By 1954, the station was Michigan's most powerful television station— even more powerful than those in the Detroit area— with 316,000 watts. That year, WOOD TV also was one of just 21 stations across the United States that broadcast the annual New Year's Day

Tournament of Roses Parade in color. In 1955, the station moved to its current address in the Heritage Hill district of Grand Rapids, and two years later, Time, Inc. purchased the thriving company.

In 1972, the television station became known by the call letters WOTV, and despite the sale of the station to LIN Broadcasting Corp. in 1983, it stayed WOTV until 1992.That year, through a marketing agreement with WUHQ (ABC affiliate channel 41), WOTV reclaimed its old call letters and became WOOD TV8 once again, and WUHQ became WOTV4. LIN Broadcasting also owns WXSP, which runs WOOD TV's 24 Hour News 8 weekday evening newscasts an hour after they are broadcast live.

WOOD TV8 offers solid news coverage with 32.5 hours of news per week including a weekly political show, 'To The Point'. And since 1983, Chopper 8 has been hovering above West Michigan, allowing reporters to cover the news from a

higher viewpoint. Technical capabilities for the station include authorized power of 316-kilowatt visual and an antenna that is circularly polarized 970 feet above average terrain, 1,015 feet above ground, and 1,835 feet above sea level.

The people of WOOD TV8 know that operating a local television station is more than just technical proficiency, however. The station sponsors more than forty area non-profit organizations. And, through its daily events calendar and the Connecting with Community program, led by Community Affairs director Eva Aguirre-Cooper, WOOD TV8 gets the word out about the accomplishments, events, needs, and resources available through area non-profit agencies, art institutes, health resources, and educational programs.

With its long and rewarding history, its active community involvement, and its forward-thinking management, WOOD TV has become the go-to station for many television viewers. It's a community tradition.

WOOD TV 8's Control Room.

WOOD TV's Web-site, woodtv.com.

WOOD TV 8 Anchors, Suzanne Geha and Larry Nienhaus.

"With its long and rewarding history, its active community involvement, and its forward-thinking management, WOOD TV has become the go-to station for many television viewers. It's a community tradition."

Unist, Inc.

Every manufacturer knows the necessity to work faster, cleaner, and better in today's global market. Newspaper

Unist, Inc. continues to have space to allow for growth and progress well into the future apparent in the size of its' modern facility.

"Our 50 years of knowledge of the metal working industry allows us to meet challenges where 'tools meet the work piece,'" Boelkins said. In addition, he noted that the company has remained strong due to "our flexibility to resolve customer concerns while improving their productivity and cleaning up the work environment on a worldwide basis."

headlines remind them of the consequences if they don't. So when a company like Unist, Inc. offers an array of air operated, low maintenance precise fluid dispensing systems, it's worth paying attention.

Since 1957, Unist has been the leading manufacturer of Minimum Quantity Lubrication (MQL) machine lubrication systems and Coolube lubricants. The company's lubricant product line has proven to be a low cost, low volume lubrication solution for manufacturing

processes involving just about any industry you could think of, including plastics, glass, wood, appliances, auto, aerospace, mining, and tire.

Begun as Uni-Mist by two Grand Rapids businessmen in 1957, the company designed, patented, and sold a pressurized spray system for coolant applications that is still marketed today. As the company explains it, "We determined that utilizing the tremendous heat absorbing properties of converting any liquid into gas could be effectively used in heat removal generated when cutting metal. Water was the liquid of choice."

Since those early days, Unist products have diversified and now include a broad range of offerings. The company has been the first to develop a number of important products in the lubrication industry.

"We have about twenty patents and three or four worldwide patents

in process," said Wally Boelkins, president of Unist.

When Boelkins purchased the small company in 1968, he was the sole employee for two years. Today, the company has about twenty-five employees including part-time workers.

"Unist is firmly planted in Kentwood," Boelkins said, "with space to allow growth ten times our size. With Unist capital, technical ability, increased markets, and an increased product line, growth of that magnitude is very attainable within ten to 15 years."

The company certainly has maintained a healthy growth over the years, with an average of approximately 20 percent annual cumulative growth in a 30-year period. Serving some 2,500 customers in North America, Asia, Australia, Europe, Africa, and South America, Unist helps

manufacturers improve their manufacturing and assembly processes in metal machining, metal forming, wood working, machine lubrication, part lubrication, air motor lubrication, and mold release application.

"Our 50 years of knowledge of the metal working industry allows us to meet challenges where 'tools meet the work piece,'" Boelkins said. In addition, he noted that the company has remained strong due to "our flexibility to resolve customer concerns while improving their productivity and cleaning up the work environment on a worldwide basis."

In one situation, a Unist customer was able to reduce coolant expenses in its fabrication production by 97 percent—and realize cleaner operations as well as

a drastic reduction in coolant disposal, which must be EPA compliant.

Unist micro-fluidization systems exceed OSHA compliance standards for oil mist exposure, according to approved environmental lab tests. The company's cooling systems feature near-dry machining, which means less fluid and fewer lubricants required to operate cutting equipment, which translates into fewer dollars spent on lubrication. In fact, Unist tells its customers to "Be Stingy" when using its Coolube lubricant, because it must be used sparingly to effectively do its job. As the company literature says, "We operate on the assumption that an extremely small amount of a good lubricant can almost perform miracles."

Maintaining a broad customer base across many industries and just about every continent is a smart way to run a business in this global market. Boelkins said operating from the West Michigan headquarters has been great because of the local availability of almost all of the support services Unist needs. In addition, family, church, and community make the community the place Boelkins wants to be.

"West Michigan and Grand Rapids have a very good cross-section of educational institutions, cultural events, sporting events, spectator and

personal involvement activities, and even some phenomenal weather—good and not so good," he added with a Michigander's understanding of the unpredictable weather in this Great Lakes state.

In addition to employing what Boelkins called "a very diversified work force that is very productive," Unist keeps active in its community through its staff members. "Our employees are primarily 'church people' and their—and my—community involvement is primarily church-related activities," he said.

In addition, the company sponsors local softball teams and has been involved with the Grand Rapids Chamber of Commerce CEO Roundtable for more than 10 years.

Ultimately, there's a lot of value in being a well-oiled machine. In looking at the smooth operations at Unist, one might say that the company ably practices what it preaches.

In addition to employing what Boelkins called "a very diversified work force that is very productive," Unist keeps active in its community through its staff members. "Our employees are primarily 'church people' and their—and my—community involvement is primarily church-related activities," he said.

Wally Boelkins, at the door of the very first Unist headquarters. In 1968, Wally purchased Unist, Inc. and became the owner as well as the sole employee. Forty years later Wally's story is a fine example of the pursuit of the American dream.

Entrepreneurial spirit and a can-do attitude really can take operating a business of their own. Today, Independent Business Owners (IBOs) span the globe from Norway

Alticor co-founders Rich DeVos and Jay Van Andel.

you far. Combining their small-town values of partnership, integrity, personal worth, achievement, personal responsibility and free enterprise with that entrepreneurial drive, Rich DeVos and Jay Van Andel began Alticor Inc., a company that's become internationally recognized and respected for a variety of reasons.

The Alticor co-founders began operating their direct selling business in Ada, Michigan in 1959 out of their homes. They based their business on providing an opportunity for individuals to achieve their goals through

to Australia, Panama to Indonesia, as distributors of the company's many products. And Alticor sales totaled $6.3 billion in 2006.

As a result of the great success of the company, which began as Amway Corporation, the West Michigan community has received many benefits from not just the corporation itself, but its founders and their families. Community projects and philanthropic efforts that the DeVos and Van Andel families sponsor include the Helen DeVos Children's Hospital, Women and Children's Center at Spectrum Health, Van Andel

Institute, Van Andel Museum Center, Grand Valley State University's downtown campus, and several foundations and charities.

"Sharing our resources with Grand Rapids has always been an easy thing to do, because we grew up here and we love this community," said co-founder Rich DeVos. "We've achieved amazing business success through the years, yet we have always kept our roots in the region. In everything we do, we strive to make a meaningful difference in the lives of West Michigan citizens."

The families also have long been active in downtown Grand Rapids revitalization. In 1979, DeVos and Van Andel purchased the Pantlind Hotel, a local landmark since 1913. The hotel was restored and reopened in September

"Sharing with Grand Rapids has always been an easy thing to do, because we grew up here and we love this community," said co-founder Rich DeVos.

The Amway Grand Plaza Hotel on the left with the JW Marriott Grand Rapids Hotel on the right.

Place Convention Center, a $216 million facility that encompasses more than 1 million square feet of convention space; and the JW Marriott Grand Rapids, an exclusive 24-story and 340-room hotel near downtown's corporate, medical and entertainment districts.

1981 as the Amway Grand Plaza Hotel, an impressive four-star hotel. The 29-story Amway tower, with the popular Cygnus 27 restaurant, and The 1913 Room, Michigan's first and only Five-Diamond restaurant, opened in 1983. The Amway Grand is generally regarded as the spark that lit interest in revitalizing downtown. Other downtown projects the DeVos and Van Andel families have been involved with include the Van Andel Arena, a 10,000-seat entertainment and sports center; the DeVos

Alticor's mission statement is "Helping people live better lives." One way it works toward that goal is through employment. The Alticor family of companies employs more than 13,000 people worldwide, including nearly 4,000 individuals in West Michigan. With such a broad array of product offerings, the company

Corporate Structure

As a pioneer and perennial leader in the direct selling industry, Alticor is the parent company of Amway Corp., one of the world's leading direct-selling brands; Quixtar Inc., a leading Web-based business in North America; and Access Business Group LLC, the corporation's manufacturing and logistics division. Alticor is also the parent of Alticor Corporate Enterprises, a company that manages Alticor's non-direct selling holdings such as Amway Hotel Corp., Gurwitch Products, and Fulton Innovation.

has staff in diverse areas including information technology, microbiology, international affairs and brand management, to name just a few.

In addition to its direct employees, Alticor also has more than three million Independent Business Owners worldwide who serve as its distributors. These IBOs include engineers, surgeons, farmers, homemakers, factory workers and many others. While some have made this their full-time profession, most IBOs sell and distribute Alticor products on a part-time basis.

"Helping people live better lives.' One way it works toward that goal is through employment. The Alticor family of companies employs more than 13,000 people worldwide, including nearly 4,000 individuals in West Michigan."

Alticor's seven main facilities span 250 acres in Ada, Michigan.

John Faye talking with students at the Visitors Center during Job Shadow Days.

"The oldest branch of Alticor, Amway, has affiliates in fifty-seven markets around the globe. Through its subsidiaries and affiliates, the company offers products, business opportunities, and manufacturing and logistics services in more than eighty countries and territories."

A shopper finds top-quality products at an Amway China store.

Alticor subsidiaries research, create, manufacture, market and distribute more than 450 company products in the areas of nutrition, wellness, beauty, home, and commercial. Over the years, the company has been granted more than 700 patents worldwide and continues product development to further serve its customers.

Nearly 80 percent of Alticor's sales come from outside the United States, with much of the business coming from Asian markets. Amway China Co. Ltd. (ACCL) is Alticor's largest affiliate, with its 2005 sales stretching past the $2 billion mark. Alticor's newest market, Russia, opened in March 2005, and has become one of the corporation's fastest growing markets.

The oldest branch of Alticor, Amway, has affiliates in fifty-seven markets around the globe. Through its subsidiaries and affiliates,

the company offers products, business opportunities, and manufacturing and logistics services in more than eighty countries and territories. Amway can be found on every continent except Antarctica. Amway products include the ARTISTRY™ line, which, over 35 years, grew from six products to more than 150 products. Today, it's one of the world's top five largest-selling prestige brands of facial skin and color cosmetics.

Another key Amway product line is Nutrilite™, the world's leading brand of more than 200 products such as vitamins, minerals, and dietary supplements. First produced and sold in California in the 1930s by Dr. Carl Rehnborg, Nutrilite vitamin and mineral supplements eventually were sold through a direct sales marketing plan that began in the 1940s. As Nutrilite distributors beginning in 1949, Rich DeVos and Jay Van Andel saw the success

of the marketing plan. In 1959 when they started Amway, they used that plan to branch out and sell household products. In 1972, Amway Corporation acquired a controlling interest in Nutrilite, and in 1994, it purchased the remaining shares of the company. The Nutrilite brand continues to grow and expand. Today, Nutrilite owns some of the largest organic farms in the world, where crops are grown for its herbal concentrates.

Alticor's North American opportunity business, Quixtar, was launched in 1999 to provide Independent Business Owners an exciting new vehicle that retained Amway's rewarding compensation plan and high-quality products, and tapped into the power of the Internet. After three years, Quixtar became the exclusive opportunity in the U.S. and Canada, although the company will rebrand by 2010 to once again align with the global Amway business. In the company's first eight years, Quixtar IBOs generated nearly $6.8 billion in sales, plus more than $500 million for

Quixtar's Partner Stores such as Barnes&Noble.com, Circuit City, and Office Depot. For their efforts, IBOs earned more than $2.2 billion in bonuses and other incentives. These kinds of numbers have not been ignored. In 2006, *Internet Retailer* once again named Quixtar the number one online retailer in the Health & Beauty category based on sales, and 22nd among all e-commerce sites.

The third branch, Access Business Group, uses sophisticated technology to develop and manufacture numerous products for the Nutrilite and ARTISTRY brands. The division also contracts with outside companies in the areas of product development and formulation, manufacturing, private labeling, logistics services, packaging design, freight, and warehousing. Some of the world's best-selling health and beauty care lines are supplied by this group. Access Business Group operates eighty-nine laboratories worldwide. The labs include kitchens from around the world with appropriate appliances,

set-ups, and water quality to test how products will perform under the conditions of various countries. The division also operates four farms in the U.S., Brazil and Mexico that are all certified organic.

Company Origin and History

This successful international corporation began after World War II when high school buddies Rich DeVos and Jay Van Andel began exploring business opportunities. The friends, both descendents of Dutch immigrants, operated numerous businesses including a drive-in restaurant and a flying school that operated on the Grand River. In 1949, they started the Ja-Ri Corporation and became distributors for Nutrilite Products.

After ten years, the partners decided to expand their product offerings and began developing ideas for a new business venture. That's how Amway Corp. began in 1959, with product stored in the basements of the co-founders, in the tiny West Michigan village of Ada.

"They were humble beginnings," said DeVos. "Jay's basement was the office, and mine was the warehouse. And to save money, we shared a common telephone line and used a buzzer to signal each other when to pick up. We struggled in those early years, yet we persevered and our little company slowly grew."

"I can remember going with my parents to pick up product from their basements," said John

Faye, Alticor Visitor Center coordinator. Only five or six years old at the time, he already had a strong family connection with the company. His parents, grandparents, and an aunt were some of the first IBOs the company worked with.

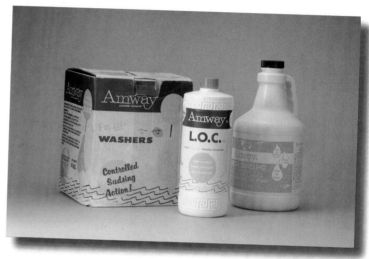

Amway's earliest products, featuring L.O.C.

DeVos and Van Andel coined the name Amway from the term "American Way," and red, white and blue have remained strong colors for the company. The fledging company's first product was a biodegradable all-purpose cleaner called L.O.C.™ (Liquid Organic Cleaner). In 1960, the operation was moved to a former gas station on the corporation's current site in Ada. In 1962, Amway became an international company when its first affiliate opened in Canada. In just five years, the company's payroll expanded from a dozen workers to more than 500, and the sales force had multiplied to 65,000.

"Our success is a testament to hard work and our unwavering belief in free enterprise and the entrepreneurial spirit," said DeVos. "I'm proud that we've inspired millions of people around the world

"They were humble beginnings," said DeVos. "Jay's basement was the office, and mine was the warehouse. And to save money, we shared a common telephone line and used a buzzer to signal each other when to pick up. We struggled in those early years, yet we persevered and our little company slowly grew."

to do what Jay and I did by starting and building a business of their own." In 1973 when the Amway World Headquarters building opened and the company expanded into the European

Above left to right: Alticor Inc. President Doug DeVos and Chairman Steve Van Andel.

"Our success is a testament to hard work and our unwavering belief in free enterprise and the entrepreneurial spirit," said DeVos. "I'm proud that we've inspired millions of people around the world to do what Jay and I did by starting and building a business of their own."

An Alticor employee harvests echinacea at a Nutrilite farm in Washington state.

market, Faye got his very first job out of high school – a tram driver for facility tours at Amway. "I've been here ever since," he added.

Distribution, sales, and production really took off during Faye's early years with the company. "It was an exciting time; every day there was something new," he said. "The running joke was that if you left your car in one spot for too long, they'd put up a building over it. We had desks in the hallways... They couldn't get the buildings up fast enough."

A Family Affair

Alticor is privately held by the Van Andel and DeVos families. By the mid-1990s, Rich DeVos and Jay Van

Andel had stepped aside and given the operation keys to their eldest sons Steve Van Andel, chairman, and Dick DeVos, president. DeVos ran the company with Van Andel until his retirement in August 2002. Dick DeVos was a key architect of Alticor's corporate structure when Amway reorganized in October 2000 under its new name.

Steve Van Andel, who became chairman in 1995 when he replaced his father (who died in 2004 at the age of 80), also helped organize the corporate restructuring, and has led the expansion of Alticor into a stronger and more diversified company. Before becoming chairman of the company, Van Andel was vice president of Amway Americas, overseeing the company's business operations in the western hemisphere, and vice president of Amway Marketing.

Today, the company is run by Steve Van Andel and Dick's younger brother Doug DeVos, who is the current president and who has spent his career building enthusiasm for the Amway and Quixtar businesses. DeVos has extensive experience with the company as well, serving previously as the senior vice president of Amway Asia Pacific, director of Amway Europe, and general manager of Amway United Kingdom.

The Alticor corporation is governed by a board of directors consisting of eight members from the families, plus three outside members who are not affiliated with the company.

Community Involvement

In addition to working to revitalize downtown Grand Rapids and support the medical facilities in the community, the DeVos and Van Andel names are prominent on many local and regional boards of directors. Steve Van Andel, a past chairman of the board of the United States Chamber of Commerce, serves on the boards of the Gerald R. Ford Foundation, Grand Rapids John Ball Zoo Society, Borgess Metro Health Alliance, Metropolitan Health Corp., and the Metropolitan Hospital Foundation in Grand Rapids. He also is a member of the Hillsdale College Board of Trustees in Hillsdale, Mich., where he received a bachelor's degree in economics and business administration, and serves on the Dean's Advisory Board for the Seidman School of Business at Grand Valley State University in Allendale, Mich.

Doug DeVos also serves on the Gerald R. Ford Foundation board, as well as the boards of Keystone Community Church and The Right Place Inc. He is a member of the Dean's Advisory Council for the Krannert

School of Management at Purdue University, where he earned a bachelor's degree in management and was a member of the Boilermakers football team. DeVos also is chairman of the advocacy committee for the World Federation of Direct Selling Association (WFDSA), and serves on the WFDSA CEO Council. He is past chairman of the board of directors for the U.S. Direct Selling Association. In addition, DeVos is co-chairman of Gospel Communications International Inc., a non-profit organization that uses communications media to spread the Gospel around the world.

Alticor is committed to making a difference in the communities where it does business. The company has a long history of giving hope: Since 1959, worldwide contributions encompassing corporate, employee and Independent Business Owner donations total approximately $300 million. To bring greater focus to its giving, the company launched the One by One Campaign for Children in 2003. The campaign rallies the resources of the entire Alticor family of companies – IBOs, employees, affiliates and customers – to make

a difference in the lives of children around the world. One by One has raised millions of dollars and generated hundreds of thousands of volunteer hours, impacting the lives of five million children in its first three years alone. Through partnerships with respected organizations including Operation Smile, Easter Seals and UNICEF, the company works to address children's issues in the countries where it does business – and beyond. It also works with smaller local groups where placing Braille textbooks in the hands of blind children and providing public health education can make all the difference.

In West Michigan, Alticor ties its volunteer activities closely to the organizations that they fund. Since 1989, Alticor has partnered with an inner city K-8 school in Grand Rapids to help students achieve academic success and provide programs that boost their self-esteem. Programs include Penpals, which matches students with Alticor employees to exchange monthly letters; Career Days and Job Shadow Days for students to get a closer look at the working world; and one on one tutoring and mentoring to boost literacy and self-esteem. Alticor also supports Special Olympics, which empowers children with intellectual disabilities to become physically fit, productive and respected members of society through sports training and competition, and Junior Achievement, through which Alticor employees

Alticor world headquarters and promenade, featuring the flags of fifty-seven nations.

visit Grand Rapids area schools to teach business concepts to students. For employees who prefer to spend their volunteer time working outdoors, Alticor sponsors team "Day Away" projects that support partner organizations such as Bethany Christian Services, a foster care and adoption center, Equest, a therapeutic horseback riding center, and children's camps across West Michigan.

"Since 1959, worldwide contributions encompassing corporate, employee and Independent Business Owner donations total approximately $300 million."

From those early days when Jay Van Andel and Rich DeVos, with their entrepreneurial spirit and can-do attitudes, took a leap of faith and formed a corporation that was based in their homes, to today, as their offspring operate a diverse, multi-product corporation that spans the globe, one thing is clear: These folks have drive.

An Alticor employee mentors a student at Southeast Academic Center in Grand Rapids.

Notice the shiny chrome finish on your new bathroom

fixtures? Or the rich, satiny quality of the handles on your kitchen cabinets? Chances are, those durable, high-quality finishes were brought to you courtesy of Master Finish, the friendly metal finisher in West Michigan's own backyard.

Master Finish plates metal surfaces for customers in the OEM automotive, hardware, and plumbing industries, which means you've probably appreciated (or overlooked) the work of Master Finish on ordinary items you use every day.

As with so many companies in West Michigan, Master Finish is homegrown and family-run. The company was founded by John Mulder in 1959 to apply that shiny, new finish to locally produced zinc die castings; forty-eight years later, Master Finish is owned

by two sons, Dale and Mike, and their cousin, Doug Roetman.

The company also employs eighty workers, several of whom are lifelong Master Finish employees, whose "years of experience and commitment to customer service are a wonderful company asset," according to Dale Mulder.

Metal finishing is an exacting process whereby a substrate metal, in this case, steel, brass, zinc, magnesium, or stainless steel, is coated with another metal, such as chrome, copper, or nickel, to protect the substrate metal and to make it more beautiful.

The process involves immersing the metal parts in a series of baths that have other metals suspended in the solution. An electric current passing through the liquid causes the suspended metal to deposit, or "plate," onto the substrate metal. In addition to this process, Master Finish offers pre- and post-plate services as well, such as polishing, buffing, electropolishing, and painting decorative highlights.

The process is exacting, and it can be environmentally hazardous. From the beginning, Master Finish has been careful to use its resources efficiently and to dispose of its waste responsibly. The company takes seriously its role as a corporate citizen and next-door neighbor in a region

that boasts extraordinary natural beauty.

Today, not only does Master Finish meet ISO 9001 quality standards for its products, but it also meets rigorous ISO 14001 environmental standards as well. Heavy metals are removed from wastewater, dried, and recycled.

While the company has succeeded in diversifying beyond plating zinc die castings for the automotive sector, it continues to improve, to expand, and to prosper. "Whether it is offering new plated colors or plating on new substrate materials, we know we can't stay in business doing what we've always done," says Dale Mulder. "We strive to be innovators who push the envelope and bring new value to our customers."

A striking feature of Grand Valley State University, with its main campus in Allendale, is that it looks

Student Services Building, Allendale.

demographic changes brought by the Baby Boom generation in the late 1950s, state leaders began exploring the option of

that an affordable college education should be available to anyone with the ability to succeed, and that it should educate the next generation of local employees. In the end, somewhat in opposition to the businessmen who envisioned graduates with practical, professional degrees, the college adopted a more classical, liberal education approach, and that academic model continues to guide the university today.

"We have to ensure that our programs are contemporary so that our graduates come out with the skills the business community wants. But we also want our students to be undergirded with an outstanding liberal education," said Thomas J. Haas, president. "We want our students to be adaptable, to have the ability to continuously learn, to think critically, and to work in teams."

Growth in Fits and Starts

Grand Valley State College opened for classes in 1963 with 226 students. For the first few years, its growth was slower than anticipated, and it began to look as though the college in the cornfields was indeed too rural and too isolated, both conceptually and geographically.

Enter Arend D. Lubbers, the young, energetic president of a small college in Iowa. Lubbers took the

"We have to ensure that our programs are contemporary so that our graduates come out with the skills the business community wants. But we also want our students to be undergirded with an outstanding liberal education," said Thomas J. Haas, president. "We want our students to be adaptable, to have the ability to continuously learn, to think critically, and to work in teams."

so new. The brick buildings haven't yet acquired the ivy-covered patina of age; the trees haven't reached the majestic girth of a century of growth. Founded in 1960, Grand Valley State University (GVSU) is a youthful institution by academic standards. In some ways, the founding of GVSU represents the ideological tug-of-war surrounding the direction higher education should take. The success of the university and the quality of the education it provides is testament to the wisdom of the course it ultimately pursued.

College in the Cornfield

Faced with the

establishing regional, four-year colleges throughout the state. Recognizing an opportunity, community leaders in Grand Rapids, led by businessman William Seidman, suggested that Grand Rapids was an ideal location, and they gathered enough local support to back up their suggestion. Following exhaustive surveys of options and locations at the state level, the decision was finally made to establish a four-year college in Allendale, Michigan, to serve an eight-county region surrounding the college.

The next challenge was to define the college's mission and educational approach. Seidman was a firm believer

helm as Grand Valley's second president in 1969 and guided the college through the next 32 years of change, challenge, and redefinition. While firmly backing the ideal of liberally educated students, he recognized the inevitability of professional degrees in fields such as education and nursing, which the local community demanded. He also indicated early on that he would broaden the college's scope to granting graduate degrees. Finally, he approved the notion, which the college had previously articulated, of creating separate, autonomous colleges that would retain an intimate quality of instruction and resist the "education factory" approach to granting undergraduate degrees.

Thus, Grand Valley for a time comprised five separate colleges each with a unique educational focus. The experiment was one of the most progressive in the nation, and the college even changed its name to Grand Valley State Colleges to reflect the nature of its school.

But enrollment declined during the 1970s and early '80s. With Michigan's economy mired in 16 percent

unemployment and deep cuts at the state level for higher education, Grand Valley was compelled to reorganize and refocus. Beyond cuts in faculty and staff positions and general belt-tightening, the college eliminated duplication of courses, worked on refurbishing its reputation in the community and establishing links with area secondary schools. It also consolidated the five colleges and began developing the professional degree programs and graduate degrees that local students wanted. By 1984, while the state was still in the midst of economic woes, Grand Valley saw a 16 percent jump in enrollment, from 6,000 to 7,000 students.

From that point, the trajectory was mostly ascendant. Enrollment continued to increase as more degree programs were added, new facilities were constructed, and planning for an urban campus in downtown Grand Rapids

was begun. In 1988, the L.V. Eberhard Center on the banks of the Grand River was dedicated.

Student Scholarship Day showcases an impressive array of academic work.

The Pew Grand Rapids Campus

Today, in addition to the Eberhard Center, Grand Valley's Pew Grand Rapids Campus comprises 37 acres. An exceptionally beautiful campus in the heart of downtown Grand Rapids, it includes the Richard M. DeVos Center, the Fred M. Keller Engineering Laboratories, the John C. Kennedy Hall of Engineering, the Eberhard Center, and the Cook-DeVos Center for Health Sciences, which houses classrooms, conference space, and laboratories as well as Grand Valley's degree programs in nursing and the health professions.

The Pew Campus creates a robust link with the Grand Rapids business community and its burgeoning health sciences corridor. It provides the technical and creative

The Richard M. DeVos Center in downtown Grand Rapids.

"The Pew Campus creates a robust link with the Grand Rapids business community and its burgeoning health sciences corridor."

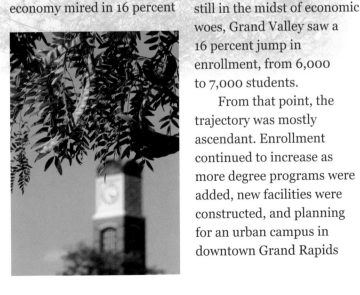

The Cook Carillon Tower sits in the center of the Allendale Campus.

The Cook-DeVos Center for Health Sciences on Medical Mile in Grand Rapids.

"The Initiative is bringing ideas from basic research through commercialization to job creation. It is a vehicle for innovation and entrepreneurship," Haas said.

A grand arch provides a welcome to the Allendale Campus.

Cell and Molecular Biology lab, Padnos Hall of Science.

environment not only for learning, but for research and new business development.

The West Michigan Science and Technology Initiative, one of the state's SmartZones, is a good example. Established in 2003, the WMSTI is a partnership of several organizations, such as Spectrum Health, the Right Place Program, and Grand Rapids Community College. Its raison d'etre is to access the rich ferment of life sciences technology underway in the "Medical Mile" in downtown Grand Rapids and to provide the space and support services to bring those innovations to market while involving students and faculty in the process. "The Initiative is bringing ideas from basic research through commercialization to job creation. It is a vehicle for innovation and entrepreneurship," Haas said.

Soy Ultima, for example, began as a business incubator in the Science and Technology Initiative. Now, Soy Ultima is an $80 million enterprise that produces nutri-ceuticals made from soy.

In another arena, the Van Andel Global Trade Center, located in the DeVos Center, seeks to increase global awareness through consulting, training, and providing resources. It creates a space that attracts international trade missions and speakers and links local resources to a global marketplace.

Sustainability on Campus

In the last decade Grand Valley has made a concerted effort to engage in the global dialogue on environmental issues and to operate as a more sustainable institution in its own right.

"Sustainability is a key factor for me personally and

for this university," said Haas, who has a doctorate in chemistry. "We've really embraced the idea of sustainability. It's very broad in its implications."

In 2004, Grand Valley's Michigan Alternative and Renewable Energy Center (MAREC), another SmartZone, opened in Muskegon to develop and facilitate research on alternative energies and to advocate for the political and cultural changes that will make alternative energies viable. "The critical issues are political," said Imad Mahawili, MAREC executive director. "We seem to be a few years away from real bottom-line realization of this from a business point of view." MAREC is working with a Ravenna dairy farm to build a biodigester to turn animal waste into electricity. The project is a commercial demonstration of an advanced biodigester technology that converts renewable dairy biomass waste into valuable methane gas and subsequently to electricity.

In 1986, the Water Resources Institute was established to preserve, protect, and improve water resources. While the infant

institute was shuffled from one location to another for many years, its floating classroom, the *D.J. Angus*, became wildly popular. In 1996, the *W.G. Jackson* was placed into service; it has visited 30 ports of call in Lake Michigan during its annual "Making Lake Michigan Great" tour. From 1986 to 2006, the research vessels welcomed some 100,000 passengers for educational cruises on Lake Michigan. In 1997, the institute was renamed the Robert B. Annis Water Resources Institute, in recognition of the long-term support and encouragement of the Indianapolis scientist and businessman.

In 2001, the institute moved to a new facility on Muskegon Lake. Since then, AWRI has significantly increased its staff and research capacity and is becoming a national clearinghouse for resources and information.

Beyond establishing research initiatives, Grand Valley walks the talk. Its new Lake Ontario Hall is LEED-certified by the U.S. Green Building Council, meaning it meets strict standards for construction and operation.

In 1990, the university began planting one tree for each ton of paper it recycled. By the end of the decade, the VanSteeland Arboretum grew to encompass seven acres with 735 trees and shrubs.

In cooperation with the City of Grand Rapids, Heartland Builders, and Westown Jubilee Housing, Grand Valley's School of Engineering designed and began monitoring a prototypical energy-efficient house in Grand Rapids, which was donated to a low-income family. Results of the state-of-the-art energy-efficient systems will be shared with other schools and businesses.

Campus Sustainability Week also brings awareness of stewardship and sustainability home to students on campus. And the message is being heard. Haas said: "We have 23,000 students and I rarely see even a cup lying on the ground. The students and faculty really do take care of the environment."

Looking Ahead

With more than 23,000 students on campuses in Allendale, Grand Rapids, Holland, and centers in Muskegon and Traverse City, Grand Valley is well-positioned both to benefit from the growth of the surrounding areas and to add value in meaningful ways to the region. Through its partnerships and resources

for technology, research, and business, it brings new energy and opportunity to the area. By providing a quality education at a reasonable cost, Grand Valley returns a trained and educated workforce to area employers.

"This is a university with outstanding principles. We want to offer relevant professional programs," said Haas. "Access and accountability are very important to this university, and they are important to me."

Students walk past Henry Hall.

"This is a university with outstanding principles. We want to offer relevant professional programs," said Haas. "Access and accountability are very important to this university, and they are important to me."

JW Marriott Hotel Concrete Frame – Grand Rapids

When Keith Granger and his sons—Alton, Ron and Jerry—started Granger Construction as a family business in 1960, they agreed that honesty, integrity, and a commitment to remarkable customer service would always be their compelling reasons for coming to work each day.

Since then, their approach to "treating others the way they would like to be treated," has remained unchanged. Today, under the leadership of Alton and his son Glenn, a field and support staff

WMU – College of Health & Human Services – Kalamazoo

"Building lasting relationships has always been as important to us as delivering on-time, under-budget, quality construction projects."

of over 200 individuals continue the family legacy.

"We've come a long way over the years," says third generation President Glenn D. Granger, "and it is especially rewarding to know that we continue to adhere to the guiding principles set forth by my grandfather, father, and uncles."

What started out as a small general contracting company has evolved into one of the country's largest construction firms. With average annual sales of approximately $250 million, Granger Construction is consistently listed among the Top 400 Contractors in America by Engineering News-Record (ENR) magazine, a division of McGraw-Hill.

"While sales volume is one way to gauge our success, the most important measurement is customer satisfaction," says Glenn Granger. "Building lasting relationships has always been as important to us as delivering on-time, under-budget, quality construction projects."

K-12, higher education, commercial, healthcare, industrial, research, government, and senior housing are just a few of the market segments that Granger serves. With corporate offices in Grand Rapids and Lansing, Granger specializes in a variety of delivery methods including general contracting, construction management, design-build services and, according to Glenn, many approaches in between. "Because our goal is to exceed the unique needs and expectations of our customers, there's no such thing as a 'cookie cutter' approach to the services we offer today or in the future."

Impressive West Michigan Track Record

Over the past 20 years, Granger Construction has managed over $500 million in West Michigan projects including the structural concrete frames for the JW Marriott Hotel and Parking Structure in the heart of downtown Grand Rapids.

Other examples of Granger's successful West Michigan track record include Western Michigan University's (WMU) College of Health and Human Services in Kalamazoo, the Granger Center for Construction and Heating, Ventilation, Air Conditioning and Refrigeration (HVACR) at Ferris State University in Big Rapids (named after Alton and Jan Granger), Hope College's A. Paul Schaap Science Center in Holland, Orchard View High School in Muskegon and the City of Wyoming's Lakeshore Water Treatment Plant, located near Holland.

"I was very pleased by the thoughtfulness and professionalism that Granger displayed throughout our project," said Dr. Janet I. Pisaneschi, Dean of WMU's College of Health and Human Services, of Granger's involvement in their new 195,000 square foot, $39 million building. "Our questions were promptly and carefully answered. Members of the Granger team were courteous and helpful and we were continually impressed with their quality of work and attention to detail. We are especially grateful to Granger for being such a great partner."

While Granger Construction has amassed an impressive library of testimonials and industry awards over the years, testaments to the company's unique capabilities are also on display throughout the state with high-profile corporate headquarters projects for the Lear Corporation in Southfield, Jackson National Life Insurance Company in Lansing, Consumers Energy Corporation in Jackson and General Motors' Service Parts Organization in Grand Blanc.

Lear Corporation's Vice-President for Global Finance and Real Estate summed up Granger's performance on their recent 140,000 square foot, $30 million project stating "Bottom line, your company's hands-on approach was instrumental in seeing to it that our difficult to build project progressed on-time and within budget with virtually no disruption to our day-to-day operations. Hiring Granger to serve as our construction management firm proved to be the right

decision and we sincerely appreciate your dedication to successfully overseeing the largest and most complex construction project in our company's history."

Advocate for the Environment

"Like all businesses, we must continually adapt in order to offer our customers every possible option to invest in projects of uncommon value. That is why we have launched an all-out effort to maximize the number of professionals on our team who are certified as Leadership in Energy and Environmental Design (LEED) Accredited Professionals by the U.S. Green Building Council," reflects Glenn Granger. "We are enthused about the number of customers who have determined that pursuing some level of LEED Certification is right for them, right for their employees and those they serve and—most importantly—right for the environment."

LEED Certification is just one of numerous educational opportunities provided by the Granger Learning Center. Founded over ten years ago, the Granger Learning Center is dedicated to offering Granger employees a wide range of training programs that improve their on-the-job skills and enhance the quality of services delivered. Over 95 percent of Granger's workforce participates in program offerings on an annual basis.

Lear Corporation Headquarters – Southfield

Consumer Energy World Headquarters – Jackson

Listening—the Greatest Skill

Glenn Granger notes that—beyond bricks and mortar—listening is the greatest skill that every Granger employee applies to each project in order to effectively understand and subsequently meet our customers' needs. "Granger Construction has always been in the business of helping our customers. To do this, we must not only fully embrace their needs and concerns but also understand the reasons for them. The best way to accomplish that is to be a great listener."

As time goes on, listening remains something that Glenn Granger and his employees are very good at. Following in the footsteps of the company's founders, they've remained committed to the company's founding principles of honesty, integrity and providing remarkable customer service. It's a formula that has always worked well for Granger Construction and, in turn, for the customers they serve.

"Granger Construction has always been in the business of helping our customers. To do this, we must not only fully embrace their needs and concerns but also understand the reasons for them. The best way to accomplish that is to be a great listener."

Ever since Gerritt Visser began work in 1926 as a mason and chimney sweep, commitment to family has been a bedrock value at the company that bears his name. That company formally began on April 1, 1960, when it was raw land through turnkey occupancy. While Visser Brothers manages many sub-contractors, it also handles multiple phases of construction in-house, from excavation to finish carpentry. Handling construction in-house allows Visser Brothers to respond to projects quickly, to manage them efficiently, and to complete them on time.

Photos credited to: Integrated Architecture & Photographer, Mark Thomas Productions, Ltd.

> *"Visser Brothers is a general contracting firm that can take a commercial building project from raw land through turnkey occupancy. While Visser Brothers manages many sub-contractors, it also handles multiple phases of construction in-house, from excavation to finish carpentry."*

incorporated by the three Visser boys, Bruce, Dale, and Jack. Visser Brothers has remained committed to its family values ever since. For the Vissers, that means hard work, keeping one's word, fulfilling obligations, and taking care of each other. Now in its third generation, those values continue to define the company.

Building Local Landmarks

Visser Brothers is a general contracting firm that can take a commercial building project from

After forty-seven years in business, Visser projects have come to dot the local landscape: the new Country Inn & Suites Hotel, Center Pointe Mall, Mercantile Bank's Headquarters, and the B.O.B. Long a downtown eyesore, the B.O.B. was completely gutted and renovated by Visser Brothers, restoring the structure to its former elegance. The company also constructed the circular, glass-enclosed David D. Hunting YMCA on Lake Michigan Drive. This is the first LEED certified YMCA building in the world, meaning that it meets stringent environment qualifications for sustainability in design, construction, and operation.

Retaining Its Roots

As the company has grown, it has incorporated the latest construction techniques to stay current with changing technologies and to meet customer expectation. "We have GPS equipment on our excavating equipment, for example, that lets the guys excavate almost without loss," says Bill Mast, president. "They can tell down to the tenth of a foot where their bucket and bulldozer blades are located on an 80-acre site. That eliminates a lot of staking and overdigging."

Yet, the company's culture remains firmly rooted in the values of its founders and the

course they continue to set for the company. At nearly 70, Bruce Visser is still CEO and still visits construction sites daily. "They lead by example, and the rest of us have a hard time keeping up with them," says Mast.

That example has resulted in a hard-charging company that stands by its commitments. "We'll have the foundations in the ground while others are still applying for financing for a project," Bruce Visser has been heard to say.

The story still circulates about the time a cement truck ran over Visser's foot. He wrapped it in duct tape and finished the day's work. "The standards set by the brothers still influence the company today," says Mast. "They're embodied in our employees who show the same passion, commitment, and dedication to hard work."

Committed to Family

For this company, its commitment to family embraces the entire firm. In an industry that is known to

be seasonal and vulnerable to fluctuating economic cycles, Visser Brothers takes care of its own. In its entire forty-seven year history, the company has never laid off an employee. "An equipment operator may be inside painting handrails in the winter, but it keeps him employed and puts food on the table," says Mast.

The company is committed to retaining that sense of family. While larger firms inevitably become more bureaucratic with multiple layers of management, more paperwork, and greater distance from the workers in the field, Visser Brothers has deliberately opted to maintain a close, family environment, flat hierarchy, and more managed growth. "We're not bureaucratic; we never will be," says Mast. "Our goal is to provide personal commitment to our employees. If we grew too big, we would lose that."

That sense of family

creates an extraordinarily dedicated workforce, some of whom have been with Visser Brothers for over 30 years. Visser employees absorb the same passion, drive, and work ethic modeled by their founders. So, in the end, the customer benefits from work done by people who care about their work.

In addition to dedicated employees, the company also has loyal customers who know that their building projects will be dealt with professionally, on time, and within budget. To that end, the company prefers to bid on local projects—within 50 miles—and to foster the same trust and familiarity with its clients as it does within the company.

Now with a third generation at the helm, the heritage established by Gerritt Visser and his sons continues to guide the company's values, approach to doing business, and future course as strongly as ever.

Photos credited to: Integrated Architecture & Photographer, Mark Thomas Productions, Ltd.

"The standards set by the brothers still influence the company today," says Mast. "They're embodied in our employees who show the same passion, commitment, and dedication to hard work."

Photos credited to: Integrated Architecture & Photographer, Mark Thomas Productions, Ltd.

I f you are familiar with downtown Grand Rapids, you know the Amway Grand Plaza values all focused on its strategic purpose to provide clients with the best construction experience.

Above and below: DeVos Place, Grand Rapids, Michigan

Hotel Tower, Calder Plaza Building, Plaza Towers, Van Andel Research Institute, Van Andel Arena, and DeVos Place Convention Center. Erhardt Construction was involved in all of these signature buildings, projects that have been the result of the company's proven capabilities and recognized performance throughout the region.

The company offers a broad range of pre-construction and construction services, and approaches all projects as a team player. Some recent building projects include the Ottawa County District Courthouse, Faith Hospice, Holland Home's Breton Terrace and Breton Ridge, and the Salvation Army Kroc Community Center.

Core Values and Team Leadership

Erhardt Construction, established in 1962 by Larry Erhardt, rests on a foundation of solid core

"With the belief that 'the best way to build something right is to get it right from the start.'"

Right: Van Andel Institute, Grand Rapids, Michigan

Erhardt is a company that is well-respected by the community—a company with a great reputation in the market. Since its inception, the company has put in place over $1 billion of construction for numerous clients and has provided employment opportunities for hundreds of people in the community.

The current leadership team is comprised of six individuals who possess a great mix of talent, depth, and experience. Larry's son, Joe Erhardt, has been president since 1989. Dale Bramer, Senior Vice President, has been with the company more than 43 years. As a boy, Bramer said he was taught that "what you are speaks aloud to those with whom you come in contact and that actions speak louder than words. As a company, we feel it is not only critical, but right, that we walk our talk."

Keith Vandenbergh, Vice President of Estimating, joined Erhardt in 1987 and

is responsible for estimating activities through all phases of pre-construction and construction. Taggart Town, Vice President of Field Operations, develops and manages field supervisors and craftspeople. Taggart also serves as the Corporate Safety Director overseeing the safety management process. Ben Wickstrom, Vice President of Construction Operations, has been with Erhardt for nine years. Ben provides supervision and management direction for all active construction projects and is an active member of Erhardt's Lean Construction Coalition, implementing Lean Construction on all new projects. And Michelle Paepke is Controller, responsible for the day-to-day financial activities of the company.

Right from the Start

With the belief that "the best way to build something right is to get it right from the start," Erhardt Construction has been constructing buildings for more than 45 years. Interestingly, although the remarkable signature buildings are often what people think of when they think of Erhardt

Construction, the firm has built up years of diversified experience that range from municipal projects, to churches, office buildings, and healthcare and manufacturing facilities.

While the company has an impressive history and a comfortable place in the market, its leaders keep the focus on their customers and the future. "We're very proud of the fact that our clients desire our services, but we don't take that for granted. We know we need to continue to deliver what we promise and more." Bramer said.

Lean Construction

Erhardt has differentiated itself from the competition by leading the West Michigan construction industry in the implementation of Lean Construction. Based on production management principles of planning and control of a project from design to delivery, Lean Construction is a win/win/win situation. First, it benefits clients by reducing costs and shortening construction durations, while maintaining quality. Second, it benefits subcontractors because jobs run more smoothly and with more reliability of work flow, which means cutting waste and reducing job duration.

Third, satisfied clients mean more work opportunities for Erhardt Construction, for whom 75% of new projects come from repeat customers.

Giving Back to the Community

Larry Erhardt's legacy of supporting the community continues to this day. Erhardt's leadership team participates with many trade and philanthropic organizations including The Right Place, Grand Rapids Area Chamber of Commerce, Grand Rapids Rotary, and Associated Builders and Contractors. Staff members volunteer in home-building projects for Habitat for Humanity and get their feet wet in the West Michigan Environmental Action Council's Adopt-A-Stream program, cleaning up, monitoring, and restoring the shoreline of the Grand River.

Diversity

"Erhardt Construction believes in diversity. The company is a member of the National Association of Women in Construction, and vice president of estimating, Keith Vandenbergh, is very involved with the West Michigan Minority Contractors Association. In fact, the firm has been mentoring Terrell Daniels of Modern Fire and Security Systems, a minority-owned fire and security company, for two years. "Diversity is good for business and it's the right thing to do." said Joe Erhardt.

LEED

Sustainability is another important consideration for

Erhardt Construction. The company endorses the efforts of the U.S. Green Building Council, which implemented LEED® –Leadership in Energy and Environmental Design.

"LEED addresses an issue that is long overdue," Bramer said emphatically. Environmental awareness and action "are critical in our society, and for future generations." In addition to LEED-certified projects like the Grace Hauenstein Library at Aquinas College and Grand Valley State University's Movement Sciences and Indoor Recreation Facility, the company is taking measures to support environmental and economic sustainability including splitting waste materials to recycle as much as possible.

Erhardt Construction has earned a solid reputation over the years by providing the best construction experience to its clients. Their people, professionalism, and integrity—coupled with an innovative attitude—have contributed to providing high quality solutions which meet and exceed customer's needs and expectations.

Aquinas College Grace Hauenstein Library, Grand Rapids, Michigan

Christ Memorial Reformed Church, Holland, Michigan

"LEED addresses an issue that is long overdue," Bramer said emphatically. Environmental awareness and action "are critical in our society, and for future generations."

Left: Holland Police Facility, Holland, Michigan

WZZM 13

WZZM 13, the ABC affiliate for Grand Rapids, has

PDAs. That same year, "Great Lakes Adventure" aired as West Michigan's first locally produced HDTV special. In 2007, new high definition cameras were put into active service, and the station launched three niche micro-web sites, with more to come.

WZZM 13 first broadcast in 1962 in a converted banquet room at the Pantlind Hotel (now the Amway Grand Plaza Hotel.)

In 1971, the station introduced the first weather radar in West Michigan and moved to a new studio. Former President Gerald R. Ford, who was then a congressman, presided over the dedication ceremonies.

There were several ownership changes over the

years. Gannett Co. Inc., the international media firm that owns USA Today, purchased WZZM 13 in 1997.

Over the next ten years, the newsroom was expanded, a new radar receiver was installed, tower cameras were erected in Grand Rapids and along the lakeshore, and community grants were established for area nonprofit groups. Many other WZZM 13 community efforts, like the annual 13 Food for Families campaign, also were started to serve area residents. And that famous Grand Rapids icon, the colorful 13 Weatherball, returned to duty in 2003. Now located at the I-96 and 131 junction north of downtown Grand Rapids, the historic Weatherball stands tall, reminding local residents of days gone by as well as of things to come.

What the colors mean:
- 13 Weatherball red, warmer ahead.
- 13 Weatherball blue, cooler in view.
- 13 Weatherball green, no change foreseen.
- Colors blinking bright, rain or snow in sight.

"WZZM 13 has been the leader in launching new news and weather products in the new millennium. These new products are being delivered on three screens – TV, computer and mobile devices."

created a strong presence over the years. The station's goal is to deliver news and information in all the ways the customers want it.

WZZM 13 has been the leader in launching news and weather products in the new millennium. These new products are being delivered on three screens – TV, computer and mobile devices. The station's web site was unveiled in 2000. Three years later, WZZM 13 launched WZZM-DT, a high definition television (HDTV) channel, and a local 24/7 weather channel in 2004. Two years later, WZZM 13's news, weather and sports began appearing on mobile devices – cell phones and

"At the end of each day, I have the knowledge and the assurance that one of our employees has made someone's life better," said Hope Network President and CEO Phil Weaver.

A lot of good happens because of Hope Network. The Grand Rapids-based organization has a mission to "enhance the dignity and independence of persons who have a disability and/or disadvantage"—and the ways they do this are as individual as the people they serve.

Hope Network programs are accredited by The Commission on Accreditation of Rehabilitation Facilities

Based on the belief that everyone is inherently worthy, Hope Network serves people who have behavioral issues, mental illness, and physical and developmental disabilities. The 501(c)(3) nonprofit organization

in service for communities that might not have the infrastructure that we do – or if an individual is unable to overcome certain challenges, we'll bring in some very creative people for problem-solving. Our goal is to allow everyone we serve the opportunity to have the best quality of life that they can."

Programs include specialized housing, crisis residential treatment, respite care, vocational services such as workshops and competitive employment throughout the community, adult and pediatric medical rehabilitation, case management, personal social services, and transportation service for individuals who are elderly, disabled, or economically disadvantaged.

Through customized levels of support ranging from 24-hour supervision to apartment living, residential and housing services help individuals live as independently as possible, depending on each person's needs and capabilities.

Whether someone has a brain injury, mental illness, or other barrier to employment, Hope Network

Hope Network Industries (HNI) has built a strong relationship with Kellogg in Battle Creek, just one of many businesses that use HNI for contract packaging or manufacturing services. HNI provides ex-offenders, economically disadvantaged, or refugees the opportunity to build a solid work history and become self-reliant members of the community.

"At the end of each day, I have the knowledge and the assurance that one of our employees has made someone's life better," said Hope Network President and CEO Phil Weaver. "Every night I go home with a smile on my face."

Hope Network serves the state through its three affiliates: Hope Network Behavioral Health Services, Hope Network Rehabilitation Services, and Hope Network West Michigan. All

also helps ex-offenders transitioning into society as well as homeless or socio-economically disadvantaged individuals. Hope Network also provides housing for low-to moderate-income people throughout the state. About 9,500 people receive some form of service through Hope Network every day.

"Our willingness to take on the most challenging cases out there makes us unique," said Weaver. "We take on problems or gaps

works with them so they can become productive members of their communities. Employment, training, and day programming have always been vital to Hope Network's mission. Vocational programs include industrial work at its own sites as well as collaborations within area businesses.

West Michigan is fortunate that it's home to Hope Network Rehabilitation Services, a leader in the rehab field. Children and adults facing the challenge of recovering from a traumatic brain injury, stroke, or birth defect receive the help they need to put their lives back together. A team of specialists offers inpatient and outpatient services including physical, speech, language, and occupational therapy, as well as vocational and therapeutic rehabilitation.

Hope Network Behavioral Health's Institute for Neurodevelopmental Differences excels at treating individuals with autistic spectrum

disorders, attention-deficit hyperactivity disorders, cognitive limitations, genetic and metabolic disorders, learning disabilities, fetal alcohol syndrome, or multiple/complex

disabilities. Begun in 2004, the Institute focuses on early intervention with an emphasis on children and adolescents. Its programs are unique in the state—and rare in the nation.

Hope Network has nearly 2,000 dedicated employees located throughout the state. "Our biggest strength is our people," Weaver noted. "We are a people-centered business with top-notch employees who all have a passion for serving others."

Hope Network is large and diverse enough that individual programs and divisions can learn from one another, too.

"We take the best practices from one part of the organization and apply them to another," said Weaver, who brought a business background to Hope Network when he joined the nonprofit in 2006.

Established in 1963, Hope Network has become an important organization to many West Michigan residents. Weaver said, "In a certain respect, we've stayed behind the scenes doing what's important in the community. Often people are surprised when they learn about all of our programs. We want people to know they can call Hope Network and find help. That's the kind of awareness we want."

The organization is constantly looking for ways to enhance and expand services. This is a hard-working group of people who know they must continue to improve and grow to serve an ever-changing society.

"We can't do what we did 30 years ago, or we'll get the same results we got 30 years ago," Weaver said. "Our organization must continue to step outside the box."

Genesis East Apartments are part of Genesis Non-Profit Housing Corporation, which Hope Network, the Inner City Christian Federation, and Dwelling Place of Grand Rapids formed in 1008. Genesis provides permanent, supportive housing for people with disabilities who are homeless or at risk of homelessness.

> **"We are a people-centered business with top-notch employees who all have a passion for serving others."**

Hope Network Rehabilitation Services is the expert in neuro-rehabilitation services. People of all ages who have challenges such as a traumatic brain injury, spinal cord injury, stroke, or birth defect/injury can receive the help they need to rebuild their lives at one of six West Michigan rehabilitation centers. Services range from one-time evaluations to supervised living options.

Left: Hope Network's Institute for Neurodevelopmental Differences serves families facing challenges such as autism, attention deficit hyperactivity disorder, fetal alcohol syndrome, cognitive impairment, and Down syndrome. It offers a full range of outpatient services, and its long-term residential program for children and adolescents is the only one of its kind in Michigan.

"GFIA is an integral part of the West Michigan community and has many mutually beneficial partnerships with civic and business organizations, such as the Grand Rapids Area Chamber of Commerce, the Grand Rapids/Kent County Convention & Visitors Bureau, and The Right Place, Inc. It has a strong, well-proven commitment to service to the residents, businesses, and visitors of West Michigan."

Groundbreaking for Kent County's first airport took place on November 26, 1919, four miles from downtown Grand Rapids. By mid summer of 1926, it offered the United State's first regularly scheduled airline service. With the opening of a U.S. Customs Bureau Office in the main terminal of the relocated airport in 1977, it became Kent County *International* Airport.

In December 1999, Kent County International Airport became the Gerald R. Ford International Airport (GFIA) in honor of Gerald R. Ford, the 38th President of the United States, who faithfully served West Michigan as a U.S. Congressman from 1949 to 1973. The airport community is deeply honored to have its airport named after President Ford, a beloved native son and long-time supporter of the airport.

GFIA is, and has always been, an important piston in the economic engine of West Michigan, providing the passenger, cargo, and general aviation services required to foster growth in the region. Today, it generates over $500 million annually in economic activity throughout its West Michigan 13-county service area.

The GFIA passenger terminal is equipped with a wireless Internet network that provides free Internet access to any wireless-enabled laptop, PDA, or cell phone. GFIA provides non-stop passenger service to numerous destinations, and amenities such as valet parking, a staffed Information Desk, and a cell phone parking lot where drivers may wait for arriving passengers until their parties call to say they are ready for pick up.

In addition to these amenities, GFIA provides other valuable services to travelers and the Grand Rapids community through its Aircraft Rescue and Fire Fighting (ARFF) unit. The ARFF's primary function is to maintain the safety of the airfield and respond to fire calls. They also respond to medical calls at the passenger terminal facility, tending to issues ranging from minor injuries to major medical emergencies. Other community service activities of the ARFF unit include providing weekly blood pressure checks to airport employees and visitors, and providing safety training to airport ground and flight staff. These efforts were acknowledged by the FAA when it awarded the unit the *FAA Good Friend Award* for instructing FAA employees on how to use a defibrillator and perform CPR.

GFIA is an integral part of the West Michigan community and has many mutually beneficial partnerships with civic and business organizations, such as the Grand Rapids Area Chamber of Commerce, the Grand Rapids/Kent County Convention & Visitors Bureau, and The Right Place, Inc. It has a strong, well-proven commitment to service to the residents, businesses, and visitors of West Michigan.

GFIA is managed and operated by the Kent County Department of Aeronautics. The Kent County Aeronautics Board—a six-member body appointed by the Kent County Board of Commissioners—is responsible for policy setting and general oversight of the airport. GFIA is a financially self-supporting public enterprise that receives no tax revenue for day-to-day operations or ongoing capital development. Airport operations and improvements actually generate net revenue, rather than consume valuable tax dollars.

As of September 2007, GFIA began work on the $118 million Terminal Area and Parking Improvement Program. The primary element in this program will be a 4,900-space, four-story parking ramp accompanied by two passenger sky bridges connecting the parking ramp to the passenger terminal, a roadway canopy, an entrance plaza, and significant utility and roadway work. The entire project is slated for completion in the fall of 2009.

Gill Industries

In the boom-and-bust, good-old-boy's world of tool and die and manufacturing, Gill Industries not only challenges stereotypes, this homegrown company

Gerald Williams and John Gill, owners, Gill & Williams Stamping; sign order for new 300 ton Minster press to increase their stamping capacity. 1972

Gill has innovative design and engineering capabilities that can offer solutions to solve customer and industry problems.

smashes them to smithereens. While other manufacturing suppliers are shrinking and even disappearing, Gill Industries is expanding. In a male-dominated industry, Gill has been under the capable leadership of a woman since 1985, when Rita Williams became Vice President and General Manager.

From a small tool and die shop, Gill Industries has become a state-of-the-art, full-service company that not only designs, tests and manufactures the products its customers need today, but also anticipates customers' future needs. From a two-person tool and die shop in 1964, Gill now employs 960 workers. Sales in 2006 were $141 million. With locations on two continents, Gill now has its eye on a third.

John Gill and Rita Williams, owners

The numbers don't begin to tell the story.

Two-Man Tool and Die

In 1964, after working for General Motors in Grand Rapids, John Gill figured he could make better dies than those he saw being produced in the company shop. So, with $4,000 in family savings, he bought some used equipment and went into business with his brother-in-law, Gerald Williams. For John Gill, the only fly in the ointment was that his wife, Rita Williams, was expecting their 10th child. Nevertheless, they decided to take the risk.

By 1985, the company had expanded the die operations to include stamping, welding and assembly. To accommodate this expansion, Gill moved to a 55,000 square foot tool and die plant on Clay Avenue and added a manufacturing plant on Plainfield Ave. Sales were $12 million, and Gerald Williams, John Gill's partner, was ready to retire. The twelve Gill children were all in school, and Rita Williams had been working for five

years at St. Mary's Mercy Medical Center as a LPN. She wanted to get into the family business just as her brother was preparing to leave.

Rita had "sat on a lot of shop stools" over the course of 20 years and had absorbed the fine points of tool and die. She felt that the business needed the organizational and interpersonal skills she had developed running a household of twelve children. "I coaxed my way in, but it took a lot of time for people to get used to the idea," says Williams about becoming Vice President and General Manager in 1985.

The first thing she did was clean house—literally. Often with scrub brush and bucket in hand, she tidied unkempt corners and insisted that others do the same. Today, safety and cleanliness are corporate values.

Over the years, several strategic moves have helped the company not only endure, but prosper. While John Gill managed the engineering and production side, Rita Williams handled

customer relations. She soon discovered that more direct relationships with their customers would improve their service levels and help the company anticipate customer needs. Gill Industries brought its Sales and Marketing department in-house rather than relying on external sales representatives.

In addition to its core business of stamping, welding, assembly and tube bending / processing, Gill differentiated itself by developing design capabilities. Now, not only could the company produce the dies and make the part, it could design the part as well, thus rounding out its palette of services. In 2001, the Gill Technology Center opened, bringing the creative talent of many fields together to generate innovative solutions. "We're hoping to be able to let our customers know what they need before they do," says Williams.

An example of this innovative spirit is seen in Gill's new design for a head restraint mechanism for passenger seats in SUVs and minivans. This "Platform Head Restraint" can be placed into production ten times faster than competitive product, and the lighter, more versatile design can eliminate hundreds of thousands of dollars in re-design and re-tooling costs. "This new head restraint mechanism is the type of innovation that the automotive industry has come to expect of our company," says Richard Perreault, President and COO.

In recent years, Gill Industries, like many companies, has focused on streamlining production and eliminating waste in order to reduce costs and stay competitive. Several initiatives are in place, such as Lean Manufacturing, the Toyota Production System and Six Sigma. "There's pressure from Asia," says Perreault, "and to combat that trend we need to be more and more competitive, offer something that isn't offered in Asia. We need to ensure that we're the low-cost producer."

While Gill Industries manufactures parts for the major automakers as well as for their suppliers, such as Johnson Controls, Lear Corporation, and Bosch, it also seeks ways to diversify by applying its core processes to other industries—for example, tilt mechanisms for office seating and suspension systems for golf cars.

The company is going global, recently opening a sales office in The Netherlands and a manufacturing plant in Mexico, which added to the existing lineup of facilities in Grand Rapids and Georgia. A presence in Asia is also a real possibility.

The More Things Change…

John Gill retired over a decade ago from the company he founded. Rita Williams, now over 70, is handing the reigns over to the second generation. While Gill Industries is expanding, diversifying and looking ahead, it still reflects and honors the values it was built upon. Not surprisingly, that includes creating a work environment that is conducive to health and well-being. Gill offers tuition reimbursement for classes, flex-time, financial incentives for health club or Weight Watchers memberships, on-site wellness programs and chair massages. At Gill, family always comes first.

The next generation of the Gill family is poised to continue the tradition of manufacturing excellence and believes the future has just begun.

Large family, large dreams. . . . John Gill and Rita Williams surrounded by their 12 children.

"We're hoping to be able to let our customers know what they need before they do," says Williams.

Manufacturing capabilities with stamping capacity to 1000 tons.

> *"P&N believes that when engineers know a client community well—its people, systems, laws, and unique circumstances—they can find effective solutions for the client's needs."*

Prein&Newhof has been meeting infrastructure needs for township, municipal, and private clients across West Michigan for nearly 40 years. The firm offers a wide range of civil engineering, environmental consulting, surveying, mapping, Geographic Information Services (GIS),

offices in Holland, Byron Center, Muskegon, and Kalamazoo, as well as its own Environmental Laboratory. The firm employs over a hundred full-time personnel, including engineers, surveyors, drafters, geologists, chemists, communication specialists, and support staff.

community well—its people, systems, laws, and unique circumstances—they can find effective solutions for the client's needs. Many of Prein&Newhof's clients have been with the firm 30 years or longer, and they can testify to the benefits of this relationship.

When H. Edward Prein and Thomas Newhof started Prein&Newhof in 1969, they set out to establish a distinctive engineering firm that provides continuous project follow-through from initial design to completion. Unlike most engineering firms, where one engineer oversees project design and another one oversees construction, P&N engineers strive to take full responsibility for all aspects of a project and see it through from start to finish. By following this holistic approach, P&N engineers stay focused on their clients as the clients' communities and needs evolve.

Prein&Newhof is lead by its Officers (from left): Tom Newhof, Mike Bergstrom, Jim Cook, Mike Fuller, Phil Glupker, and Bob Vander Male.

and laboratory testing. Today, Prein&Newhof (P&N) is the engineer of choice for over fifty communities across West Michigan. Some of the firm's well-known clients in the Grand Rapids area include the Gerald R. Ford International Airport, Grand Valley State University, and the North Kent Sewer Authority.

Headquartered in Grand Rapids, Prein&Newhof is 100% employee-owned and has branch

Building Relationships

Prein&Newhof's focus is on building long-term relationships with its clients. The firm strives to grow with its clients, understanding and anticipating their evolving needs. P&N works closely with its clients to fully understand their existing systems and create long-term, sustainable solutions that will adapt to meet their needs for years to come.

P&N believes that when engineers know a client

Building Expertise

Because technology is constantly and rapidly changing, Prein&Newhof actively encourages its employees to participate in professional associations so that they can further their education and remain at the top of their respective fields. As an incentive to pursue this goal, P&N pays employee membership dues and conference fees to over twenty professional organizations including the Michigan Society of Professional Engineers, the Water Environment Federation, the American Water Works Association, and the American Chemical Society. P&N also compensates its employees for time spent participating in professional organization activities.

In 2006, Prein&Newhof was awarded the Employer Recognition Award from the American Society of Civil Engineers (ASCE) Committee on Younger Members. The award recognizes P&N's dedication to building employee expertise and advancing the engineering profession by encouraging young engineers to be active participants in the ASCE and other professional associations. Prein&Newhof was one of only twenty-five companies nation-wide to receive the award. At P&N over 90 percent of young engineers (under 35 years old) belong to at least one professional organization.

Over the years, P&N has earned numerous awards from organizations such as the American Society of Civil Engineers, the American Public Works Association, the Michigan Municipal League, the Michigan Concrete Paving Association, the Michigan Department of Transportation, and the Consulting Engineers Council of Michigan.

The firm earned these prestigious awards for work performed on projects as varied as river restoration and dam removal for the Muskegon River in Big Rapids, the Lake Michigan Intake & Pump Station in South Haven, and site

development for the Gerald R. Ford International Airport Cargo & Trade Center in Grand Rapids.

Building Our Community

Through engineering excellence and a commitment to honesty and personal attention, Prein&Newhof has been helping build and strengthen Grand Rapids for over 35 years. This is done primarily by developing long-lasting client relationships.

Prein&Newhof's relationship with Gerald R. Ford International Airport began in 1982 and still is going strong today. Some highlights of P&N's award-winning work performed for the airport include reconstruction of both major runways, site development for the Air Cargo & Trade Center and Remote Rental Car facility, a storm water management program, and wetland mitigation.

A more recent relationship began in 1995, when Grand Valley State University (GVSU) contracted Prein&Newhof to perform the site development for its new campus in downtown Grand Rapids. Since then, Prein&Newhof has performed site development and designed roads, sidewalks, and parking lots for the Richard M. DeVos Center, the Cook-DeVos Center for Health Sciences, and the Pew Campus Student Housing, among others.

In 1998, Prein&Newhof began working with the recently-formed North Kent Sewer Authority. The firm is currently working with the NKSA to design and construct the $50-million PARCC SIDE Clean Water

Plant, which will treat wastewater with innovative Membrane Bioreactor technology. Other projects have included a number of pipeline reconstructions and the award-winning Four Mile Lift Station.

Prein&Newhof is proud to have aided the success of its many private and community clients throughout West Michigan. The firm hopes to continue improving the infrastructure and quality of life in West Michigan for years to come.

The Kent County Board of Aeronautics has relied on Prein&Newhof to design runway and site improvements at Gerald R. Ford International Airport for over 25 years.

M-01 in downtown Greenville received a face-lift in 2002 with engineering help from Prein&Newhof and a Transportation Enhancement Grant from the Michigan Department of Transportation.

With its mandate to "go where the needs are,"

rehabilitation, a Wellness Center, transportation services, and in-home care. In 1993, the Village was the first in West Michigan to receive national accreditation from the Continuing Care Accreditation Commission (CCAC), meaning that it can provide residents with all the services necessary to support them from independent living through end-of-life care.

In the late 1990s, Porter Hills grew beyond the Village. In 1997, it acquired Meadowlark Retirement Village in Sparta, with independent residential and assisted living services; Cook Valley Estates soon followed, offering a selection of freestanding homes, townhouses, and apartments as well as the Meijer-Hadley Wellness Center, all situated in an upscale environment. In 1997, Porter Hills

began constructing several "affordable retirement" apartment communities for low-income residents. Presently, six such affordable Porter Hills Communities are dotted throughout Grand Rapids. Soon, a new community will open in Caledonia—Station Pointe, targeted toward middle-income residents.

All Porter Hills communities are set in pleasant surroundings with support services, such as transportation, meals, laundry, and help with daily tasks, available on campus or near by. A resident in any Porter Hills Community also has access to the Martindill Wellness Center at Porter Hills Village, which houses the organization's most comprehensive health and wellness resources in addition to an out-patient rehabilitation center.

In-home Care

In addition to residential care, Porter Hills has significantly increased the assistance it offers to seniors who choose to live in their

1968 Ground Breaking Ceremony at Porter Hills Village.

"All Porter Hills communities are set in pleasant surroundings with support services, such as transportation, meals, laundry, and help with daily tasks, available on campus or near by."

1968-1969 Construction at Porter Hills Village.

Porter Hills serves the senior population in West Michigan with a comprehensive range of services, from pleasant residential communities to hospice care. As new programs are developed, Porter Hills is becoming an important—and expanding—resource serving some elders at all levels of its "continuum of care" throughout West Michigan.

The Village

In 1970 its first community, Porter Hills Village, offered both independent residential living and skilled nursing care for elders no longer able to live independently. Over the years, the residential choices and services at Porter Hills Village expanded to include hospice care,

own homes. In fact, it is organizations like Porter Hills Home Care that often enable the elderly to stay at home. From in-home nursing care to simply running errands or preparing a meal, Porter Hills tailors the assistance to the person's needs.

Recently, the organization was pursuing a federal contract to care for the low-income elderly in their homes. Under the LifeCircles Program of All-inclusive Care for the Elderly (PACE), Porter Hills will cover all the support services the PACE recipient might require for the remaining years of his or her life, enabling the individual to reside in the comfort of home.

Innovative Programs

Two Porter Hills communities already incorporate elements of the Eden Principles, which advocate a pointedly compassionate approach to caring for the elderly. The Eden Principles are meant to counter the "three plagues" of the elderly—boredom, helplessness, and loneliness—by incorporating meaningful activity, human contact, and elements such as plants, animals, and children into daily life.

Now, the organization is more deliberately adopting the Eden Principles in an innovative new facility, THE GREENHOUSE PROJECT®. Based on a "social model" rather than the familiar nursing home concept, which is focused on medical care, the Greenhouse Project is more like a family home than

a nursing home. The intent is to create a small, homey community in which the residents contribute to the upkeep and decision making of the household, all gather at one table for meals, and have private rooms, while still receiving the assistance and medical oversight they need.

Good Governance; Good Employer

Stereotypically, working in a skilled nursing center ranks near the bottom of desirable jobs, usually involving low pay, demanding work, and a marginal environment. Complicating that scenario, labor costs are extremely high in the industry, amounting to about 80 percent of operating costs, which motivates communities to cut corners on those costs wherever possible.

Porter Hills, however, resoundingly challenges that stereotype. For four consecutive years, 2003, 2004, 2005, and 2006, Porter Hills was named one of West Michigan's *Best*

Cook Valley Estates

and Brightest Companies to Work For, awarded by the Michigan Business and Professional Association.

This recognition not only reflects the quality of the work environment Porter Hills provides for its employees, but it also speaks to the environment and level of care it offers residents. A good work environment necessarily spills over into quality of care.

Additionally, Porter Hills remains on solid financial footing while consistently expanding its services and moving into innovative models of care because its Board of Directors is fiscally conservative and socially progressive in fulfilling its mission. The last two decades has ushered in a period of growth for the organization to meet the changing needs of seniors. Porter Hills is committed to providing comprehensive, quality care to meet needs at all levels, from pleasant surroundings that support an active lifestyle to intensive care for those who need memory support and the growing need for home care services.

Porter Hills Village
Photo by Carol Meekhof

"Porter Hills remains on solid financial footing while consistently expanding its services and moving into innovative models of care because its Board of Directors is fiscally conservative and socially progressive in fulfilling its mission."

317

Larry Andrus, CEO, bonds the Trivalent Group through his strong leadership and vision.

I t's hard to remember a world without the technological conveniences we use on a daily basis, but it wasn't that long ago when a postage stamp – not an Internet connection – was required to send mail. Today, companies like Trivalent Group specialize in solutions to communications issues unimagined 20 years ago.

The company began in 1991 as Trivalent LAN Concepts, (Trivalent stands for the bonding of three integral components –"our

The crown jewel of Trivalent's organization are the Data Centers. From here they connect thousands of customers to the Internet, and support hundreds of servers and many terrabytes of data.

clients, our people, and our partners"). CEO Larry Andrus, who first became involved with the company as a silent investor, acquired

controlling interest in 2002 and soon began broadening its scope. Under the umbrella name of Trivalent Group, its family of companies now includes Remex Systems Group of Kentwood, which began in 1971 and merged with Trivalent in 2003, Entré of Mt. Pleasant, CD&H Support Services of Grand Rapids, Reiughes of Kalamazoo, ACCN of Allegan, A5.com of Peoria, and created Trivalent Capital.

Combined, these companies offer an impressive depth of networking and core technology solutions, along with financial management and lease financing for its clients. In fact, Trivalent has coined a phrase for these solutions: "DEMAND driven services." DEMAND is an acronym for Design, Engineering, Managed Services, Assessment, Networking, and Data Management. Many solutions that client organizations need will cut across every letter of DEMAND in one way or another. Clients benefit from this robust offering by knowing they can depend on Trivalent to be their Internet Service Provider, connect their remote sites, manage the health of their systems, ensure their systems and data are secure, keep track of and control the mountains of data being stored, and do all this and more either on the client's site or in one of the Trivalent Group data centers.

As technology continues to evolve to support business complexity, more and more businesses are turning to outsourced technology solutions. Headquartered in Grandville, Trivalent Group operates with a mission of "providing our clients continual access to their mission critical network applications and business data by combining the talents of our people and our partners to help our clients succeed," according to Andrus.

In such a high-tech enterprise, the people of Trivalent Group understand the need for good client

The Trivalent engineers take the time to design and explain, in business terms, the concepts and solutions that help clients capitalize on their technology investments.

network operations, account management, project management, engineering, and service desk personnel, the company is "large enough to have sufficient depth yet small enough to be responsive," he added.

Andrus and the rest of his team also thrive on the family-oriented environment at Trivalent, where, as he said, the company provides "opportunities that challenge our members to grow and develop their skills." Some of those opportunities come in the form of community service. "We do many things for our greater community, as employees and as a company, that are below the radar, but really help to build our collective character," he added. Projects include helping out families in need during the holidays, assembling and sending packages to Iraq, and working on Habitat for Humanity homes.

Trivalent Group is able to operate with agility in a very fast-changing industry. A large part of the value Trivalent provides is in "our unique capability to bundle all technology deliverables into one monthly payment," Andrus

relationships. When thinking about what's most rewarding about being involved with the firm, Andrus said, "establishing long term relationships with our clients that 'help them to succeed'" goes at the top of the list. He takes particular pride in the willingness of his team to truly do what it takes to get the job done, as well as the diversity of skills and experience within the company. With its experienced and intelligent

said. Part of that capability comes from partnerships and wholesale agreements with technology giants that provide telecommunications, infrastructure, software, and systems support.

The West Michigan based company has seen plenty of economic ups and downs over the course of its existence. As Michigan faces further change, Andrus said he sees West Michigan as a "business oasis" in the state, with growth, diversity, and overall culture continuing to evolve.

"Relationships of trust and mutual benefit can be established and sustained. West Michigan is a great place to raise and nurture a family," he added.

Ultimately, Andrus said he finds great satisfaction in "creating a current business model that works and seeing our vision become a successful reality!"

The hub of Trivalent's business is the Service Desk organization where Client Service Engineers provide remote support for our clients according to ITIL best practices.

> *"Relationships of trust and mutual benefit can be established and sustained. West Michigan is a great place to raise and nurture a family," he added.*

Confident, proactive support is provided by the Trivalent Group managed services team. They tirelessly monitor and support clients both in the data center and across the region through our unique blend of technologies.

A DAC Automotive, headquartered in Grand Rapids, is a direct supplier

"Employing just over 1,000 people, ADAC designs, develops, and manufactures interior and exterior door handle assemblies, lighting applications, exterior trim, and cowl grille assemblies."

of automotive products to Chrysler LLC, Ford Motor Company, General Motors, Honda and Nissan. Employing just over 1,000 people, ADAC designs, develops, and manufactures interior and exterior door handle assemblies, lighting applications, exterior trim, and cowl grille assemblies. Chairman Ken Hungerford and President and CEO Jim Teets lead the corporation. In 2006, ADAC realized

combined revenues of $230 million and has continued to hold steady in an uncertain economy through its focus on innovation, quality, and continuous improvement. The company has five manufacturing facilities in Grand Rapids, Kentwood, Muskegon, and Saranac; a separate innovation and engineering centers in Grand Rapids; a joint venture molding and assembly operation in Juarez, Mexico; and, a sales and engineering office in Troy, Michigan. Each manufacturing facility is highly specialized and dedicated to its own product lines. The company uses state-of-the-art equipment, featuring injection-molding presses, advanced robotic manufacturing processes, facilities for fully automated product-specific painting, automated assembly equipment, statistical process control (SPC) technology, and certified testing labs and equipment.

ADAC's Future— Driven By Innovation

In 2006 ADAC joined the VAST (Vehicle Access Systems Technology) Alliance, along with STRATTEC Security Corporation of Milwaukee, Wisconsin, and WITTE Automotive of Velbert, Germany. VAST brings together ADAC's expertise in door handles, STRATTEC's knowledge and experience in keys and locksets, and WITTE's experience in

latch and handle systems. Through VAST, ADAC and the alliance members have manufacturing operations not only in North America but in Europe, China and Brazil, to serve the ever-expanding global needs of their customers. By channeling global opportunities through the VAST Alliance, ADAC can continue to refine and improve its higher value added operations in its West Michigan home base. In conjunction with this new business model, ADAC changed both its name and its logo: ADAC Plastics is now ADAC Automotive.

Entrepreneurial Instincts Paved the Way to the Future

ADAC draws from a rich history of success. In 1972, Dan Trapp and four associates started A-Line Plastics, an injection molding operation in Grand Rapids. Three years later, Trapp purchased the company, and began operating under the name ADAC Plastics, Inc. With six employees and three machines, the company specialized in producing plastic molded parts for appliance and furniture manufacturers in West Michigan. Soon, Trapp began to expand the business. The company grew to include twenty-two employees and six injection molding machines. In 1977, the company relocated to Union Street SE. By 1985, that facility had grown to 60,000 feet with 20 machines, including a new 1,000-ton molding machine. By the end of its first 10 years, ADAC was a well established custom injection molder and Trapp sold a majority of his interest to Richard Lacks, Sr. and Ken Hungerford. Hungerford, as president and general manager, began positioning ADAC as a supplier to the North American automotive marketplace. During the mid-1980s, ADAC moved to a new facility on 36th Street and organized its product base into four groups: exterior lighting, nameplates and ornamentation, functional parts and assemblies, and interior decorative parts and assemblies. In 1989, ADAC added the Design and Development Center. The central engineering facility employed some of the most talented people in the industry, including product designers and engineers, program managers, and tool and quality engineers. A year later, ADAC launched its operation in the Port City Industrial Park in Muskegon, producing door handle assemblies. The Muskegon facilities feature the latest in molding, robotic, and material handling and drying technologies, in addition to proprietary paint systems. The company began producing cowl grilles and functional assemblies in 1995 in Saranac. This operation uses the latest molding press and assembly technology and boasts the company's largest injection molding presses, at 1,500 tons each. Complete lighting systems were developed at

the ADAC Lighting Design Center in Livonia in 1992 and later consolidated with the ADAC Detroit sales office. In 1998, ADAC established ADAC Paintbox Group in Birmingham, England, to manufacture components for Rover and other customers. A year later, ADAC purchased the door handle and trim division of Dura Automotive, Inc., adding Honda and Toyota to ADAC's list of OEM customers.

The Essence of ADAC

ADAC was awarded both ISO-9000 and ISO- 9001 certification for its high quality standards by The International Organization for Standardization (ISO) in 1997. In 2005, ADAC upgraded its certification to comply with standard TS 16949. In addition, the company has been recognized by major customers for continued product and service excellence, including Chrysler's Gold Pentastar Award, GM's Mark of Excellence and Ford's Q1 Preferred Quality Award. In 2002, ADAC received its first Clean Corporate Citizen Award from the State of Michigan. By 2003, the company had received this same award for each of its facilities and the facilities continue to hold these designations. ADAC has also been recognized as one of the "101 Best and Brightest Places to Work in West Michigan" by the Michigan Professionals Association. Critical to ADAC's success is the belief that its people are the source of its strength, intelligence, vitality, and reputation. ADAC believes

it must provide the very best in servicing customer needs, and that profits are the measure of how efficiently those needs are met. ADAC's prosperity can be attributed to its guiding principles of creating and maintaining high standards of quality; providing products and processes that are cost-competitive in the world marketplace; providing consistent on time delivery to customers; and developing and maintaining technological capabilities consistent with the design, development, and manufacture of best-in-class automotive products. In addition, ADAC treats customers, employees, and other stakeholders with fairness and integrity; and works continuously to improve performance.

"ADAC's prosperity can be attributed to its guiding principles of creating and maintaining high standards of quality; providing products and processes that are cost-competitive in the world marketplace; providing consistent on time delivery to customers; and developing and maintaining technological capabilities consistent with the design, development, and manufacture of best-in-class automotive products."

Suspa, Inc.

Adjust your office chair. Open the hatchback of your car. Raise the baby changing table in the mall restroom. You might not be aware of it, but each of those ordinary activities relies on gas-filled cylinders for smooth and effortless operation. Many of those gas cylinders were manufactured right here in West Michigan by Suspa, Inc.

SUSPA's Management Team

Right: SUSPA's most valuable assets......manufacturing leadership.

"We've worked on literally hundreds of applications," says Steve Garvelink, president. "We look around and say, 'We can do that!'

of its handy location near the world's car capital.

In the U.S., Suspa soon discovered that it would need to diversify beyond the automotive industry in order to survive. Fortunately, the applications for gas and hydraulic springs are limitless: a door that needs to open easily; a mechanism that raises and lowers; equipment that

Who knew?

While Suspa was founded in Altdorf, Germany, in 1950 to make shock absorbers for bicycles and motorcycles, it expanded to Grand Rapids in 1974 to manufacture gas springs for the hatchbacks of the small, energy-efficient cars that were becoming popular at the time due to rising gasoline prices. Grand Rapids was chosen because

needs to be stabilized or to absorb shock. From lift mechanisms on airline doors to height-adjustable tables to stabilizing washing machines, Suspa has developed mechanisms to open, raise and lower, stabilize, and dampen. "We've worked on literally hundreds of applications," says Steve Garvelink, president. "We look around and say, 'We can do that!' With those broad

applications has come a broad customer base as well as a steady influx of business. From manufacturing 100 or so cylinders a week for the automotive industry in 1975, the company now produces about 170,000 cylinders a week divided into several business units, of which the automotive industry now comprises about 10 percent. Another important application is office seating: Suspa manufactures the gas cylinders that raise and lower task chairs. It sells the suspension cylinders that prevent washing machines from walking across the floor. Another business unit manufactures hydraulic cylinders that raise and lower tables for, among other things, medical and office applications. Its industrial unit, which amounts to about 42 percent of Suspa's sales, produces a variety of product for a grab bag of applications, from the service doors on jukeboxes to the food tray tables in hospitals.

Suspa's strength is its flexibility. Its two main U.S.

Investment in automation has kept SUSPA ahead of the competition.

competitors focus on big customers and orders of 100,000 cylinders or more. Suspa is "happy to run 100 pieces or 500 pieces of a product," says Garvelink. While that agility gives Suspa a very diverse customer base, it also requires a high degree of organization.

To accommodate this range and delivery schedule, Suspa runs three assembly lines. Two are fully automated robotic lines. "We set them up, and they runs 5,000 to 20,000 pieces," says Garvelink. With the ability to very quickly switch from one product to another, a process that takes minutes

and occurs about 75 to 90 times a week; these lines allows Suspa to manufacture a variety of products quickly and efficiently. The third line, which is mostly hand-operated, produces small, specialized orders. Additionally, a prototype room does nothing but build samples for customers. "We have as many sample orders in a month as we have production orders," says Garvelink.

This capability to efficiently capture this mid-sized market has given Suspa an edge against fierce domestic and international competition. While sales growth has plateaued somewhat, Suspa is holding steady at 170 employees and $56 million in sales. Today, Suspa's German parent company, with three plants in Germany, has additional manufacturing locations in the Czech Republic, India, and China. It, in turn, was acquired in 1998 by PPM Capital, a holding company headquartered in London.

These global connections give Suspa's Grand Rapids location a global perspective and access to information, resources, customers, and materials that are beyond

the capability of all but the largest local companies. Due to this perspective, Garvelink is well aware that Suspa must continue to be agile and innovative in order to remain a viable player.

"The key for us is to continue to diversify with new customers and products," says Garvelink. "And to be efficient. Our company has done a lot to squeeze the cost out of our system. But we have to keep developing new markets and niche applications."

Robotic technology in action.

Competition Engineering, Inc.

I n 1976, Competition Engineering, Inc. (Competition) was started from a 400 square foot garage in Marne,

Michigan. By 1997, its sales had tripled and the company employed 18 people. Today, Competition Engineering employs more than 37 highly trained workers and remains located in Marne, a small town just northwest of Grand Rapids.

Competition is a modern 27,000 square foot, ISO/ 9001:2000 certified tool and die shop that focuses on designing and building small to medium size progressive and line dies for the automotive industry. Competition's success has come from meeting and exceeding its customers' need for high quality, production-ready tooling.

Competition specializes in providing the tooling (complete set of dies needed to make a part) for manufacturing stainless steel parts used in catalytic converters and mufflers for

"Competition is a modern 27,000 square foot, ISO/9001:2000 certified tool and die shop that focuses on designing and building small to medium size progressive and line dies for the automotive industry. Competition's success has come from meeting and exceeding its customers' need for high quality, production-ready tooling."

cars, trucks, and off-road vehicles. Competition has become an industry leader in working with stainless steel, which is difficult to form and trim for the same reasons it has great ability to handle heat and resist rusting.

The need to conquer the "rust belt" syndrome and make vehicles last longer has led to an ever-growing increase in the use of stainless steel components in the automotive industry. This trend has created a stable niche for Competition because, with its decades of knowledge and leading-edge technology, Competition has become an industry leader in providing long-lasting, cost-effective tooling for stainless steel components that hold up in demanding production environments.

Competition's tryout presses are equipped with coil feed lines, tonnage monitors, and die sensors that enable Competition to run sample "tryout" production runs in "continuous mode." This process enables Competition to test its dies before they are implemented in actual production environments—a

value-added service that saves Competition's customers time and money.

Unlike many of its competitors, Competition has significant experience in integrating "in-die-tapping" and "pierce nut and pierce stud" units into its progressive dies, which offer tremendous labor savings for high-volume parts.

In addition to designing and building world class progressive and line dies, Competition maintains all the state-of-the-art equipment needed to offer transfer dies, self-contained compound dies, roll form cut-off dies, weld and assembly fixtures, computer numerically controlled (CNC) machining, and wire electrical discharge machine (EDM).

Competition provides extensive on-the-job training to keep its employees up-to-date on ever-changing technology and enjoys very low employee turnover. Most of Competition's employees have worked there for more than 10 years and take deep satisfaction in knowing that they are the best at what they do.

Dane Systems, LLC

Dane Systems, LLC (Dane) was founded in 1990 by a small group of dedicated engineers and tradesmen who envisioned a better way of designing and building custom automation and test equipment.

Offering innovative solutions, Dane quickly outgrew its original plant and built a 45,000-square-foot facility in Stevensville, Michigan. Since 1990, Dane's team of associates grew steadily from fewer than 20 to more than 85 today, and the process of mechanical design progressed from the drafting board, to AutoCAD® to 3D design on the SolidWorks® platform.

Dane applies cutting-edge technologies like robotics, machine vision, laser welding, DC welding, non-synchronous and synchronous platforms, and automatic testing to solve the age-old manufacturing challenges of maintaining high quality and continuous throughput while minimizing costs.

Dane specializes in designing and building automated assembly and test equipment for the automotive, computer products and peripherals, and electronics industries throughout North America. Dane's expertise coupled with long-term support and strong financial backing have made it an industry leader in providing custom-automated solutions such as automated vision inspection, robotic welding, and non-synchronous assembly and tests for high volume production.

Dane has the in-house capability and resources to build equipment through each stage of conception, design, build, wire and plumb, programming, debug, installation and service. However, Dane's approach is to make prototypes and critical contact tooling in its machining department and focus its direct labor energy on integrating components purchased from the best automation suppliers available.

For more than 16 years, Dane has cultivated relationships and developed solid partnerships with automation suppliers that maintain the highest level of reliability for robots, bowl feeders, conveyors, valves, motors, sensors, controls, vision, 3D software and management software.

Dane leverages its vendor partnerships to bring its customers the best combination of equipment and services needed to solve their problems. By taking this approach, Dane manages the risk, time, and resources necessary to integrate multiple technologies into one system, which enables Dane's customers to concentrate on other productive activities within their enterprises.

Dane has more than 16 years experience in custom automation, custom machine building and process development and processes more than 100 orders a year for automated systems, assembly and test equipment, special tools, process development, integration to existing equipment and retrofitting existing tools for new product releases.

Dane is a full-service company and offers additional services, such as project management and data collection systems, to provide turnkey solutions. Unlike many of its competitors, Dane has the expertise and resources to provide these services and does not outsource them to other companies. These services are becoming increasingly valuable to Dane's customers.

"For more than 16 years, Dane has cultivated relationships and developed solid partnerships with automation suppliers that maintain the highest level of reliability for robots, bowl feeders, conveyors, valves, motors, sensors, controls, vision, 3D software and management software."

Datum Industries, LLC (Datum) is a 38,500-square foot, state-of-the-art, ISO/9001:2000 certified tool and die facility located in Grand Rapids, Michigan. With a focus on medium to large size line dies, transfer dies, and progressive dies, Datum has been providing cost-effective, world class stamping dies since 1997.

Datum specializes in designing and building the tooling for manufacturing the steel structural members used in automobiles and trucks, such as the brackets used to mount the chassis to the frame. (Tooling is the complete set of dies needed to manufacture a part that requires more than one die to make it.)

Tool and die making for the automotive industry is a blend of art and technology that makes it possible to form metal into the desired shapes that satisfy the designer's requirements and meet the manufacturer's need to assemble world-class cars and trucks using automation while meeting the consumers' need for safe, solid vehicles.

Through the years, the growing need for lighter, yet stronger vehicles led to the development of a variety of complex raw materials—first of high-strength low-alloy (HSLA) steel and, more recently, of advanced high-strength steels (AHSS). These materials provide many advantages over most carbon steels. With its highly trained staff and cutting-edge equipment, Datum excels at engineering and fabricating sophisticated tooling that consistently produces tight-tolerance, defect-free parts.

Datum prides itself on the talent, skill, and experience of its employees, who have undergone extensive on-the-job training and, in some cases, have served long apprenticeships in the die-making trade. Datum also prides itself on its solid record for providing 100 percent on-time delivery and continuous improvement to all aspects of its quality assurance systems.

To ensure ongoing delivery of world class products and services, Datum uses a full array of state-of-the-art equipment, including the latest in computer aided engineering (CAE), computer aided design (CAD), computer numerically controlled (CNC) machining centers, wire electrical discharge machines (EDMs), a coordinate measuring machine (CMM), and its seven tryout presses with coil-fed lines that enable Datum to handle heavy workloads and manage multiple tooling packages simultaneously.

Unlike many of its competitors, Datum provides simulated production runs to "try out" its dies before they are implemented in the customer's production environment. This value-added service saves Datum's customers the headache of conducting multiple time-consuming tryout tests on their expensive production lines.

> *"Datum prides itself on the talent, skill, and experience of its employees, who have undergone extensive on-the-job training and, in some cases, have served long apprenticeships in the die-making trade. Datum also prides itself on its solid record for providing 100 percent on-time delivery and continuous improvement to all aspects of its quality assurance systems."*

Since its founding in 1980, JR Automation Technologies, LLC (JR) has become one of the leading special machine suppliers in the Midwest, providing automated manufacturing equipment and process development solutions to manufacturing companies throughout North America.

Today, its 120,000-square-foot facility located in Holland, Michigan has more than 190 employees. Most of JR's employees have earned college degrees, a process that is made easier as a result of the partnerships that JR has developed with local and state universities. These partnerships are a win-win situation for everyone involved. They keep college professors informed of the latest trends in the industry, keep JR's staff up-to-date on technological advances, and provide internship opportunities for the brightest students.

JR builds equipment for manufacturers throughout North America. From labor reduction and process-improvement robotic systems to stainless steel FDA-compliant machines and heavy-metal welding systems, JR partners with its customers in supplying equipment that meets ROI requirements and yields competitive advantages in the marketplace.

Twenty-five years of history, coupled with dedicated engineering, development and manufacturing personnel, enable JR to provide cost-effective, cutting-edge equipment solutions today. Whatever manufacturing equipment needs exist, JR has the ability to partner in addressing those needs.

JR offers research and development and design engineering services, and it maintains a dedicated research and development lab to develop, prototype, and validate the concepts and methods needed to achieve its customers' goals.

JR's internal machining and fabrication capabilities include computer numerically controlled (CNC) boring mills, drill presses, grinders, lathes, paint booths, sheet metal and welding equipment, and vertical mills. This vertical integration enables JR to control the quality and timing of every project and ensures the most robust, highest quality machinery possible.

JR's project managers control every aspect of the design-and-build process, including mechanical and controls engineering, machining, fabrication, painting, assembly, programming, and installation. And JR's lean manufacturing experts provide on-site assistance in order to evaluate current operations, identify cost reduction opportunities, increase throughput, and improve efficiency.

"Twenty-five years of history, coupled with dedicated engineering, development and manufacturing personnel, enable JR to provide cost-effective, cutting-edge equipment solutions today."

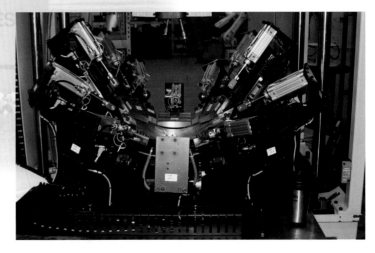

The idea for Monroe, LLC of Grand Rapids began in 1971

"Today, Monroe is a world leader in the design and manufacturing of precision plastic injection-molded parts and components."

when General Motors (GM) encouraged Howard Schuitema to establish a company to supply stamped metal automotive pointers for its full line of cars and trucks. By 1972, Monroe was tooled up and producing pointers in addition to developing its Machine and Engineering departments for the production of prototypes, assembly equipment, and fixtures.

The industry standard for pointers—used in speedometers, tachometers, and other gauges—had always been the painted metal pointer, but in 1973, Monroe introduced the concept of plastic pointers. By 1976, injection-molded, plastic pointers had passed all of GM's engineering, environmental, and aesthetic tests. They were in full production and quickly became the new industry standard.

Building on its reputation for innovative engineering and creative design, Monroe was instrumental in introducing the light pipe (an internally lit pointer) and led the industry in the development of tip-to-tail-lit pointers.

From the beginning, Monroe worked closely with its customers' engineering groups to develop new technologies and methods to improve quality and efficiency and to reduce costs. However, in order to further enhance its superior customer service and support, in the early 1990s, Monroe increased its engineering staff and began its still-current practice of providing an engineer for each customer.

Today, Monroe is a world leader in the design and manufacturing of precision plastic injection-molded parts and components. It molds, decorates, and assembles more than 60 million pointers a year and holds a significant share of the automotive instrumentation market.

Monroe pointers are shipped to locations all over the world, many of which are the renowned tier-one automotive suppliers. Monroe pointers go into almost all of the leading domestic and foreign brands of automobiles, trucks, tractors, motorcycles, boats, snowmobiles, and other industrial and recreational vehicles.

Monroe has been in the pointer business for more than 35 years, but also designs and manufactures a wide variety of other plastic components. Its core competencies of engineering, manufacturing, decorating, and assembling precision-molded plastic components apply to any small, injection-molded part.

In addition to shipping more than a million pointers each week, Monroe produces a variety of other precision plastic parts, including reset knob assemblies, light pipes/dials, buttons, and decorative rings.

Monroe employs 275 loyal and talented people. Turnover is extremely low and Monroe often has a backlog of applicants. Monroe's facilities include three production facilities, a warehouse in Grand Rapids, and a distribution center in Mexico.

The story of Parkway Electric & Communications, LLC (Parkway) begins in August 1945 at the end of WWII when Fafnir Bearings, like so many other defense contractors, closed its doors. At that time, Elton Achterhof (1913–2000) found himself out of work and began using the skills he fine-tuned at Fafnir as a plant electrician to start his own business wiring local homes and businesses from his home in Holland, Michigan.

Elton had studied almost every night while working seven days a week at Fafnir and understood the value of education. The company continues to value education today by providing tuition reimbursements and encouraging employees to further their educations. The result is a well-educated and highly skilled work force that has allowed Parkway to build a reputation of reliability and long-term relationships with its customers. Through the years, the three R's of Parkway—relationships, reliability, and reputation—have become the company's core values, all of which have grown from its value for education.

At Parkway, on-the-job experience is also

highly valued. The 80-plus electricians and technicians as well as the engineers, estimators, CAD designers, project managers, and other support staff at Parkway have longevity with the company and many years of experience.

To stay on top of the most recent developments and the newest technologies, Parkway concentrates on what it does best—commercial, industrial, and educational projects. Parkway's Power Division provides a full range of electrical contract services to West Michigan businesses. Its Communications Division develops complete, customized solutions that range from audiovisual systems to security systems and Voice over Internet Protocol (VoIP). Its Controls Division builds full control systems that make managing processes safer, more accurate and productive.

In 2006, Parkway helped to design and it installed all the electrical, sound system, video projection, theatrical lighting, voice/data cabling, and fire alarm systems for the Resurrection Life Church in Grandville, which has a 4,300-seat auditorium and offers live television broadcasts of its services.

In 2007, Parkway designed and installed the audiovisual system for Alticor's 24-story JW Marriott Grand Rapids hotel, which is centrally located near Grand Rapid's

corporate, medical, and entertainment districts.

Parkway has worked with two of West Michigan's billion-dollar, global workspace and furniture companies beginning with Haworth, Inc. in 1948 when it was founded. Most recently, Parkway provided complete electrical design-build services for the expansion of Haworth's North American headquarters in Holland. Parkway has provided services for Herman Miller since the 1970s, including its Miller SQA building and, most recently, the design-build of its National Design Center in Atlanta, which achieved the Gold LEED rating.

Companies and communities all over West Michigan look to Parkway as a single point of contact for the latest technologies and the most progressive thinking on power, communications, and controls.

"Companies and communities all over West Michigan look to Parkway as a single point of contact for the latest technologies and the most progressive thinking on power, communications, and controls."

Robert Grooters is proud to be a part of the Grand Rapids community, and is excited about playing a role in the city's future growth. Robert Grooters Development Company has developed over 25 million square feet of office and industrial space over the past two decades, making Bob's vision a reality.

Looking for some space of your own? Robert Grooters Development Company (RGDC) has been specializing in helping companies find real estate that works for them for more than 30 years.

Founded by Robert D. Grooters, President, along with his wife Sharie, RGDC has grown to become the area's largest privately owned developer of industrial and manufacturing buildings. Robert Grooters said they still operate as a small

core service of providing affordable, quality space and property management, RGDC also offers its customers planning, phones, computers, warehousing, material handling, light assembly, transportation services, marketing, and the ever-popular business growth networking. Networking opportunities for RGDC tenants include Breakfast Boosts, holiday tenant celebrations, personal introductions, and other ways for clients to meet one another.

to keep abreast of the various incentives, tax abatements, and other programs that will benefit its clients. With several of its properties already located in designated Renaissance Zones and tax abatement districts, the company has a solid understanding of the ins and outs of tax breaks.

While RGDC has many properties across the region, the company is widely known for three highly visible projects: Bridgewater Place, River House Condominiums, and Union Station.

Bridgewater Place, the largest office building in Grand Rapids, is an award-winning, 400,000 square foot, 17-story office tower located downtown along the Grand River. Recognized as a world-class building, Bridgewater Place houses premier legal and financial offices as well as numerous other companies. The $60 million building was constructed to be half of a two-tower structure.

In 2007, the second half of the building started to become a reality. River House, being constructed at Bridgewater Place on Bridge Street, will be the tallest building in the city at 400 feet high, with 34 floors. The luxury condominium complex will also be ranked as the fourth tallest building in the State of Michigan but the tallest residential building in the state. More than 200 units will range in size from 850 to 1,900

Virtual picture of River House luxury condominiums. This 34-story residential living facility will be the tallest building in West Michigan. It will reside along the banks of the Grand River in downtown Grand Rapids and will be the second tower to the prestigious Bridgewater Place building.

company, making fast decisions and remaining agile in the ever-changing Michigan marketplace.

This attitude benefits RGDC clients, because the firm knows the importance of value-added services. In addition to delivering its

Also key to a healthy business is knowing—and taking advantage of—available tax breaks. The Robert Grooters Development Company team works closely with the State of Michigan and regional government offices

square feet, not including larger penthouse suites. More than 60 percent of the units were already sold in the summer of 2007.

The third major project for RGDC is the 500,000 square foot commerce and distribution facility known as Union Station. It's considered to be one of the most successful Renaissance Zone development projects in the nation, according to RGDC literature.

"We took a tough area and really turned it around," Robert Grooters said. "Really, that project is one of the prides of our company." Located between highway 131 and railroad lines south of downtown Grand Rapids, Union Station was designated a Renaissance Zone property. This Renaissance Zone property not only needed drastic work to get it up to speed, but it also offered its tenants virtually tax-free operations for a set number of years.

"It's so expensive to develop a Renaissance Zone," Grooters said, listing fiber optics, train tracks, sewers, easements, and contaminated land as a few of the challenges his company faced

when it took on the property.

But it was all worth it in the end. Grooters said Union Station, with its steam locomotive and railroad caboose prominently displayed along highway 131, put 800 people to work and today has about 15 thriving companies operating from the facility. "I consider this a shining example of making it work. You really need to be community minded to do it, because there is a lot of risk involved."

Active in supporting local nonprofits, RGDC personnel believes in giving back to the community, Grooters added.

The company has fourteen people on staff who specialize in real estate, construction, financing, marketing, and management. RGDC also has more than 450 acres of property ready to be developed for its clients.

One of its core offerings involves building facilities to suit its clients' specific building requirements. By handling the entire development and construction process, the company allows its clients to focus on their businesses.

From the industrial space at Union Station, to the many industrial and manufacturing facilities conveniently located near the Gerald R. Ford International Airport, to the elegant Bridgewater Place and soon-to-be-completed River House, Robert Grooters Development Company has really left its mark in West Michigan. And that's not just a figure of speech.

"We've developed about 25 million square feet of buildings," Grooters said.

The 500,000 square foot facility known as Union Station is considered to be one of the most successful Renaissance Zone projects in the nation.

The original Union Station in 1875. Later restored by Robert Grooters Development Company in 1999.

"We took a tough area and really turned it around," Robert Grooters said.

Aerial taken of Grand Rapids and RGDC's Union Station in 2006.

At the turn of the last century, Grand Rapids was a thriving town, and the Pantlind

Exterior of Glass Tower.

"This is the centerpiece of downtown, and people continue to point to it."

Historic Pantlind Lobby.

Hotel, on the banks of the Grand River, was a crown jewel in the center of its bustling downtown. In fact, by 1925, it was ranked one of the ten finest hotels in America with a 7,000 square foot gold leaf ceiling in the Pantlind Lobby that is still the largest in the world.

By the 1970s, however, like many Midwestern cities, the downtown had seen better days, and the Pantlind Hotel was looking threadbare. Years of economic uncertainty in the state along with the centrifugal force of people moving to rural and suburban areas had drained the downtown area of its vitality and had transformed classic landmarks like the Pantlind Hotel into dusty relics.

In 1978, seeking to revitalize Grand Rapids' downtown, Rich DeVos and Jay Van Andel, the co-founders of Amway, acquired the old Pantlind Hotel. They not only restored and revived the beauty of the original structure, but they also built a gleaming, 29-story "Glass Tower" beside it, adding shops, restaurants, convention and meeting rooms, and 300 guest rooms, creating one of the most recognizable structures on the Grand Rapids skyline.

Their intent was to invest in the downtown and by that personal vote of confidence, to encourage other investment, perhaps even to spark a renaissance. They also wanted to create a destination in its own right—something that was worth coming to Grand Rapids to see.

The historic Pantlind, now rechristened the Amway Grand Plaza Hotel, has indeed presided over a slow, steady renaissance of downtown Grand Rapids. And it still occupies a premier spot as a downtown destination for West Michigan and beyond. A 2000 Condé Nast Traveler survey ranked the Amway Grand as the 12th best hotel in North America and among the top 100 in the world.

Dining Room of The 1913 Room.

Its 1913 Room, an exclusive restaurant with a French flair, is the only five-diamond restaurant in Michigan. And it is only one of seven restaurants in the Amway Grand, from Cygnus 27, high atop the Glass Tower to the Starbucks® in the historic Pantlind lobby. Other amenities include a fully-equipped fitness center with a pool, tennis and racquetball courts, hot tubs, sauna, and steam room to luxurious suites overlooking the city skyline.

The hotel has forty-two meeting rooms to accommodate events of all sizes, while a climate-controlled skywalk leads to the DeVos Place Convention Center with 250,000 square feet of convention space as well as DeVos Hall, a world-class performance space.

While retaining the elegance of a former time, the Amway Grand Plaza has far surpassed its predecessor in scope and grandeur. "This is the centerpiece of downtown, and people continue to point to it," says Tomaselli.

When Mom told us to clean our rooms, she never meant quite like this. Since 1982 Clean Rooms International (CRI), located in Grand Rapids, has specialized in designing

and providing cleanrooms, workstations, air handling equipment, and cleanroom components to industries that require work space with as few airborne particles as possible.

While pharmaceutical, semiconductor, and electronics industries are three major fields the company serves, "there isn't any one industry that really stands out for us," said company president Nelson Werkema. Other industries served include aeronautics, automotive, healthcare, and plastics, as well

as universities and government agencies.

Some of these projects can be rather secretive, too. "A lot of times we supply the cleanrooms," Werkema noted, "but we don't always know what's going to go

on inside them." That's because projects that require exceptionally clean air are often involved with research and design, be it in the

aerospace or pharmaceutical industry, for example.

Not surprisingly, many of these industries must meet cleanroom air standards regarding the quantity and size of airborne particles. As explained in an informational CRI brochure, the United States Federal Standard 209 has been the most commonly used standard for years, classifying air quality by the number of 0.5 micron particles found per cubic foot of air. But today many organizations, especially those with ISO 9000 certification, now use the ISO 14644-1 standard, which categorizes air quality into nine classes based on the size (from 0.1 microns to 0.5 microns) and the concentration of particles.

What's in all that dust, anyway? The most common airborne contaminants include atmospheric dust, bacteria, skin pigments, oil smoke, paint pigments, pollens, various nuclei, and sulfuric acid fumes. And whether a company is focused on

"There are very few of us who put it all together," said Werkema, who has been with the company since 1992. "We have so many product offerings; we really offer one-stop shopping."

growing mushrooms or manufacturing optical equipment or aviation instruments, removal of these contaminants clearly benefits everyone concerned.

Cleanroom products range from items as straightforward as a fan with HEPA filtration to more complex, self-contained cleanrooms that can be reconfigured to meet changing customer needs. "There are very few of us who put it all together," said Werkema, who has been with the company since 1992. "We have so many product offerings; we really offer one-stop shopping."

Major CRI product groups are the Legend modular cleanroom system, Flexible Solutions Softwall cleanrooms, SAM® fan filter units, Tru-Clean workstations and clean benches, ceiling systems, terminal diffusers, air handling units, Cleanmaster air purifiers, custom isolation

with a solution, that's really the fun part of this business," Werkema added. Designing customized products has been a longtime CRI tradition, along with exceptional customer service. The CRI staff takes great care to provide not only great service and custom-made systems, but also exemplary technical support and accuracy in every step of the process.

While the need for cleanrooms remains unchanged, product demands have changed over the years. Clean areas once typically encompassed up to several thousand or several hundred thousand square feet, but that has largely become a thing of the past. "We have seen a tremendous increase in demand for

has more than 150 distributors and representatives around the globe. CRI cleanroom products are installed in the United Kingdom, Germany, Ukraine, Australia, Korea, Hong Kong, China, India, Singapore, and Vietnam, to name a few countries.

The late David Toering acquired Clean Rooms International in 1990. Keith Weber joined the company in 1994 and serves as vice president and director of engineering. Timothy Werkema joined in 1997

"When we're working with a customer to come up with a solution, that's really the fun part of this business."

systems and workstations, and pass-through cabinets and tables. In addition, CRI also offers delivery, installation, and consulting and design services to meet its clients' rigorous, precise cleanroom needs.

"When we're working with a customer to come up

smaller cleanrooms and clean benches which are desk-sized workstations," Werkema said. The average size of a cleanroom today is around 1,000 square feet, he estimated.

CRI employs twenty-six individuals at its Grand Rapids location and

and serves as vice president and director of sales. The company has been at its current location in Grand Rapids since 1997. In 2006, it more than tripled its office space, and it still has plenty of room to expand its design and assembly facility in the future.

Cambridge Partners takes apartment living in West Michigan to the next level. Not only are its apartment communities beautiful and convenient, but Markwat, marketing director. "That allows us to make decisions that are in the best interest of our residents."

Woodland Creek Apartments is the

Woodland Creek is Cambridge Partners' largest luxury apartment community; its 756 apartment homes are situated within 98 acres of scenic countryside, yet the community is conveniently located only 1/2 mile south of 28th Street in Kentwood where ample shopping, dining and entertainment are found.

The Woodland Creek Guest Suites feature all the comforts of home for business travelers or families in transition between homes. The fully furnished apartment suites come with a fully-equipped kitchen, washer & dryer, complementary continental breakfast and a health club membership.

Cambridge Partners sets a high standard for service and personal attention in each one of them.

Cambridge Partners owns and manages six apartment communities located throughout Grand Rapids and ranging from affordable efficiencies to luxurious two-bedroom apartment homes with all the amenities. All are beautifully landscaped, nicely accessorized, and managed with the attentive service that residents have come to expect from Cambridge Partners.

"Our apartment communities are locally owned and managed, which gives us an advantage in our market," says Karen

cornerstone of the Cambridge Partners family. The resort-style community is tucked away on ninety eight rolling, wooded acres with ponds and hiking trails set amidst West Michigan's abundant natural beauty. Yet, despite its tranquil setting, the community is only a half mile from the shopping, restaurants, and hustle-bustle of 28th Street.

Besides spacious and unique one- and two-bedroom apartments, Woodland Creek offers extras such as a carport, washer & dryer, an oversized deck or patio, and community features such as free continental breakfast, outdoor pools, tennis and volleyball courts, a carwash station, a community garden, and an exquisite clubhouse with a fitness center, indoor pool & hot tub, an expansive sundeck, and a business center equipped with fax and copy machines, high-speed Internet and a video/DVD library. Residents and guests enjoy free wireless Internet access throughout the clubhouse as well as sixty channels of free Dish Network TV in their home.

All these amenities are available to the long-term resident or to the business traveler, who may be in town just for a few days, a few weeks or a few months. In addition to apartments, Woodland Creek has sixty Guest Suites available

for a stay of any length. These suites are beautifully furnished complete with high speed internet and everything from linens in the closet to silverware in the drawer. "Our Guest Suites are a wonderful alternative to a hotel, whether you need accommodations for a few nights, months, or even for a year," says Markwat. "We'll even prepare a continental breakfast for you every morning."

These conveniences make Woodland Creek a popular home-away-from-home for those who are between houses, newly

relocated to the Grand Rapids area, or traveling for business.

In fact, Woodland Creek has a special program that caters to just such business travelers: Its Elite Employer Program contracts with local companies to assist their valuable employees who are traveling or relocating. "Our Elite Employer Program is perfect for companies who are growing or who frequently provide accommodations for their travelers. We are committed to offering customized rates and services to best suit the company's needs."

And that kind of

commitment is the bedrock of the Cambridge Partners Satisfaction Guarantee & Diamond Club Service. Need dry cleaning picked up? No problem. Expecting an important package? It's in good hands. New to the area? Joins us for coffee and bagels in the morning and we'll introduce you to your neighbors.

Residents in any Cambridge Partners community are treated to similar outstanding levels of service, such as complementary membership to a local health club, for example, to promote healthy living. And opportunities to get to know the neighbors through regular, community get-togethers, from a fall wine-tasting event, Toys for Tots fundraiser, casino party, and even a Cambridge "American Idol" competition.

The social gatherings and the personal attention are all designed to help people feel right at home. "When people choose our communities, we are careful to remember that this is their home," says Markwat.

"Our vice president, Shannon Brandon, attends community events. You will see our upper management getting involved in the daily

activities and talking to the residents. We get to know our customers personally and take the time to find out what is important to them." she says.

The high-quality lifestyle offered by Cambridge Partners communities is not a well-kept secret, but has received recognition statewide. In 2006, the Property Management Association of Michigan awarded Cambridge Partners its highest honor of Management Company of the Year. The community manager of Woodland Creek also received top honors in his category. This annual competition is held each year among more than 700 apartment communities throughout Michigan. Cambridge Partners won a total of seven awards, more than any other company in the state.

So, whether you're looking for a pleasant, well-appointed place to stay while you're traveling or for a picturesque, friendly place to live without the hassle of mowing the lawn, Cambridge Partners communities offer exceptional value, great locations, and all the comforts of home.

The staff of Cambridge Partners, Inc. was honored with 7 Awards of Excellence by the Property Management Association of Michigan in 2006. Among these was the top honor of Management Company of the Year for the state of Michigan.

Wyndham Hill Apartments is located near the popular Knapp's Corner shopping district. Residents here enjoy a heated outdoor pool, picturesque views and a convenient location within 10 minutes of downtown Grand Rapids. Wyndham Hill is the choice destination for those who commute to downtown hospitals, colleges and corporations but who prefer to live in a relaxed, peaceful setting.

"The high-quality lifestyle offered by Cambridge Partners communities is not a well-kept secret, but has received recognition statewide."

The Right Place, Inc.

The Right Place, Inc.

The Right Place, Inc. was founded in 1985 out of a shared vision to

"The mission of The Right Place is to promote economic growth in the areas of quality employment, productivity and technology in Greater Grand Rapids by developing jobs through leading business retention, expansion and attraction efforts."

establish Greater Grand Rapids as a premier location for business. The result: a private/public partnership dedicated to enhancing the regional economy by fostering job creation, sustainable growth strategies and innovative business practices. Supported by forward-thinking investors, The Right Place collaborates with business and community leaders to fulfill its mission to promote economic growth in the areas of quality employment, productivity and technology in Greater Grand Rapids by developing jobs through leading business retention, expansion and attraction efforts.

This more-than-20-year commitment to growth and innovation has made Greater Grand Rapids a leader among mid-size communities. With one of the most advanced manufacturing infrastructures in the world, billions invested in life science research and patient care, and a diversified, vibrant economy, the region has become an internationally recognized center for excellence. Since its founding, The Right Place has helped to secure hundreds of millions in new investment and new payroll, as well as thousands of new jobs. More importantly, it has collaborated with the region's businesses to retain thousands of jobs and hundreds of millions in investment.

As a central resource for economic development, The Right Place provides retention and expansion services to hundreds of area firms each year. Its comprehensive portfolio of services includes:

- Site selection
- Guidance in accessing local and state incentive programs and services
- Guidance in identifying financial providers, potential partners and customers
- Customized research services
- Access to workforce development and training resources
- Enterprise development programs and services
- Opportunities to collaborate with peers in the Greater Grand Rapids business community as well as regional and national business leaders.

Working with its customers to satisfy both immediate and long-term strategic needs, The Right Place is continually identifying the next new resource, technical partner, or innovative idea that will help the region sustain a competitive advantage. It provides access to the best minds and technical advancements from around the U.S. and around the world, offering area businesses opportunities to collaborate, exchange ideas, and gain new expertise.

The organization also works with local, regional and international partners to raise the profile of West Michigan as a leader in life sciences, technology and advanced manufacturing. In the years to come, The Right Place will continue to provide the best strategies and services to facilitate the region's adaptation to an ever changing global economy, and lead its extraordinary development as one of the country's premier communities.

These days, companies are exposed to a wide variety of risks, such as a volatile business environment, unexpected business expenses, or even global warming. How those risks are managed can make or break a company. This is where Marsh comes into the picture.

Marsh, part of the MMC family of companies, is the world's leading risk and insurance services provider, with clients in more than a hundred countries. Its services include risk management and consulting, insurance brokerage, financial solutions and insurance program management. The company has more than $5 billion in annual revenues and employs almost 30,000 professionals.

Marsh's West Michigan division employs more than fifty employees and brings an

Matt Wey, Managing Director, Marsh USA Inc.

"Marsh's West Michigan division employs more than fifty employees and brings an impressive average of more than 20 years experience to the firm."

impressive average of more than 20 years experience to the firm. The office provides risk management services such as insurance brokerage; risk control; claims management; captive design, implementation, and management; alternative risk financing; e-business risk consulting; global risk management; and employee benefits through its sister company, Mercer.

To best serve its clients, Marsh takes a proactive approach to risk. Methods used include identifying a client's overall business risk profile, analyzing data and developing performance measures, identifying and designing the best solutions for its clients, and executing a risk and insurance program to support the unique situation of each individual client. Once the program is in place, Marsh continues to support its clients by

measuring and monitoring performance and continually improving each program.

Although this level of detail and service might lead one to believe the company only serves major international corporations, the fact is, Marsh serves a varied clientele. For example, the Grand Rapids office provides risk management programs to industries such as manufacturing and construction, as well as education and financial institutions. It also offers the Academy of Risk, a series of courses designed to help both current and prospective clients understand the ins and outs of risk management and the company keeps its clients abreast of risk management issues such as climate change with its publication, Risk Alert.

Clients are not the only ones who benefit from the efforts of Marsh employees. The Grand Rapids office is actively involved in the community, both as a company and through its employees. It supports area nonprofit and economic organizations that focus on improving the region for business as well as residents. Individually, company employees support more than twenty-five cultural and nonprofit groups with both their time and money.

From philanthropy to insurance and risk management services, Marsh has and will continue to make a positive impact on West Michigan.

When it comes to buying, selling, and leasing commercial property, S.J. Wisinski & Company emerges as a leader in West Michigan real estate.

"Hard work, commitment, and the dedication of the sales associates and support staff have made the company a success. We are proud of the business that happens every day at our facility," says Stan Wisinski.

"Stanley J. Wisinski's business philosophy is simple, yet effective: All clients, large and small alike, deserve the same level of professionalism and service."

Agents at S.J. Wisinski work to gain a thorough understanding of their clients' business, learning how to best meet their needs while forming long-standing relationships.

Professional Service From Knowledgeable Associates

Stanley J. Wisinski's business philosophy is simple, yet effective: All clients, large and small alike,

Just a glance at the firm's extensive portfolio of clients is proof enough of its superb knowledge of commercial properties. No matter the size of the transaction, the associates at S.J. Wisinski & Company are known for catering to the specific needs of their clients. From leasing to tenant concerns, from negotiations to accounting, S.J. Wisinski & Company covers the entire gamut of commercial real estate services.

deserve the same level of professionalism and service. It's what he believed when he started his company in 1986 and it's what he and his associates uphold more than 20 years later.

S.J. Wisinski & Company is a full-service brokerage company specializing in the sales, leasing, and site selection of commercial, industrial, and office properties throughout West Michigan. The company markets vacant land, existing structures, conversions, new construction, and build-to-suit properties, in addition to offering complete property management services. The company's focus on brokerage has built a stellar reputation, establishing strong relationships with many local, regional, and national developers and owners. Regional and national associations extend the expertise of S.J. Wisinski & Company agents into markets both near and far.

S.J. Wisinski & Company's professionals, supported by a full administrative and research staff, provide their clients with the highest level of service and representation. They thoroughly understand the market and they put that understanding to use,

"Clients find that the associates at S.J. Wisinski & Company are the key to reaping the highest returns on their property."

coupled with the most relevant statistics about the premier properties, the environmental concerns and requirements. The brokers have an in-depth knowledge of the community and know what it takes to bring buyers, sellers, owners, tenants, lenders and investors together.

As real estate brokers, S.J. Wisinski & Company brings a wealth of expertise in representing individual owners and users of real estate. Agents provide counsel on all phases of the buying process, from finding the property and comparing

its cost-effectiveness to supervising building inspections and negotiating contracts and leases. S.J. Wisinski & Company helps each client conduct a thorough assessment and build a customized strategy for achieving the best real estate investments.

Clients find that the associates at S.J. Wisinski & Company are the key to reaping the highest returns on their property. Nothing is overlooked; securing tenants, negotiating leases, responding to tenant concerns, accounting, and reporting are all handled

with the professional courtesy on which S.J. Wisinski & Company stakes its reputation.

S.J. Wisinski & Company has been West Michigan's premiere commercial real estate firm since 1986.

Although many of S.J. Wisinski & Company's clients call West Michigan home, its investors come from all over the globe. For those looking to expand their business locations or investments in Michigan, they will find an excellent business partner in the firm of S. J. Wisinski & Company.

The high level of attention to the needs of all parties – real estate users as well as owners and investors – has gained S.J. Wisinski & Company a strong reputation for real estate management professionalism.

"We work in a company that actually gets to change our

Davenport University W. A. Lettinga Campus.

Middle Right: Rally for Hope and Hunger.

Right: Grand Rapids Art Museum.

"We have a group of employees who are extremely proud to be part of the company," Wheeler said. "People start here when they are 22 years old and after a year or so say, 'I'm going to retire from here.'"

community," said Rockford Construction Company CEO and chairman John Wheeler. And the company certainly does that, whether it's building the Davenport University W.A. Lettinga campus in Caledonia or working with internationally renowned architects Workshop Hakomori Yantrasast to construct the new Grand Rapids Art Museum in downtown Grand Rapids, to name just two major projects.

John Wheeler and Mike VanGessel, President of Rockford Construction, founded the company in 1987. Today, Rockford Construction and Rockford Development Group, LLC, are under the umbrella of Rockford Companies. Based in Grand Rapids, Rockford is building in 20 states across the country in large part due

to its retail clients Meijer, Inc. and Family Video Stores.

The company has around 200 employees, many of whom have been with the company for more than a decade.

"We have a group of employees who are extremely proud to be part of the company," Wheeler said. "People start here when they are 22 years old and after a year or so say, 'I'm going to retire from here.'"

No doubt, part of the recruiting and retention success comes from corporate support of employee volunteerism outside the office, a Rockford tradition. "They sit on boards, they do charitable work, they volunteer and make a real difference in West Michigan," he said.

"We want employees to find balance in their lives," said Mike VanGessel. "We really do rally around one another to support each other's passions."

Those passions cover a broad range of charitable organizations that benefit from such generosity. "We

have been blessed to have a profit each and every year of business and we want to share our good fortune with the non-profits," VanGessel added. "Everyone here wants to be involved."

Rockford has long-term relationships with God's Kitchen, a non-profit program run by Catholic Social Services in Grand Rapids, and the Van Andel Institute, which is

dedicated to world-class cancer research. These organizations have benefited from the motorcycle Rally for Hope and Hunger, a fundraiser Rockford developed and manages each year. The Hammer for Hope, another Rockford fundraiser, benefits local charities including the Inner City Christian Federation.

"We don't see ourselves as builders; we look at ourselves as agents of change," Wheeler noted. That perspective is apparent not only in the company's charitable efforts, but also in its building and renovation projects across the country.

Locally, Rockford Construction signs have

popped up at construction sites as diverse as the JW Marriott Grand Rapids hotel, designed by internationally renowned architects

Goettsch Partners, and the eight-story Steketee Building renovation project in downtown Grand Rapids that sparked Monroe Center's revitalization. A 15-year plus relationship with Meijer, Inc. stores has yielded more than 250 completed projects in five states that include new stores, gas stations, distribution centers, and existing store remodels. Other notable projects include Hackley Health at the Lakes – a joint project with sister company Rockford Development Group, ongoing development and construction of projects in Cherry Street Landing – a multi-year renovation effort in the heart of downtown Grand Rapids, and nearly 400 Family Video stores in sixteen states.

Rockford offers "one-stop shopping," which means the company can manage a construction project from design to completion, including guidance regarding land purchase and development, site and municipal approvals, financing assistance, and subcontractor and supplier decisions.

In addition, "Our goal as a company is to incorporate sustainable construction practices into each project while maintaining an awareness of the needs, desires, and available resources of our clients. We strive to strike that delicate balance of project cost versus environmental impact," as stated in the Rockford mission statement.

To that end, the company is a corporate member of the United States Green Building Council, which developed the LEED (Leadership in Energy and Environmental Design) Green Building Rating System™. By following this voluntary, consensus-based standard for developing high-performance, sustainable buildings, Rockford has a number of projects that have either attained LEED certification or are in the process of acquiring it. They include Inner City Christian Federation at 920 Cherry St., Davenport University W.A. Lettinga Campus as well as Keystone Community Church and the new Grand Rapids Art Museum – the first LEED certified church and art museum in the world, respectively.

Looking at their company, Wheeler and VanGessel see much to be proud of, whether it's exceptional employee retention, the company's continued growth and success in a changing economy, or "the community letting us build landmark buildings," as Wheeler said. "It's a tough business. But we've been able to keep our free-spirit atmosphere. We don't belabor negativity; we stay positive and, because of that, opportunity finds us."

JW Marriott Grand Rapids hotel.

It's that kind of attitude that has made Rockford Construction a strong presence in the growing West Michigan area, a place Wheeler and VanGessel are proud to call home. "It's a whole lifestyle. West Michigan has so much to offer; philanthropy, geographic amenities, the honesty and integrity of the workforce. And the religious and cultural background is huge. At the end of the day this is a place that good and honest people call home."

"Rockford offers "one-stop shopping," which means the company can manage a construction project from design to completion, including guidance regarding land purchase and development, site and municipal approvals, financing assistance, and subcontractor and supplier decisions."

Jon Rooks

Wharf Marina at Grand Haven.

Waterfront Homes at Norton Shores.

Bayou Meadows at Spring Lake.

At age 15, Jon Rooks was quoted on the front page of The Grand Rapids Press saying, "I like taking something old and useless and making it functional again." He wasn't talking about a broken bicycle, but the first two dilapidated multi-family properties he purchased on Grand Rapids' west side. He put the deal together with the help of his former Boy Scout master as an investor and by leveraging his construction experience. This young Grand Rapids entrepreneur later sold the units for a profit and helped pay for his education at Calvin College and his degree from the University of Michigan business school, with a special focus on real estate. During college breaks, he also dabbled in import cars, venturing overseas to take advantage of the strong dollar and his ability to speak German, and selling 22 German sports cars out of his fraternity house parking lot.

Two decades later, Rooks returned to that same Westside neighborhood to transform the city's oldest high school building into hip urban condominiums. By 2007, Parkland Properties, Inc. marketed 460 condominiums, attracted some 830 new residents, and achieved more than $80 million in condo sales in Grand Rapids' urban core, representing 85% of all downtown Grand Rapids condo closings in 2006 and 2007. His company's marketing campaigns including sales materials and www.UnionSquareGR.com and www.BoardwalkGR.com won prestigious Addy Awards for marketing creativity and effectiveness.

Rooks' company has a reputation for selling out projects and getting things done, including passing along savings to enthusiastic downtown homebuyers—fulfilling the intent of tax break-driven economic development tools like Ren Zone and Neighborhood Enterprise Zone (NEZ). In fact, Parkland Properties set sales records with three properties, all located in Renaissance Zones: Monroe Terrace, CityView Condominiums at the Peoples Building, and Union Square Condominiums.

Live A Little

That phrase is the tagline for Boardwalk Condominiums at 940 North Monroe Avenue, a project that contrasts historic architectural character with modern design and construction materials, and where urban neighbors enjoy friendships and convenience. The building, when renovated in 2001, won the Governor's Historic Preservation Award, the Neighborhood Business Award, and is featured in the book "Buildings of

Monroe Terrace in Downtown Grand Rapids.

Cityview in Downtown Grand Rapids.

Union Square in Downtown Grand Rapids.

Boardwalk in Downtown Grand Rapids.

"I like taking something old and useless and making it functional again."

Interior of a Monroe Terrace condo in Downtown Grand Rapids.

Interior of a Cityview condo in Downtown Grand Rapids.

Rooftop pool & hot tub at Union Square condos.

Courtyard pool & hot tub at Boardwalk condos.

Michigan." Finally, under Rooks' leadership, the original Berkey and Gay furniture factory—turned mixed-use property—got a modern facelift and many new amenities to attract yet more generations of urban homeowners. It became the fastest selling condo development in the state in 2007.

Passion for Places and People is Inspiration for Business Success

Traveling (41 countries to date) and his other hobbies are sources of inspiration. "You could argue that I'm always working because my favorite hobbies are boating, overseas travel, and keeping a constant eye out for amazing old buildings and cool new architecture. But, my hobbies stimulate creative ideas that easily overlap into my business. I love what I do."

Parkland Properties success creating real estate options for people of all ages, interests, and economic means, has also reinvigorated West Michigan lakeshore economies from Spring Lake to Montague.

At 29 years old, Rooks was developing three marinas and two lakeshore condo projects, creating properties that gave small communities in North Muskegon County their highest tax base increase in decades. That year, Rooks was named the U.S. Small

Business Administration's *Young Entrepreneur of the Year*.

"We seek properties where we can create recreational and residential opportunities for people who desire an urban or lakefront lifestyle within a certain price range. We've sold some of the most expensive condos in downtown Grand Rapids, and some of the least expensive, ranging from $69,000 to $1,200,000. We've done the same with condominium homes in lakeshore communities along Lake Michigan."

What next? Rooks is focused on a 100-year-old downtown bank tower in a recently extended Ren Zone further up the shore in Muskegon. This combines both the lakeshore and urban lifestyle themes upon which he's built a successful career. In some projects, Parkland may function as either the developer, investor, consultant, marketer, or whatever is needed. Regardless of his role, Rooks maintains that a careful combination of on-site lifestyle amenities that help friendships form faster, low price point per square foot, custom finishing, historic architecture combined with hip design ideas, and end-user tax or interest rate incentives, are the marketing mix behind Parkland Properties' success stories and those properties hip reputations.

Weathervane Inn at Montague.

Ellenwood Estates at Montague.

Ellenwood Landing Marina at Montague.

"You could argue that I'm always working because my favorite hobbies are boating, overseas travel, and keeping a constant eye out for amazing old buildings and cool new architecture. But, my hobbies stimulate creative ideas that easily overlap into my business. I love what I do."

Compatico, Inc.

With the goal of providing simple, high quality office furniture systems and parts at affordable prices, Compatico, Inc. has become a strong player in the competitive office furniture industry. In fact, amid a very challenging West Michigan economy, company President and CEO Dick Posthumus said, "We're an American manufacturing company that is growing."

Credit the staff for much of the company's success, Posthumus said. "Our strength is in the people that work here. We have a tremendous group of associates. Without them, this company wouldn't be anything." One area where that's evident is customer service, which Posthumus considers the company's number one strength. "Our 'Customer First Service' is the best in the country," he said. It isn't one department at Compatico, but rather a part of every department, from accounting and operations to sales and transportation.

"Our strength is in the people that work here. We have a tremendous group of associates. Without them, this company wouldn't be anything."

Compatico manufactures full systems and parts and employs fifty individuals, including regional sales managers in Texas, California, Georgia, and Wisconsin. The company also has more than a dozen independent sales representatives across the United States and Canada. Its sales reach extends to every state in the U.S., as well as Puerto Rico, Dominican Republic, Canada, and South America.

Sixty percent of the company's products are new furniture systems sold to dealers. They are designed to integrate with select systems created by some of the office furniture giants or stand alone as independent office designs. Compatico has five complete new systems: Genesis, a tile and frame system that gives high quality, contemporary design at a low cost; Compatico AO1 and AO2, compatible with Herman Miller Action Office 1® and Action Office 2® systems; Compatico CMW, compatible with Steelcase Avenir®; and Compatico PolyPanel, a

stackable system unique to Compatico.

The other 40 percent of the company's products are new parts sold to office furniture recyclers and refurbishers who revitalize systems that could be two or 20 years old. Posthumus said Compatico appreciates this role in helping reduce waste. "It's important to contribute to recycling – and it provides a nice diversification for us."

Posthumus hasn't always been a furniture man. He also has a long history in farming and agribusiness. However, it was during his twenty years of public service that he developed a good understanding of Michigan manufacturing. He was a state senator from 1983 to 1998, the Senate majority leader from 1991 to 1998, and lieutenant governor of Michigan from 1999 to 2003. In 2004, Posthumus joined Compatico as executive vice president and a minority partner. Two years later he led a group of business and community leaders to buy the company from Glenn Steil, Sr.

The four partners, including Posthumus, William Boer, Peter C. Cook, and Patrick Mullen make up the board of directors that oversee the company. All four also take leadership roles in their communities.

Posthumus is on the boards of the Greater Grand Rapids YMCA, Metro Health Hospital, Gerald R. Ford Boy Scout Council, and US BioEnergy, a company involved with the production of ethanol as an alternate fuel source.

Boer is on the board of directors for Spectrum

Health Hospital and the Gerald R. Ford District of Boy Scouts of America, the chairman of DeVos Children's Hospital Board Committee, and a member of the Calvin College Investment Committee.

Cook and his wife Pat have contributed to numerous Grand Rapids organizations, including John Ball Zoo, the Public Museum, the Butterworth-Blodgett Healthcare Foundation and Spectrum Hospital, Van Andel Institute, Hope Network, Hope College, Grand Valley State University, Davenport University, Cornerstone University, Calvin College, Aquinas College, and Grand Rapids Community College.

In Chicago, Mullen serves on the boards of Shedd Aquarium and MSTV (Maximum Service Television Association), and he is chairman emeritus of the Fox Affiliate Board of Governors and founding chairman of the Michigan Association of Broadcasters Foundation. His Grand Rapids involvement included serving on the boards of Aquinas College, Lake Michigan Academy, Lions Club, and Davenport Foundation.

Compatico was founded in 1989 and soon after purchased by Glenn Steil, Sr. He laid a strong foundation

for the company before selling it to Posthumus and his partners. Now, with new ownership there is a new focus, and a strategic plan to thrive in a new global manufacturing industry.

"To succeed in the 21st century American manufacturers must think differently. We must think of ourselves as 'the manager of the making of products', not just 'the maker of products'." according to Posthumus. "This means being very agile as an organization, while thinking and acting globally," he concluded.

It is this strategy that has led Compatico to bring increasing value to its customers and new jobs to West Michigan.

"To succeed in the 21st century American manufacturers must think differently. We must think of ourselves as 'the manager of the making of products', not just 'the maker of products'." according to Posthumus. "This means being very agile as an organization, while thinking and acting globally," he concluded.

These days you hear every bank in town talk about personal service. But Founders Bank & Trust has been doing a lot more

Beard and senior vice president and chief lending officer Gregory Conway.

Offering people in the West Michigan marketplace a full range of premier quality, innovative banking services and products delivered with a distinctively superior level of personal attention, Founders Bank & Trust prides itself on an environment where every visitor feels welcomed when entering its doors.

To best serve its customers, shareholders, employees, and community and to stay healthy and dynamic in the competitive banking industry, the bank remains true to its strategic growth plan. The strategy includes several key components: developing consistent, steady growth while remaining an independent, local, and community-based organization; building long-term relationships with customers who appreciate

and value exceptional service; offering a comprehensive range of products and services while remaining flexible and responsive to technology and new niches; and expanding its presence throughout West Michigan. Current branches are in Cascade, downtown Grand Rapids, Grandville, and Plainfield Township.

The Board of directors represent leaders from a variety of local businesses, including industry, health care, and finance. The bank prides itself on being a Michigan financial partner, offering local decision-making and community leadership.

Specializing in relationship banking, Founders Bank & Trust has a vision statement that offers, "To be the bank of choice for financial products and services in the communities we serve, driven by a passionately dedicated team of employees committed to developing valued relationships and having a positive impact on the financial success of our customers."

"To be the bank of choice for financial products and services in the communities we serve, driven by a passionately dedicated team of employees committed to developing valued relationships and having a positive impact on the financial success of our customers."

than talking about it, they've been setting the standard for banking that has only one focus - the customer. Founders Bank & Trust has been a personable presence in the local financing business since 1991. Begun as Founders Trust Personal Bank, it became Founders Bank & Trust in 2006 to better reflect its full-service capabilities. From commercial lending and investment services to online personal financial management, the bank serves individuals, businesses, and nonprofit organizations.

Founded as a de novo (new) state-chartered bank in late 1991, Founders Bank & Trust today has four full-service locations in the greater Grand Rapids area and one trust office in Traverse City. Its eighty employees are led by the executive leadership team of president and CEO Laurie

In the heavy manufacturing industry, there are only three ways to move objects—air power (pneumatics), hydraulic

The owners from left to right: Dave Grimm, Roger Betten Jr., Rod Kowalski, and Roger Betten Sr.

oil power (hydraulics), and mechanically (wheels and sprockets, etc.)— Michigan Fluid Power is a master of utilizing pneumatics and hydraulics. Located in Grandville, Michigan Fluid Power (MFP) has always been and continues to be a leader and innovator in hydraulic and pneumatic systems design and manufacturing.

Founded in 1991 by Roger L. Betten, Sr., David M. Grimm, and Rodney R. Kowalski, MFP has grown from three employees and $200,000 in sales in 1991 to forty-seven employees with over $15 million in sales.

All three original partners got their start in the hydraulics business at Fauver Co. where they learned the fluid power business from John Fauver. However, when Fauver sold

"Founded in 1991 by Roger L. Betten, Sr., David M. Grimm, and Rodney R. Kowalski, MFP has grown from three employees and $200,000 in sales in 1991 to forty-seven employees with over $15 million in sales."

MFP's over 20,000 ft. facility located in Grandville, Michigan.

his company to Sunoco, the three men decided to start their own business. Working for a public corporation headquartered in Philadelphia where management decisions were driven by quarterly earnings rather than long-term growth did not appeal to them. So, they formed Michigan Fluid Power, Inc.

Betten had worked at Fauver for 29 years. When he and his partners left Fauver, many customers followed them and have stayed with them ever since. In 1992, Roger Betten, Jr. joined the company and together the owners represent over 75 years of experience in the fluid power industry.

MFP is a major fluid power & motion control components distributor. MFP holds franchises from and is a leading distributor for Parker Hannifin, a cutting-edge hydraulics components provider, Lincoln Lubrication, and Ace Controls.

Parker Hannifin makes custom pumps for MFP that idle at 100 pounds of

pressure and offer additional energy cost savings in MFP-designed systems. Lincoln Lubrication manufactures automatic grease systems for tractor-trailer trucks and heavy construction equipment that dispense precise amounts of grease at regular intervals to every bearing, and MFP offers both onsite and in-house installation of those systems. Ace Controls supplies industrial shock absorbers and deceleration devices.

Besides selling a high volume of these components, MFP uses them in the manufacture and assembly of the systems they design and build. Although MFP's main business is as a fluid power sales distributor—MFP maintains over a million dollars of fluid power components in inventory—it has the in-house capability to design and manufacture fluid power systems and custom manifold assemblies. Over 40 percent of MFP's employees are involved in the design, manufacturing, and installation of entire hydraulic and pneumatic

control systems.

MFP is the leading source for heavy-duty machines that require the strength that only fluid power can provide. MFP engineers and builds hydraulic systems for demanding customer applications. For instance, a customer may need a system with 10 tons of force to push a part through a machine in a second and a half that also has part loading and clamping capabilities. MFP builds over 500 custom hydraulic systems a year and specializes in big industrial systems with 50-, 75-, 100-, or 200-horse power. Its typical customers use MFP's hydraulic systems to make and supply the widgets that, for example, go into automobiles or large appliances.

MFP provides custom power units, custom manifolds and valve packages, engineered assemblies, hydraulic/lubrication system installation, air/liquid filled gauges, and unparalleled customer support through its Hydraulic Tech Center and Pneumatic Tech Center. In addition to hydraulic and pneumatic capabilities, Michigan Fluid Power also offers a full line of electro-mechanical solutions. Whether your industry involves heavy duty industrial or clean room environment the Parker electro-mechanical product line has a solution for your motion application.

MFP's 20,000 square foot facility houses an engineering office, a machine shop, a manufacturing and assembly area, a staging and testing area, and a warehouse holding over a million dollars of parts in inventory.

MFP also offers onsite customer service and installation of fluid power equipment and components, including repairs and upgrades, at customer facilities. And, in January, 2007, MFP opened a fluid power retail store to offer its customers immediate access to over 3,000 parts in stock, onsite services such as "while you wait" hose assemblies and custom tube bending, and face-to-face engineering assistance and systems evaluation. Adjacent to the Grandville facility, the store, called the Parker Store, is sponsored by Parker Hannifin.

Michigan Fluid Power rewards its employees with performance bonuses, a pleasant working environment, and a great compensation package that includes excellent training and cross-training opportunities. MFP pays 100 percent of employees' trade school programs and provides some reimbursement for related college or university courses. MFP rarely advertises its job openings—their future employees are referred by current employees or hear about openings from them. MFP prefers to recruit its employees right out of college or high school and have them complete a two-year, in-house apprenticeship program to learn the hydraulic business.

Highly rated by Dunn & Bradstreet, MFP remains privately held and is still run by its three cofounders and Roger Betten, Jr.

In recognition of its solid growth, ingenuity, innovation in workforce recruitment, development and retention, and contributions to the community, the Grand Rapids Chamber of Commerce named Michigan Fluid Power, Inc. as one of four recipients of its 1999 Small Business of the Year award.

One of many installation vehicles for Michigan Fluid Power.

"In recognition of its solid growth, ingenuity, innovation in workforce recruitment, development and retention, and contributions to the community, the Grand Rapids Chamber of Commerce named Michigan Fluid Power, Inc. as one of four recipients of its 1999 Small Business of the Year award."

Michigan Fluid Power's customer service department.

353

There's always something interesting going on at Reagan Marketing + Design, LLC. On a typical day the company's talented, multi-tasking employees might

Reagan Marketing + Design has achieved success by combining flexibility with consistency. "We're constantly adapting as individuals and project teams to produce excellent

Steelcase Inc., Virginia Tile, Vos Glass, Zanco, and Zondervan.

Reagan Shapton founded the company in 1991, after a career at Steelcase. Her former employer soon became her biggest client. Initially she worked out of her home and had no employees, drawing on the strong relationships she had formed with talented freelancers to complete the creative side of the work. Consistent with her vision, she gradually expanded her workforce, diversified her client base and moved up through a series of office spaces.

RM+D offices are in a converted warehouse at 820 Monroe in the Monroe North Business District. Windows offer a view of the Grand River, and the interior

produce a newspaper insert celebrating a local firm's anniversary, finish an office furniture brochure, shoot footage for a regional health care provider's video, develop a Web site, find a location for a major conference, design centerpieces for an elegant fundraising event, and write and produce, with local musicians, an inspirational song. All of this creative activity is supported by a unique work culture committed to producing the best possible solutions for clients while meeting the needs of the staff and their families.

work and meet deadlines," explains RM+D President Mary Reagan Shapton. "We're able to work quickly and creatively because we have defined processes and the essential skills in place. Details make the difference."

A full service agency, RM+D has created marketing communications and design solutions for local, national, and international clients, including American Leather, Belco, Haworth Inc., Herkner Jewelers, Ideasphere, Milliken Fabric, the Netherlands American Commission for Educational Exchange, Paoli Furniture, Performance Systematix, Rico Vida, Spectrum Health,

"We're able to work quickly and creatively because we have defined processes and the essential skills in place. Details make the difference."

Custom furniture and an abundance of natural light make it a pleasure to work in the design area at Reagan Marketing + Design.

retains many elements from the building's industrial past. "We moved here in 1994, and so we've been able to watch and be involved in the revitalization of this part of town."

Today RM+D employs a staff of more than twenty. Many of these employees have held high-level positions in other marketing firms or corporate communications departments, and several are former freelancers who worked with Reagan Shapton when she launched the business.

Reagan Shapton is able to attract and retain excellent employees because she recognizes and respects the need for balance between work and life. As a small, privately owned company, RM+D can support the work/life balance for each member of the staff. Flexible schedules accommodate the needs of working parents and enable employees to take care of personal matters. Maternity leave is generous. Extra time off may be granted to staff who have put in long hours to meet a deadline. Employees are encouraged to develop new skills and are given educational opportunities that make it possible to take on additional responsibilities. The office closes between Christmas and New Year's, to give everyone a chance to recharge their creative batteries.

Deeply committed to the Grand Rapids community, RM+D supports a variety of local organizations financially and/or by active involvement in pro bono projects, and Reagan Shapton has sat on the boards of several local nonprofits.

"We're about being productive, financially sound and personally responsible to clients, the community, each other, and family," says Reagan Shapton. "And, we also make sure we have fun." This approach continues to make Reagan Marketing + Design a dynamic and successful small business in West Michigan.

"We're about being productive, financially sound and personally responsible to clients, the community, each other, and family," says Reagan Shapton. "And, we also make sure we have fun."

From the first time you walk through our doors, you'll know that with us, you come first. Others may give lip service to this idea, but we practice what we preach. Whether it's a friendly greeting by our staff or the "real person" answering the phone, mmpc is *putting patients first.*

therapy, mmpc aspires to improve health through high-quality, affordable, integrated health care. We are distinguished by our strong social purpose, physician responsibility for clinical care, and enduring cooperation between our specialty groups.

Our physicians are our shareholders ... each participating in the success of the entire group. In addition, we are governed by a board of directors that emphasizes pride and concern for the patient, family and community, and the value of teamwork.

At mmpc, we are committed to providing our patients with quality, cost-effective health care. Our physicians and managers work together to improve care, service, and the overall performance of our organization.

Our Team Approach

Physicians at mmpc practice together as a group; each focusing on his or her specialty while being able to consult with trusted peers as necessary. This makes it simpler for patients to

"Founded in 1995, mmpc's 300+ providers serve the health care needs of patients in Coopersville, Grand Haven, Grand Rapids, Grandville, Greenville, Holland, Rockford, and Zeeland."

Area's Largest Physician-Owned Multi-Specialty Group

Michigan Medical, P.C. (mmpc) is West Michigan's leading multispecialty group. Founded in 1995, mmpc's 300+ providers serve the health care needs of patients in Coopersville, Grand Haven, Grand Rapids, Grandville, Greenville, Holland, Rockford, and Zeeland.

With over thirty specialties and on-site services such as laboratory, imaging, and physical

get referred to one of our specialists. In addition, we typically provide many types of medical services under one roof, making it more convenient to get care.

A common electronic medical record for each patient also helps simplify the seemingly ever-growing complexities of today's medical world, as well as our strong working relationships with area hospitals and insurance providers.

Our Practitioners

Our outstanding medical professionals are dedicated to providing comprehensive and compassionate personal care. Selective hiring processes help ensure that we partner with highly skilled medical professionals with whom our patients will want to build long-term relationships.

Once they become a part of mmpc, our physicians receive ongoing training in their specialties as well as in general patient care. This includes cultural sensitivity training, new technology education, and education in our accepted best practices.

A Focus on Wellness

The philosophy at mmpc centers on keeping our patients healthy, not just treating them when they are ill. We continually promote wellness by combining preventive care and health education with appropriate clinical intervention.

A Tradition of Community Involvement

At mmpc, one of our core values has always been to improve the health of the community, as well as the health of our patients. We accomplish this through a variety of programs and activities.

We know that good corporate citizenship benefits the community at large. Social responsibility and community involvement are part of our legacy, and are crucial to our mission— caring for the communities we serve and making them better places to live and work.

Whether it's preventive care, health education classes, or providing appropriate treatment, we support good health by providing personalized care every step of the way.

Investing in the Community

All of us at mmpc are acutely aware of the uninsured and indigent populations in our area, and we strive to reach out in a number of ways: in annual donations of administrative services to the Holland Community Health Center for the uninsured; by our participation in Project Access and the Kent Health Plan; through individual efforts of voluntary physician services at the Cherry Street Clinic and Health Intervention Services in Grand Rapids, as well as Medicaid participation and care in our offices and local hospitals.

Putting Patients First

Our goal is simple: to provide quality health care services to all patients. The mmpc Board of Directors, administrative team, and physicians continually explore new ways to ensure we deliver the best possible care and service, driven by our ongoing commitment to *putting patients first.*

"Our goal is simple: to provide quality health care services to all patients. The mmpc Board of Directors, administrative team, and physicians continually explore new ways to ensure we deliver the best possible care and service, driven by our ongoing commitment to putting patients first."

Would the Medical Mile exist in downtown Grand Rapids without the

Cascades of glass provide natural light to both offices and laboratories within.

"The collaboration of research and education is critical to advances in science," said Institute Chairman and CEO David Van Andel.

presence of Van Andel Institute (VAI)? With its collaborative focus melding research and education and promoting local, regional, national, and international partnerships, the Institute has helped drive the expansion of the life science industry in West Michigan.

"The collaboration of research and education is critical to advances in science," said Institute Chairman and CEO David

Van Andel. "At Van Andel Institute, this combination not only enhances our fight against today's diseases, but also allows us to inspire tomorrow's scientists, ensuring our future workforce."

Established in 1996 by Amway co-founders Jay and Betty Van Andel, VAI supports Van Andel Research Institute (VARI) and Van Andel Education Institute (VAEI) to fight disease through research and inspire future scientists through education. The Institute is dedicated to preserving, enhancing, and expanding the frontiers of medical science, and to achieving excellence in education by probing fundamental issues of education and the learning process.

VARI conducts biomedical research focusing primarily on cancer and Parkinson disease. It also focuses on translating that scientific research into clinical applications. Research done at VARI has resulted in advances in diagnosis, treatment, and prevention.

"The Institute has been successful in competing for NIH grants, a testimony to the talents of our research staff," said VARI Director George Vande Woude, Ph.D., a cancer research pioneer whose own lab discovered the human gene that causes the transformation of normal cells into cancerous ones in the 1980's. "The number

of major awards that we have received is impressive for an Institute of our size, especially considering that we started only seven short years ago."

Vande Woude leads a truly collaborative, international team of over 200 researchers representing 19 different nations. In only a few, short years, investigators have made great strides in a number of different areas. In 2006, the Program for Translational Medicine was established under the leadership of Scientific Investigator Craig P. Webb, Ph.D., to move research findings into clinical practice with the aim of "personalized medicine" founded on molecular-based individual diagnosis and treatment. Using a database his lab developed to analyze tumor genes and

compare them to a patient's normal genetic makeup, Dr. Webb has been able to match tumor cells with the most compatible treatment option. It is too early to fully determine the accuracy of the system, but there are signs that lead to cautious optimism.

In another recent study, Senior Scientific Investigator Arthur S. Alberts, Ph.D., and his team recently discovered that a naturally occurring protein changes the way cells move. This is significant because cancer patients most often do not die from their original tumor, but from those that metastasize (spread to other organs). This discovery has strong potential in future applications that may one day prevent the spread of cancer.

Scientists led by Senior Scientific Investigator Bart O. Williams, Ph.D., have found a pathway for molecular signals in bone cells that increase bone density in

mice. Because this pathway is intimately related to normal bone growth and development, understanding it may provide insight into how and why some tumors metastasize to and grow in bone. Such spreading is frequently found with common cancer types such as lung, prostate, and breast cancer. Dr. Williams' studies may point the way toward treatments to prevent bone loss in humans as they age, and may also provide clues to fighting cancer metastasis to bone.

VARI scientists collaborate with one another to share findings and resources and to create a synergy and unity of purpose, but collaboration does not end within the walls of the Institute. Van Andel Institute collaborations extend to the local, regional, national, and international

levels and involve scientists, consortiums, institutes of higher learning, and private businesses.

"Collaborations complement the strengths of our scientists, thus increasing the pace of progress in research, opening up new opportunities for discovery," Vande Woude said. "They help to translate discoveries into therapies that may one day conquer illness and enhance lives."

The Institute has partnered with Spectrum Health to create the Center for Molecular Medicine, which offers resources that enable personalized medicine to help patients suffering from cancer, heart disease, mental illness, and other conditions by finding solutions individualized at the DNA, RNA, and protein levels. ClinXus, an alliance between several West

"Collaborations complement the strengths of our scientists, thus increasing the pace of progress in research, opening up new opportunities for discovery," Vande Woude said.

Rendering of Phase II expansion to be completed in 2009

Every dollar of every donation to the Institute goes directly to research and education.

"Rather than reading about research in a textbook or listening to a professor, students will be active participants in ongoing research focusing on the genetic and molecular components of cancer, Parkinson, and other diseases," said Steven Triezenberg, Ph.D., scientific investigator and VAI Graduate School dean.

Michigan healthcare and life science organizations including the Institute, was created to deliver cutting edge biomarker (personalized) treatments to local patients through innovative clinical trials seven to eight years sooner than the rest of the patient population, who must wait for approval by the Food and Drug Administration.

Other collaborations include the Core Technology Alliance (CTA), which provides services in specialized research areas; the Antibody Technology Development Program, a collaboration with Nanjing Medical University, China, that focuses on the development of antibodies for clinical diagnostic/prognostic and therapeutic applications against cancer and infectious diseases; the Good Manufacturing Practices Facility, established by VARI and Grand Valley

State University, which will produce biological agents for early-phase clinical testing; the Pediatric Cancer Fellowship Program, which partners VAI with Helen DeVos Children's Hospital in a program focused on the diagnosis and treatment of pediatric cancer and blood disorders; and a collaboration with the National Cancer Center, Singapore, which focuses on the biology behind varying drug responses in Asian versus non-Asian patients with specific types of cancer.

Van Andel Education Institute (VAEI) is dedicated to strengthening science education and preparing and motivating individuals to pursue science or science-related professions, ensuring that there are scientists to continue this vital research in the future. Current programs that work to accomplish this include VAEI's Science Academy and VAI

Graduate School.

"The Science Academy studies how students learn science and what sustains their interest in science. It also provides professional development opportunities for classroom teachers," said VAEI Associate Director Marcia Bishop. "The goal is to have an impact on science education nationally."

The inaugural program of the Academy is an out-of-school-time program for fourth and fifth grade students. The students get hands-on experience gathering and interpreting data, predicting outcomes, and testing hypotheses. All students are eligible to participate; the Academy seeks to represent the ethnic and socioeconomic diversity of the Grand Rapids community. VAEI staff analyzes how students learn science; the goal is to share this knowledge with other educators.

The Science Academy recently piloted Classroom Science Investigation in 2007, a program that targets specific needs identified by the teacher, invites both teacher and students to the Science Academy where staff model lessons that address those needs, and follows up with classroom visits to continue to model the new concepts and methods.

VAI Graduate School welcomed its inaugural class in the fall of 2007. The school, which has received an independent charter from the State of Michigan to confer advanced degrees, trains Ph.D. scientists as leading scholars in cell, molecular and genetic biology relevant to human diseases through a novel, problem-based curriculum that closely represents the way scientists conduct research.

"Rather than reading about research in a textbook or listening to a professor, students will be active participants in ongoing research focusing on the genetic and molecular components of cancer, Parkinson, and other diseases," said Steven Triezenberg, Ph.D., scientific investigator and VAI Graduate School dean. "Our niche is unique enough that we are considered by universities as a potential partner rather than a competitor."

Educational opportunities are available to students at many levels of educational development. Programs include laboratory internships, training programs for Michigan State University graduate and veterinary students, a postdoctoral program that gives graduates a start on their research careers, and participation in the Grand Rapids-Area Pre-College Engineering Program (GRAPCEP) for underrepresented minorities and women.

Van Andel Institute has grown quickly in just a few short years. According to Vande Woude, "The establishment of 20 laboratories since the Institute opened its doors in 2000 has provided a critical mass of scientists and a good cross section of biomedical cancer research. The success of this first phase in VAI's existence is reflected by international peer recognition for our progress

on several research fronts over the past seven years."

More growth lies ahead. A 240,000 square foot Phase II expansion, designed by famed architect Rafael Viñoly and estimated at $178 million, is scheduled to be completed in late 2009. Viñoly also designed the original 160,000 square foot building that Phase II will adjoin. The expansion will allow VAI to broaden its research focus to include other neurological disorders and chronic illnesses, provide a new home for VAI Graduate School, as well as host students of the new regional medical school, Michigan State University's College of Human Medicine. The building design will also incorporate several features that lessen its environmental impact and will be LEED certified.

"Our Phase II expansion is the continuation of the vision we were founded on: 'An independent medical research institution unencumbered by bureaucracy that encourages collaborative and novel approaches to medical research within its own labs, with organizations here in West Michigan and with institutions throughout the world.'" said Van Andel.

As the Institute and nearby life science organizations expand, more employment opportunities will be generated for local employees. In total, once Phase II is complete, some 800 staff members are

expected to work at the Institute, representing 550 new jobs. And through the numerous collaborations and partnerships with institutes of higher learning, VAI has a greater ability to attract research dollars and recruit future scientists, thereby keeping the intellectual capital in the state. In addition, world-class scientists have been and continue to be attracted to the Medical Mile, bringing their science expertise to the region. This dynamic growth has the potential for a ripple effect that will impact everything from the housing market, to local colleges and universities, to the prosperity of local businesses.

From atop the Michigan Street hill in downtown Grand Rapids where VAI is located, the future looks bright for West Michigan, according to David Van Andel.

"West Michigan is a community willing to embrace new ideas," he said. "It is proving that it can adapt and blend its tradition of manufacturing technology and R&D with the growing demand for products and services to support the health sciences industry."

Scientists at the Institute work to find genetic and molecular origins of cancer and other diseases.

From elementary to high school, college to postdoctoral work, Van Andel Institute provides opportunities for tomorrow's scientists.

Students in the Institute's Science Academy program use the tools of science to conduct investigations.

"West Michigan is a community willing to embrace new ideas."

The Grand Rapids office is located at 51 Ionia S.W., just south of the Van Andel Arena.

Banks are important parts of communities and fill a role in serving their business, cultural and social needs. They are meant to appear secure and trustworthy—rock solid. Unfortunately, they often appear to be goliath in size and unapproachable.

Beginning in 1998, The Bank of Holland has been different from a marketplace full of one-size-fits-all banks with headquarters miles away. It is a homegrown neighborhood bank built on the premise of delivering the services of a big bank with the personal and responsive service of a community bank. From a friendly "hello" when you stop in to an exceptional level of competent service, The Bank of Holland has built a culture of knowing its clients by name and exceeding their service expectations.

The footprint for The Bank of Holland was founded on a different paradigm than that of most banks. A single location in each market serves their clients without the expensive network of branch locations. They focus on providing superior Internet, electronic and ATM banking services and offer unique services, such as a personal courier service for business customers. They believe that in the future banking customers will not rely as heavily on traditional branches for their banking needs but on a variety of traditional and electronic banking products. Their vision allows them to focus on competitive rates and services instead of bricks and mortar. "We recognize that our bank can't be all things to all people, so we strive to be the best at providing a broad range of banking products delivered with personalized service," says Phil DeVries, Senior Vice President of The Bank of Holland, Grand Rapids.

The heart of the bank, however, is their people. Each bank location is managed by a true community leader with a focus on building strong, lasting client relationships. They have also cultivated an environment of giving back to the community. "We genuinely care about our community and, as a neighborhood bank, see it as our responsibility to invest in the cities where we do business," says DeVries. The Bank of Holland provides not only financial support but has donated hundreds of hours of hands-on volunteer time to a variety of community organizations.

They also remain true to their roots as a small business and can identify with the special financial needs of the business client. Their products—traditional savings and checking accounts, loans, leases and mortgages—are tailored to the needs of small-to medium-sized businesses, individuals and municipal/governmental entities. The products are straight-forward and transparent, without pages of fine print or unnecessary fees. "We did not want to provide any product that included hidden fees or that offered little value to our clients," says DeVries. "Our product offerings have increased over the years as the needs of our clients have changed, but they are still transparent and competitive."

Since the company is nearly ten years old, The Bank of Holland has taken advantage of current technology and designed a highly technical backroom support system. With no antiquated legacy systems to replace, they designed an operating system to ensure high-quality customer service, efficient processes and maximum flexibility to meet client needs. They have capitalized on the new technologies and outside service providers to effectively compete with any other financial service providers in the market.

"We did not want to provide any product that included hidden fees or that offered little value to our clients," says DeVries.

H ow does a region develop and grow? Is it innately organic? Are concrete strategies enacted? How closely do business, government, and non-profit organizations have to work together to best serve the broader community? As the West Michigan area continues to develop, the West Michigan Strategic Alliance (WMSA) is keeping tabs on everything from land use to collaborative business efforts and governance. The organization is actively working toward creating a shared vision for the region for the next 25 years.

Formed by business and community leaders in 2000, the WMSA encompasses a seven county region surrounding Grand Rapids, Muskegon and Holland. The WMSA follows the guiding principle "that the most successful future will come from regional decisions that balance economic prosperity, environmental integrity and social justice."

In March 2006, Michigan Governor Jennifer Granholm designated the WMSA as one of seven Centers for Excellence in Michigan. That year, the organization was involved with three major projects.

WIRED (Workforce Innovations in Regional Economic Development), a program established by the U.S. Department of Labor, awards the West Michigan Workforce Innovation Lab $15 million over three years to promote economic transformation through regional collaboration; the WMSA was selected to oversee the activities.

The Green Infrastructure program was created to help protect, preserve and manage the region's natural features and resources, such as area waterways and open space. It has received significant funding from People and Land (PAL), a state public policy group, the Wege Foundation, and grants from community foundations in Fremont, Grand Haven, Grand Rapids, Holland/ Zeeland, and Muskegon.

The *Vital Signs*, a third major project, has developed a set of indicators to measure social, economic, and environmental trends. The goal of this project is to identify and define standards to measure quality of life and sustainability through aggregated data gathered in Kent, Ottawa, Muskegon, Allegan, Ionia, Barry, and Newaygo counties.

Led by president Greg Northrup, the WMSA Board of Directors includes chair Steve Heacock, CAO of Van Andel Institute; vice-chairs Nancy Crandall, retired Mayor, Norton Shores and Al Vanderberg, Administrator, Ottawa County; Treasurer, Jim Dunlap, President, Huntington National Bank; and many other community leaders.

The WMSA has produced a number of detailed reports, including *The Common Framework*, a 28-page document published in 2002 that, as the introduction states, "provides a snapshot of West Michigan that can be used as a tool for creating a shared understanding of our Metro Tri-plex, its complexities and interconnections, its strengths and weaknesses and its opportunities and threats." More recently, in April 2007 WMSA hosted a State of the Region presentation and shared its Action Report, discussing 2006 results and 2007 plans. For years to come, the WMSA is dedicated to being a catalyst for collaboration that helps make the West Michigan region a best place to live, work, learn and play.

"Ensuring West Michigan's position, nationally, is in good hands. Setting the best practices benchmarks for successful collaboration is making a competitive difference for Michigan's West Coast."

Whether you're visiting the Grand Rapids area for business or pleasure, the Staybridge Suites, Grand Rapids offers great short- and long-term accommodations. The

extended stay hotel, open since December 2001, features ninety-four spacious studio, one-bedroom, and two-bedroom suites at its southeast Grand Rapids location.

Guests are folks in need of a place to stay for just a night or up to as long as a year, although a typical visit lasts a month or two. The hotel's extended stay percentage, which consists of a visit of five or more nights, ranges around 50 to 60 percent, general

"While those important amenities allow guests to enjoy a home-like atmosphere, other offerings provide that pampered environment so appreciated in a hotel."

manager Renae Kennedy said. "The nature of our business comes from several different sources, primarily corporations," she added.

People stay with the Staybridge Suites when they're in the area for corporate training classes or temporary business projects. In addition, "we work with some local companies who are relocating new recruits to the area. We also work closely with local hospitals and insurance claims divisions in Grand Rapids," Kennedy said. Other visitors include families transitioning due to relocation, wedding groups, and guests seeking a relaxing weekend getaway.

The spacious suites have been planned to feature all the amenities of home, so that guests will, as the company says, "Get Comfortable." All suites have a kitchenette, living area, bedroom, and work area. The kitchenette includes a full-size refrigerator, range top stove, and microwave, and is fully stocked with dishes and utensils. All-inclusive accommodations also offer free on-site laundry facilities and business services like high-speed and wireless Internet access.

While those important amenities allow guests to enjoy a home-like atmosphere, other offerings provide that pampered environment so appreciated in a hotel. The Staybridge Suites provides guests with a full, hot breakfast buffet

at no charge. Tuesday through Thursday, a free evening reception with hors d'oeuvres is also offered. And in the summer months guset are pemitted to use the grills at their leisure and on Wednesday evenings the Staybridge Suites fires up the grill for their guests.

The hotel is just three miles from the Gerald R. Ford International Airport,

five miles from the Frederik Meijer Gardens, and twelve miles from downtown attractions including museums, the Van Andel Arena, and DeVos Place Convention Center. Also, the hotel is within walking distance to numerous restaurants, shopping areas, and entertainment.

The hotel's cost-efficient rate for accommodations is based on the length of stay, and package rates are also available.

The right person. The right job. The right company. When those three stars align, organizations run smoothly, and employees are productive and happy. WilliamCharles Executive Search makes the stars align. The firm's partners and veteran associates have occupied both sides of the desk and know first-hand how critical the right fit between a candidate and a job can be.

The stars aligned for WilliamCharles in 2001 during the trough of the post-9/11 economic meltdown. During that unlikely period, Chuck Smeester, after working for 15 years in various senior management positions within the financial services industry, joined forces with Bill Benson, who had over 20 years of recruiting experience including running a profitable division in West Michigan for one of the world's largest specialty recruiting firms.

Together, they thoroughly understand the view from both sides of the desk. Benson has the resources and the operational know-how of the recruiter, and Smeester understands what companies are looking for from a cultural and organizational fit perspective. Additionally, they bring a seasoned local presence to the West Michigan area. "When I was working in human resources, no one in search work was physically located in West Michigan," says Smeester. WilliamCharles is still the region's only executive search firm with the expertise to fill the range of positions that it specializes in. WilliamCharles specializes in search work for positions in human resources, marketing and sales management, as well as general executive levels in a variety of industries. The firm also specializes in the banking industry with expertise filling positions ranging from Branch Manager and Loan Officer to CEO.

In addition, the company has a strong niche in accounting and financial positions ranging from senior staff through CFOs. In fact, they established a subsidiary, Financial Edge, which focuses solely on filling key accounting and financial positions on either a permanent or project basis.

From the depths of the economic downturn, WilliamCharles has not only survived, but has grown beyond the West Michigan region. The company now has satellite offices of its Financial Edge division in Rochester and Buffalo, New York and is a member of a world wide network of search firms that pools resources allowing them to place candidates regardless of geography. It has also moved into placing employees on a contractual as well as direct hire basis. "We feel as though there will be a continued acceptance, and even a necessity, for organizations to hire on a contingency basis," says Chuck Smeester.

"We're always looking at the trends and considering what our clients might need in people services," he says. "We want to be in a position to serve our clients now and well into the future. We're committed to contributing to the growth of this region."

The WilliamCharles Search Group lobby, where putting the right person in the right place all begins.

The WilliamCharles Sales Team specializes in Human Resources, Banking, Executive Management, Executive Support & Sales/ Marketing; as well as Accounting & Finance thru the Financial Edge division.

"We want to be in a position to serve our clients now and well into the future. We're committed to contributing to the growth of this region."

Right: WilliamCharles Search Group founding partners, Chuck Smeester and Bill Benson.

We will never have the cheapest hourly rate in town," says Darren Brown, president and founder,

> "We deliver management consulting through writing technology. We really try to understand what an organization needs—how does the technology need to work, who's going to use it, what processes will it support?" says Brown.
> "Then we figure out the right software and the right platform. We aren't focused on the technology; we're focused on the right solution."

Darren Brown, Founder, at the WMSTI 2007 Showcase event.

Arivium. "But if you look at the total cost of building, rolling out, and supporting your technology over a three-year period, we'll beat anyone in town."

That's because Arivium isn't in business just to write software programs for companies—that technology, he says, is a commodity anyone can sell. What Arivium offers is the depth of experience to clearly understand a client's organization in order to compile or create a technological package that supports its business. The edge that differentiates Arivium from commodity software developers is just that business acumen—the fact that they are consultants

as much as they are experts in technology.

"We deliver management consulting through writing technology. We really try to understand what an organization needs—how does the technology need to work, who's going to use it, what processes will it support?" says Brown. "Then we figure out the right software and the right platform. We aren't focused on the technology; we're focused on the right solution."

Arivium seeks to establish partnerships with its clients, to understand the big picture. And often, that process expands into a level of consultation that goes beyond technology. "In some cases, our clients invite us to the table because they want our input on their strategy, and it may have nothing to do with the systems we're writing," says Brown. "Our MO is about helping the client, not just installing a cool piece of technology."

The partners at Arivium are well-suited to such an enterprise, having spent many years in larger firms learning the fine points of business and how to hone technology to support business processes. Brown,

for example, spent ten years with Accenture, the international consulting firm, in addition to working for several years with a smaller company.

In May, 2002, he decided it was time to exert more control over his business and personal life and to apply that skill and training at the local level. "By working locally, I could drive home for dinner with the kids instead of living on an airplane," says Brown. Eventually, he persuaded a few colleagues to join him, and today Arivium comprises five partners and three locations in Grand Rapids, Ann Arbor, and South Bend, Indiana. The company also brings together diverse experience and expertise in areas such as life

sciences, business processes, scientific research, and the pharmaceutical industry.

From the outset, the company aimed for controlled, deliberate growth that was driven by client demand. "I set a very conservative goal of hiring about one consultant per year," says Brown. Over the past five years, however, the company's growth has outpaced expectations, and currently is above the 10 consultant mark. The recruiting and hiring process is also conducted with great care and is based on two criteria.

The first is that enough project work is available to last for several months. "Then I can be fairly confident that another project will be in place," says Brown. The second is the right fit. Arivium is very painstaking about the consultants it hires. Characteristics the company

Rob Kellner, Partner, presenting a concept.

looks for is the ability to interact well with customers and what Brown calls "a fire in the belly," someone with motivation and initiative—qualities that best serve the client.

Indeed, leveraging the diversity and depth of experience Arivium partners and consultants bring to the table only benefits Arivium clients—and sometimes it saves them money. For example, Arivium had two consultants assigned to separate divisions of a large company. In the course of sharing their experience, they realized that both divisions were using the same technological tool, but that they were paying separately for licensing fees and training. By combining fees and training classes, the company saved a significant amount of money.

Arivium clients range from small non-profits to a $50-billion international corporation, but most fall within the small- to mid-range size, the needs and vulnerabilities of which Arivium understands well. "We're a small company now, just like many of our clients," says Brown. "We know that each decision is significant, and that one bad decision could put them out of business.

And since most clients hear about Arivium through word of mouth, it is essential that that word is positive. Especially in places like West Michigan, where reputation matters, and many companies have deep roots and long memories.

"We are very, very diligent about making sure that our clients are pleased with our work."

James Bund, Technical Consultant, working on client projects.

"Arivium had two consultants assigned to separate divisions of a large company. In the course of sharing their experience, they realized that both divisions were using the same technological tool, but that they were paying separately for licensing fees and training. By combining fees and training classes, the company saved a significant amount of money."

As the leading economic development entity for the in the areas of Holland, Zeeland, and Saugatuck. It began in 2003, when, Thelen said, "a group of

lakeshore area, Lakeshore Advantage plays a crucial role in the area's efforts to attract and retain growing, successful companies.

"Lakeshore Advantage is important to West Michigan because we act as a catalyst to the local economy by helping to attract new companies to the region, retaining and expanding existing companies; and by helping to grow new, high growth potential ventures into successful businesses and employers," Lakeshore Advantage president Randy Thelen summarized.

The nonprofit organization in Zeeland, Michigan, has four full-time employees and offers services

local business leaders who were concerned about the downturn in the economy decided it would be a good idea to implement a local economic development organization with a vision of growing good paying, knowledge-based jobs.

"Our fundamental job is to be an agent for positive change in our region," he added. "We work to influence the business and civic leaders to make decisions that are favorable to the long term economic health of our region."

More than fifty investors and numerous community leaders support the organization's mission, which states, "Lakeshore Advantage will foster and implement innovative strategies for sound economic development in the lakeshore area to enhance the region's quality of life."

One way Lakeshore Advantage achieves that mission is through its Business Garden, which serves as an "incubator" for entrepreneurs during the early stages of their companies. Begun in 2004, the Business Garden is one of about 1,100 business incubators across the U.S., according to the National Business Incubator Association.

"Lakeshore Advantage will foster and implement innovative strategies for sound economic development in the lakeshore area to enhance the region's quality of life."

Located in the historic Colonial Clock building in Zeeland, the Business Garden can accommodate about ten companies in its attractive renovated loft space and has the capability to help another twenty companies through its virtual tenant program. All tenants, who pay rent for one to three years,

receive business advisory assistance, roundtable events where they can network and share resources and ideas, quarterly reviews, and other services that were designed to help them succeed. On-site tenants also have the use of telephone service, voice mail, copier, and Internet services, as well as office furniture, private conference rooms, and 24/7 access to their offices.

"There is still nothing like a job to help someone move up the economic ladder," Thelen noted about his work. "Lakeshore Advantage seeks to provide services that lead to job growth in the region. When we drive by a new business we helped start or a major business that is expanding, we take note of all the cars in the parking lot that represent all the families that have bettered themselves

as a result of the new job opportunities we helped create."

Lakeshore Advantage also offers, in a partnership with the Holland Young Professionals, the Lakeshore e2e Series (entrepreneur to entrepreneur). This regularly scheduled evening program includes ample time for people to network, and to learn from area business leaders, successful entrepreneurs, and other experts. Past e2e lectures have been led by G.W. Haworth, the founder of Haworth Corporation; Fred Bauer of Gentex; Rich Lievense of the Bank of Holland; Mike Lanser of Innotec; and Gary Krouse, the former COO of Johnson Controls.

While Lakeshore Advantage offers great support for new companies, don't think it only focuses on entrepreneurs. When it comes to economic development, the organization helps companies of all sizes. Thelen said they've helped with expansions at major local companies including Haworth, Gentex, Tiara, and Siemens. As the lakeshore area continues to grow in population, Lakeshore Advantage is ready to play a role in helping companies remain or relocate to the region, too. They can provide valuable services to large corporations by being experts in their own field: keeping up-to-date on the ever-changing state and local incentives that can make the difference in how—and where—a company grows.

Lakeshore Advantage also serves as a resource

clearinghouse with information available on its Web site regarding population trends, demographics, labor availability, communities, schools, tax incentives, commercial real estate, and other topics pertinent to new or growing companies.

Since its founding, Lakeshore Advantage has played a central role in attracting thousands of new jobs and millions of dollars in new investments to southern Ottawa County"

"We are able to work with numerous companies pursuing incredibly exciting growth opportunities," Thelen said. "Finding ways to help these companies expand into new markets, invest in new technology, and pursue new innovations keeps us energized."

"We are able to work with numerous companies pursuing incredibly exciting growth opportunities," Thelen said. "Finding ways to help these companies expand into new markets, invest in new technology, and pursue new innovations keeps us energized."

Residence Inn Holland

Whether you're on the road for business or for pleasure, whether you need a suite for a night or for a month, whether you're

traveling solo or with the whole family plus the dog, the Residence Inn in Holland is your home away from home. Conveniently located off I-196 and M-40, the Residence Inn is minutes from downtown Holland as well as from local attractions, lakes, golf courses, and most local corporations.

Guests traveling to Holland can enjoy the golden sands of Lake Michigan just minutes away. "We're located between Saugatuck and Grand Haven, so our guests come to visit the beaches and nearby towns," says Cherri Dukes, General Manager. In Holland, visitors can be immersed in Dutch culture and heritage at the Holland Museum, the Dutch Village, or Windmill Island, which features the only working windmill in the U.S. Not to

"We're located between Saugatuck and Grand Haven, so our guests come to visit the beaches and nearby towns," says Cherri Dukes, General Manager.

mention Holland's Tulip Festival, when the city bursts into masses of multicolored blooms, drawing visitors from miles around.

Rates for the suites at the Residence Inn are comparable to ordinary hotel rooms, but the suites are about 50 percent larger, so, besides the added value, guests have plenty of space to spread out and relax after a long day at work or play. Suites are available in three floor plans: studio suites with a queen-size bed and pull-out couch; one-bedroom suites with two televisions; two bedroom suites with two separate full-size baths and three televisions. All suites have separate areas for living, working, eating, and sleeping. They all have fully-equipped kitchens with a full-size refrigerator, dishwasher, stove, microwave, and utensils for eating and cooking. Many have fireplaces.

"This is a great option for families," says Dukes. "We can comfortably accommodate a family of six without needing an adjoining room." And if Fido

travels with the family, the Residence Inn also welcomes pets for a reasonable, nonrefundable fee.

Many additional amenities make a visit to the Residence Inn easier and more homelike. Start the day with a complementary breakfast buffet and end it with a relaxing evening social with beverages and hors d'oeuvres. In addition, the Residence Inn provides guests with on-site laundry facilities and same-day dry cleaning services. Workout facilities include a Sport Court and a nicely equipped workout room, indoor pool and whirlpool, and complementary access to an off-site fitness facility for real workout buffs.

Amenities for business travelers include high-speed Internet, voicemail, and complementary local calls. And with five golf courses within 30 miles, evening and weekend relaxation is close at hand.

So, whether a guest is traveling for work or pleasure, the Residence Inn Holland offers all the comforts of home. And more.

A few years ago, Crayon Interface was just a good idea. Wouldn't it be great to be able to start your car from a greater distance than most remote controls allow? To turn off the lights or to unlock it? And what about the house? Wouldn't it be awesome to be able to lock the doors, turn off lights, or monitor the babysitter from the restaurant across town or the hotel across the country?

And couldn't a cell phone, that ubiquitous and utterly mobile accessory, serve as the command-and-control center for these functions? And what if the cell phone interface was so easy to use that a child could do it?

With those daydreams, Garrick Pohl, Corbin Collet and Budd Bentley, began two years of conceptualization and development of the interface software for cell phones that came to be called Moshi. In 2005, they took the leap as Bentley and Pohl left their day jobs and never looked back. For one thing, they haven't had the time.

The notion of using cell-phone-based technology that's as easy to use as a child's crayon has piqued the interest and imagination of several partners. The beauty of the concept is that it is so easily adapted to numerous applications. "Initially, we thought we'd be controlling cars and homes. Now we're applying the same technology to many uses, and it's not a huge departure," says Pohl. "Our technology is extremely flexible." Companies including FedEx and Sprint, for example, have called on Crayon to support development of new mobile applications, which are focused on unleashing the power of cell phones to serve the needs of customers everywhere.

While Crayon is creating a few "private label" products that customers can download from its Web site, other applications, such as the new HomeRemote system, are sold by the hardware manufacturers who install the equipment. Customers then pay Crayon to activate the service.

Crayon may be a relative newborn as companies go, but it has created significant buzz in technology circles and has attracted some nice seed money. In 2006 alone, Crayon's CellStart product won Best in Show for automobile technology from DigitalLife, an Innovations Design and Engineering Award from the Consumer Electronics Association, and the New Product Award from the Specialty Equipment Market Association. In 2007, Crayon was recognized as one of "Michigan's 50 Companies to Watch."

Despite the fanfare, Crayon has benefited from West Michigan's relatively obscure geography in the technological scheme of things, which has allowed the company to develop and market its products without attracting undue attention from potential competitors in Silicon Valley, for example. "I like to think of West Michigan as the Third Coast," says Pohl. "There's Silicon Valley in the west and MIT in the east, and we're on the Third Coast. This location has been a good thing for us."

"I like to think of West Michigan as the Third Coast," says Pohl. "There's Silicon Valley in the west and MIT in the east, and we're on the Third Coast. This location has been a good thing for us."

Boatwerks

Boatwerks

Picture this: The sun setting over Lake Macatawa in Holland. You've

been trolling around the lake, enjoying a soft, spring day with friends. As a perfect day winds down, you pull up to the dock at Boatwerks, thoughts of a frothy cold one and maybe a rib eye steak or Lake Superior whitefish on your mind.

Welcome to Boatwerks!
Open since summer 2006, Boatwerks joins the pantheon of memorable Holland restaurants and the only one right on the Lake Macatawa waterfront. As such, the restaurant not only has a great lakefront view, but it also boasts one of the largest outdoor patios in all of West Michigan.

And Boatwerks caters parties, either on the

spacious front lawn or in its private Macatawa Room with seating for up to 70 guests. It also caters parties at customer locations with ample menu choices ranging from casual backyard BBQ's to elegant plated dinners. The menu, which changes seasonally, is described as "upscale comfort food." So in addition to a variety of salads, burgers and sandwiches, house specialties also feature summer vegetable risotto and wild mushroom crostini—all made from scratch with as many local, organic ingredients as possible. The restaurant's philosophy is "better ingredients make better food that is better for you." Not to mention better tasting, too.

Boatwerks is the labor of love of a local businessman and former owner of a marine construction

company, who used this site for many years for his business. When he sold his contracting business, he wanted to "give back to the Holland community, where he grew up and was able to succeed."

Not surprisingly, the restaurant harks back to the glory days of boatbuilding in the Holland area, where the old Chris Craft factory produced its fast, graceful motorboats. And it also celebrates those fun summer days of waterskiing and picnicking by the lake. A classic 1954 Elgin motorboat is the decorative centerpiece in the restaurant, and it is complemented by a collection of vintage outboard motors, wooden water skis, and artwork on a boating theme.

Also featured is The Runabout Lounge. With floor to ceiling windows and a mahogany topped bar, it is the perfect spot to celebrate happy hour, or to enjoy cocktails and live music.

> *"Open since summer 2006, Boatwerks joins the pantheon of memorable Holland restaurants and the only one right on the Lake Macatawa waterfront. As such, the restaurant not only has a great lakefront view, but it also boasts one of the largest outdoor patios in all of West Michigan."*

Marge Beaver

Marge Beaver is an aerial photographer based in Muskegon, MI with over 25 years experience flying and shooting custom aerial photography jobs all over the country. Her plane is equipped with camera ports for both vertical and oblique photography. Marge has a coffee table style book in its second printing titled *Above the North*, and a second book titled *Above West Michigan* should also be available in book stores by the time you are reading this.

Randa Bishop

From Australia to Zimbabwe, Randa Bishop has photographed in over 60 countries and 50 islands throughout the world. She has particularly large colorslide archives of Canada, Greece, Las, Vegas, Mexico, and the Caribbean. Her travel images appear regularly in leading American and International magazines and newspapers—publications such as *National Geographic, Travel & Leisure, Geo, Stern, Los Angeles Times, Junior Scholastic, Geo Mundo*, and many, many others. Her feature stories cover a wide variety of subjects from solar-powered airplanes to young children learning how to be astronauts.

Michael Buck

Seasoned photographer Michael Buck began his eclectic photography career in 1993 after graduating from The Center for Creative Studies in Detroit, Michigan. In 1996, M-Buck Studio opened and so did new opportunities for Mike, beginning with Amway Corporation as his first major client. His polished catalog work soon branched into family portraiture and wedding photography. At the same time, his keen eye and creative, interpretive approach to his subject matter made him a favored regular contributor to Grand Rapids Magazine and its sister publications. Mike realized instinctive skills in particular as a food and commercial photographer, but his out-going personality and polished people skills made him a reliable event photographer as well.

Dianne Carroll Burdick

Dianne Carroll Burdick, a Western Michigan University graduate with a BFA in Photography, is a free-lance photographer in Grand Rapids. Dianne Carroll Photography clients include The Grand Rapids Press, Grand Valley State University, the Grand Rapids Art Museum, the Grand Rapids Symphony, and Opera Grand Rapids. She is a continuing Studies Instructor at Kendall College of Art and Design where she teaches Photography/Darkroom. Dianne is the recipient of twenty-four awards in Photography and she has participated in over fifty art exhibitions and her work is included in six books. Her newest book was just released in August of 2006, called "*Listen to the Landscape*", a collection of twenty-eight hand-colored photographs, with haiku by Linda Nemec Foster.

John Corriveau

For over 27 years, the Grand Rapids based photographer has been there. He started as news photographer for small weekly papers on Michigan's east side. After studying at Ohio University's graduate Visual Communications program, he worked as a staff photographer for the College of Wooster and Oberlin Colleges in Ohio. Four years later, he moved his family to Grand Rapids where he specializes in editorial/corporate photography. He has photographed Presidents Gerald Ford, Ronald Reagan, George H.W. Bush and George W. Bush, Governors John Engler and Jennifer Granholm, Secretaries of State Madeline Albright and General Colin Powell, former Prime Minister of Pakistan Benazir Bhutto, Queen Noor of Jordan, authors Kurt Vonnegut, Garrison Keillor, Brain Greene, Harlan Ellison, Jonathan Kozol, musician/activist Bono and most recently former President William Clinton.

Julie K. Flietstra

Julie K. Flietstra, of Grandville, Michigan, is a 28 year old photographer. She has always enjoyed spending her time surrounded by nature and tries to capture those amazing moments in time with her photographs. She strives to appreciate the natural beauty of God's Creation, and also tries to compose interesting images of man made urban structures. While paying great attention to the smallest of details, Julie puts forth a daily effort to find the beauty in everything.

Photographer biographies

Laura Hollander

Laura Hollander is a recent graduate from Kendall College of Art and Design with a B.F.A. in Photography and a minor in graphic design. Laura now operates her own studio, Laura Hollander Photography, specializing in photographing weddings, families and children. One of her passions is photographing landscapes and outdoor subject matter while using and manipulating the natural light available.

Annie McFarland

Annie McFarland is an artist living in Grand Rapids, Michigan. She is a 2007 graduate of Kendall College of Art and Design where she received her BFA in photography. She is exhibiting her artwork regionally and is currently commissioned to do photography and graphic design work at Open Concept Gallery. Ms. McFarland does freelance work for a diverse variety of commercial and individual clients. Her senior thesis work was centered around visual representations of mother-daughter issues.

Thad Pickett

A freelance graphic designer and photographer, Thad graduated with a degree in visual communications from the Art Institute of Fort Lauderdale in 1990. Living in rural southern Iowa where he works from his studio, he uses state-of the-art Mac computers and professional Canon digital camera equipment for his design, photography and videography business. Specializing in book design, he has designed upwards of 100 or more books of diverse subject matter and each custom to the publishers needs. Integrity in business, quality craftsmanship, the love of the art, and treating others as you would like to be treated is the model Thad uses for success.

Christopher M. Potter

Christopher M. Potter was born and raised in Grand Rapids, MI. Following graduation from Northern Michigan University in Marquette, he made his home for many years in Michigan's upper peninsula. He eventually returned to Grand Rapids to pursue a career in photography. In addition to photography Chris enjoys music, bicycles and travel.

Johnny Quirin

Johnny Quirin has always been a photographer, even in his high schools days from the 1980s. He has worked in the photography fields of senior high school portraits, editorial and photo journalism, as well as commercial photography. One of his passions is shooting for publications, he says that it can be one of the most exciting photography assignments to receive especially if it involves photographing people at their best. Johnny and his family moved to West Michigan from San Diego, California five years ago and currently live in the city of Grand Haven.

Frederic A. Reinecke

Frederic A. Reinecke has a BFA in Art & Photography from Central Michigan University. For the past 17 years Reinecke has operated FAR Photography in Muskegon Michigan, producing commercial photography for area businesses and industry. As a fine artist Reinecke's work has been exhibited in several Michigan galleries and museums, including the Muskegon Museum of Art, Grand Rapids Art Museum, Lansing Museum of Art and the Krasl Art Center in St. Joseph, Michigan.

Chris Tack

At age 18, Chris began his college career at Delta College in 2002, where he earned an Associates Degree in Graphic Design. Continuing with a three-year run at Kendall College of Art & Design in 2004. While at Kendall, he earned dual BFAs in the areas of photography and digital media. While attending college, Chris held internships for both a graphic designer, & a commercial photographer, and currently works at the Apple Computer Store in Grand Rapids, Michigan. He is also an exclusive photographer for iStockphoto.

Lori Turner

Lori Turner has been a professional photographer since 2000. She earned a Bachelor's of Fine Art degree with an Illustration emphasis from Grand Valley State University. She has since founded DaVinci Photography & specializes in weddings, portraits & fine art photography.

Profile